CURRICULUM*-IN-THE-MAKING

CPC

CRITICAL PRAXIS AND CURRICULUM GUIDES

Shirley R. Steinberg and Priya Parmar
Series Editors

Vol. 5

The Critical Praxis and Curriculum Guides series
is part of the Peter Lang Education list.
Every volume is peer reviewed and meets
the highest quality standards for content and production.

PETER LANG
New York • Washington, D.C./Baltimore • Bern
Frankfurt • Berlin • Brussels • Vienna • Oxford

WOLFF-MICHAEL ROTH

CURRICULUM*-IN-THE-MAKING
A POST-CONSTRUCTIVIST PERSPECTIVE

PETER LANG
New York • Washington, D.C./Baltimore • Bern
Frankfurt • Berlin • Brussels • Vienna • Oxford

Library of Congress Cataloging-in-Publication Data
Roth, Wolff-Michael.
Curriculum*-in-the-making: a post-constructivist perspective / Wolff-Michael Roth.
pages cm. — (Critical praxis and curriculum guides; vol. 5)
Includes bibliographical references and index.
1. Curriculum planning—Philosophy.
2. Postmodernism and education. I. Title.
LB2806.15.R67   375'.001—dc23   2014005849
ISBN 978-1-4331-2474-7 (hardcover)
ISBN 978-1-4331-2473-0 (paperback)
ISBN 978-1-4539-1326-0 (e-book)
ISSN 2166-1367

Bibliographic information published by **Die Deutsche Nationalbibliothek**.
Die Deutsche Nationalbibliothek lists this publication in the "Deutsche
Nationalbibliografie"; detailed bibliographic data is available
on the Internet at http://dnb.d-nb.de/.

The paper in this book meets the guidelines for permanence and durability
of the Committee on Production Guidelines for Book Longevity
of the Council of Library Resources.

© 2014 Peter Lang Publishing, Inc., New York
29 Broadway, 18th floor, New York, NY 10006
www.peterlang.com

Printed in the United States of America

CONTENTS

	Preface	vii
	Epigraph	xi
Chapter 1.	The Ground of the Image	1
Chapter 2.	Event*-in-the-Making	27
Chapter 3.	World*-in-the-Making	55
Chapter 4.	Understanding*-in-the-Making	85
Chapter 5.	Subject*-in-the-Making	105
Chapter 6.	Relation*-in-the-Making	121
Chapter 7.	From Response-Ability to Responsibility	141
Chapter 8.	The Planned, Living, and Enacted Curriculum	171
Chapter 9.	Researching the Living Curriculum as Event*-in-the-Making	195
	Appendix A	215
	Appendix B	217
	References	219
	Index	227

PREFACE

Everything requires change and rebirth. Everything is shown in a moment of unfinalized transition....And in fact polyphony itself, as the event of interaction between autonomous and internally unfinalized consciousnesses, demands a different artistic conception of time and space; to use Dostoevsky's own expression, a "non-Euclidean" conception. (Bakhtin, 1984, pp. 167, 176)

In education, the practice of writing curriculum plans that are subsequently to be realized in the classroom continues to be everyday common practice around the world. Evaluators of pre-service and in-service teachers alike assess the difference between the curriculum as planned (planned curriculum) and what actually happened in the classroom (enacted curriculum). This, however, does not take into account the gulf between plans and situated actions, a gulf for which there is no remedy even when someone enacts his/her own plans. More importantly, this approach does not theorize the curriculum as living, for the "enacted curriculum" is something finished, which, only as object, can be compared to another object. But a living curriculum, understood as an event*-in-the-making – where the asterisk marks that the participants do not know what they witness (e.g., a successful lesson, teacher learning, an altercation or a relation that leads to learning, etc.) – leads to a very different appreciation of just what is happening in a classroom.

In this book, I use concrete lesson fragments and other materials to develop a post-constructivist perspective on curriculum that is grounded in a phenomenological approach concerned with understanding the never-ending movement of life. This post-constructivist position developed here counters the constructivist fallacy, which assumes that things are objectively present, represented, rather than handy and invisible. Aesthetic activity and theoretical cognition, which think of the world as thematically present in human activity, are "powerless to take possession of that moment of Being which is constituted by the transitiveness and open event-ness of Being" (Bakhtin, 1993, p. 1). Theoretical cognition, as aesthetic activity, is unable "to apprehend the actual event-ness of the once-occurrent event, for its images or configurations are objectified...they are placed outside actual once-occurrent becoming" (p. 1). In this book I develop a perspective that takes us back into the unfolding event*, which we can only witness in participation but not grasp in a theoretical manner.

What comes to the foreground in Bakhtin's philosophy of the act is the absolutely new, that which has never been, and which cannot be repeated – it is the event-ness of the event, pure flow of life. This life can be understood with and from the perspective of consciousness coming from participation (učastie, Ger. *Teilnahme*) and sympathy / commitment / interest / concern (učastie, Ger. *Anteilnahme*). That is, thinking (knowing and learning) characteristic of participation is committed rather than disinterested and emotionally uncommitted as it appears in constructivist approaches, where, at best, this dimension is a mediating factor external to the raw act of thinking itself. Bakhtin's work is interesting because he specifically thematizes the emergent quality of the event generally and discourse specifically in terms of their dialogical and polyphonic structures, which allows us to understand each act in terms of the figure of the response (Shchyttsova, 2003). Responsivity leads us to response-ability and responsibility, and, therefore to ethics. This is the underlying thread from which this book is woven and arises.

Events* are understood as in the making so that we cannot know the precise nature of what we witness until after some completion has been achieved. Some gatherings become revolutionary social movements that uproot and change societies (May 1968, France); others become almost forgotten tidbits of history (Kent State shooting, 1970), and still others become uprisings squashed by brutal crackdowns by dictators and dictatorial states (e.g., Hungarian Uprising of 1956). While we witness, however, we do not know whether we ultimately understand the period as a revolution, as a tidbit of history, or a brutal crackdown. Similarly, looking at the curriculum through the lens of something in the making, we know the *what* is happening only when the happening has come to an end. This leads to radically different forms of understanding of curriculum issues such as the subject, ethics, the role of possibility and passivity, the nature of the response, and the learning paradox.

Aspects of chapter 2 appeared in *Curriculum Inquiry* (Roth, 2013c). The text of chapter 3 is based on a presentation following the conferral of an honorary doctorate on the author (University of Ioannina, Greece) and on one of the author's four John Dewey Lectures organized by the Centre de Recherche sur l'Éducation, Apprentissage, et Développement (CREAD) and the Institut universitaire pour la formation des maîtres (IUFM, Université Rennes 2). A version was published in *Éducation et Didactique*. Fragments of chapter 6 had a very different life in an editorial published by *Mind, Culture, and Activity* (Roth & Radford, 2010). Chapter 7 was developed from materials first published in *Pedagogies: An International Journal* (Roth, 2013d). In chapter 8, I draw on the modified description of a classroom event that originally appeared in *Learning and Instruction*.

Throughout this book, I draw on non-English original works or on their translations into a language than English that in the opinion of experts on the topic are better and do more justice than the ones available in English. For example, the English translations of Bakhtin's work do not do a good job of recovering the author's reading of the French linguist Ferdinand de Saussure, who is the subject of critique in *Marxism and the Philosophy of Language* (e.g., Roth, 2013a). The French translation, however, does, in most situations, precisely that (as per the Russian original Vološinov, 1930). The Russian text "Avtor i geroi v esteticheskoi deyatel'nosti" (in Bakhtin, 1979) is much more faithfully rendered in the French "L'auteur et le héros" (in Bakhtine, 1984), in content and form, than in the English "Author and Hero in Aesthetic Activity" (in Bakhtin, 1990). English translations frequently render Vygotsky's and Leont'ev's Russian adjective obščestvennij by means of "social," when in fact the correct adjective would be "societal." From the perspective of their Marxist critiques, it is important to retain societal aspect rather than making it unpolitical in choosing social. German translations maintain the distinctions made between the two adjectives. Thus *Denken und Sprechen* (Vygotskij, 2002) is considered – see, e.g., the introduction to the German version, which also acknowledges the Italian version as more accurately rendering Vygotsky in a Western language – a better translation than *Thought and Language* (Vygotsky, 1986). Unless otherwise indicated, all translations are mine.

The names of authors are spelled differently in different languages. Within the text, I use the most common English spelling, for foreign names are often spelled differently within the same language (e.g., Leont'ev and Leontyev in English, Leontjew in German; Vygotsky in English but Wygotski and Vygotskij in German; Bakhtin in English, Bachtin in German, and Bakhtine in French). However, in references to a particular text, the spelling as per the byline is used.

Victoria, BC
November 2013

EPIGRAPH

Against determinism and teleology... "Mechanical necessity" is not a fact: *We* have interpretively imputed this to events. We have interpreted the *formulable* nature of events interpreted as a consequence of a necessity that reigns over events....Only because we have interpretively imputed subjects, "*agents*," into things the impression is created that all events are the consequence of a force/constraint that a subject exerts – who exerts? Again an "agent." Cause and effect – a dangerous concept when we think of some *thing* that *causes* and some thing *affected* by it.

a) Necessity is not a fact but an interpretation.
b) As soon as we understand that the "subject" is nothing that *effects* but only a fiction, a lot follows.

    ...If we no longer believe in the *effecting* subject, then the belief in the *effecting* thing crumbles, as does interaction, cause and effect between those phenomena that we call things.

    The "*thing in itself*" crumbles: because this is in principle the conception of a "subject in itself." But we have grasped that the subject is a fiction. The opposition between "thing in itself" and "appearance" is untenable; the concept of "appearance" thereby also crumbles.
c) When we drop the effecting *subject*, then also the *object* that is *affected*. Duration, self-sameness, Being inheres neither in what we call subject nor in what we call object: These are event-related complexes, seemingly lasting with respect to other complexes – thus, e.g., a difference in the temporality of events.

d)   When we drop the concept of "*subject*" and "*object*," then also the concept of "*substance*" – and, consequently all of its different modifications, e.g., "matter," "mind," and other hypnotic beings, "eternity and immutability of matter," etc. We ridded ourselves of *substantiality*. (Nietzsche, 1954c, pp. 540–541, original emphasis)

Regarding invention generally speaking, which nevertheless is the starting point of activity, our intelligence does not arrive at capturing it in its *gushing forth*, that is, in its indivisibility, in its *genius*, that is, in its creativity. Explaining it always consists of resolving it – the unforeseeable and new – into known and old elements arranged in a new order. Intelligence does not admit total novelty any more than it does admit radical becoming. It is here, too, that it lets escape an essential aspect of life, as if it were not made to think such an object.

[...] We would see that intelligence, so skillful in manipulating the inert, displays its clumsiness as soon as it touches the living. Whether it concerns dealing with the life of the body or that of the mind, it proceeds with the rigor, the rigidity, and the brutality of an instrument that was not destined for such a use. ...We could easily discover its origin in our obstinacy to treat the living like the inert and to think all reality, as fluid as it is, in the form of a solid definitely at halt. We are only at ease in the discontinuous, in the immobile, in the dead. *Intelligence is characterized by a natural incomprehension of life*. (Bergson, 1907/1908, p. 178–179, original emphasis)

· 1 ·

THE GROUND OF THE IMAGE

We live our lives inscrutably included within the streaming mutual life of the universe. (Buber, 1937, p. 16)

Once-occurrent uniqueness or singularity cannot be thought of, it can only be partic-ipatively experienced or lived through. (Bakhtin, 1993, p. 13)

We live within the streaming, mutual life of the universe. This stream never returns. The universe we inhabit therefore is once-occurrent and singular – a fact that natural scientists express by means of the law of entropy, which, taken over the entire universe, can only increase. The movement therefore is irreversible, in contrast to (non-entropic) representations, where movements are reversible. This once-occurrent uniqueness of life cannot be thought of, as Bakhtin states, but only participatively experienced and lived through. As Bergson (1907/1908) suggests in the quotation that appears in the epigraph, this living aspect of life, its generativity, is the most difficult phenomenon for the human mind to think; mind, he says, is characterized by a natural incom-prehension of life. Failing to capture what is living about the curriculum is what characterizes much if not all of curricular thinking. Even when educa-tors say they are thinking about the living curriculum, they tend to do so with inert categories. The very construction "to think *about...*" opens up a gap between the thinking and its object (content), here, the curriculum, which cannot be alive because it is already objectified. Life then has to be breathed into the result, animating the movement from one state to another, much like life is breathed into the sequential arrangement of photographic images on a reel, which is animated by the motor of the movie projector. This approach fails to capture, as Bergson says in the epigraph to the book, an essential aspect of life, its very aliveness, its gushing forth, its innovation, the production of the new, for example, when students learn something that they have not known before and could not have envisaged precisely because what they now see previously was unseen and therefore unforeseeable. The only way to come close to the *living* curriculum is to think participatively, as Bakhtin suggests in the opening quotation to this chapter, requiring us to use the verb "to think" as transitive verb with a direct object, which itself is living and unfinalized.

The fundamental problem in curriculum theorizing lies in the fact that learning and development – of students and teachers alike – become specific targets. The instructional process is held responsible and accountable for achieving the stated objective and the successful achievement of the planned curriculum. Inherently, there is a cause–effect figure at work, whereby the production of the new (future knowing) is to be achieved by means of educative and educational mechanisms. There is finalizing thinking at work that does not dare to theorize the living curriculum in terms of innovation and in terms of the possibility that something other than the planned target arises. This finalism has cause–effect thinking as its fundamental figure. Finalism thereby comes close to mechanism: learning can be planned ahead of time in all its detail. But the doctrines of finalism and mechanism "refuse to see in the course of things, or simply in the development of life, the unforeseeable creation of form" (Bergson, 1907/1908, pp. 48–49).

From the perspective of the learners, teachers and students alike, the new that arises for them by participating in the living curriculum, that which they know and which *they* did not and could not have anticipated because it was invisible, does in fact constitute the emergence of an unforeseeable form. The living curriculum can be thought in terms of the figure of the meeting, which goes with the figure of the generativity of life: "Creation reveals, in meeting, its essential nature as form" (Buber, 1937, p. 26). This form cannot be anticipated even by the teacher – as I show in this book – because from the perspective of the unfinished event*-in-the-making, the nature of causes and effects is inherently inaccessible. Causes are attributions that are made once effects are known. But this attribution is the problem, because it fails to recognize the living, creative, generative, and renewing dimensions of the living curriculum. The objective sciences as well as formal analysis fail to capture what is alive in life, the Heraclitean flux that has no ultimate elements and relationships, because the nature of their concepts and categories, which reduce phenomena to elements (Husserl, 1980). Even biology, intended to be the science of life, does not get at the living in life (Henry, 2000).

But failing to capture the living dimension of life in the making does not prevent us from producing, after the fact, narrative accounts of the past, which includes events in their finalized form. The inherent unpredictability of life – the beginning of wars, family crises that may or may not end in divorce, the success or failure of a planned lesson – should tell us that life generally and any unfinished and unfinalized event*-in-the-making resists representation and attribution of cause and effects. This figure of causes and effects, as Nietzsche points out in the epigraph to the volume, is a dangerous concept when we attempt to understand the very eventness of an event, where the future is unseen and therefore unforeseeable and unforeseen. In this chapter, I prepare the ground for the subsequent elaboration of a perspective on the living curriculum, which is living precisely because unfinished and changing, that takes the figure of the event*-in-the-making as its fundamental motive. The motive is extended to other moments[1] of the living curriculum, which are thought as unfinished and in the making: subject*-in-the-making, object*-in-the-making. In adopting the motive of the event*-in-the-making, we may then eschew the problems arising from the cause–effect figure that underlies the constructivist approach to the curriculum. This allows us to adopt a post-constructivist perspective, in which there is nothing like an event, curriculum, subject, object, cause, or effect as thing or phenomenon in itself. This perspective leads us to the pure mobility of life generally and the unfinalized and living curriculum more specifically.

In painting it is understood that a figure does not just exist but that it always exists against some ground. It is always against a ground that a figure can exist. This implies that there is no figure as such but always already a figure–ground configuration. The idea of a figure-in-itself – in the same way as the idea of the thing-in-itself that Nietzsche (1954c) critiques based on his analysis of the eventness of events – is a fiction. The ground of the image

---

1   To avoid confusion, I use the term moment throughout this book in the dialectical materialist sense: a concrete manifestation of a higher order phenomenon that is irreducible to all other, potentially infinite manifestations of the phenomenon. I use the term instant to mark a point in time.

against which my proposal of a post-constructivist perspective on the curriculum – understood as a living curriculum through the lens of the event*-in-the-making, as something unfinished and therefore ungraspable – is the current ideology of thinking curriculum issues such as teaching, learning, and researching curriculum. The very emergence of the image as a phenomenon, which arises in a movement from the unseen to the visible, embodies the movement we require in thinking about curricular issues from the perspective of the living curriculum that inherently is in the making. In this chapter, I articulate some of the basic premises that come with a constructivist way of thinking about knowing and the curriculum.

The Origin of the Cause–Effect Figure

The cause–effect figure is a pervasive feature that is exists in most languages (Lakoff, 1987). There are prototype effects of different kinds of causation, and the effects tend to be "relatively uniform across languages" (p. 54). The prototypical figure of the relation between cause and effect, the CAUSE → EFFECT schema, is that of direct manipulation of objects (Lakoff & Johnson, 1980). It embodies, as Nietzsche (1954c) says, the human will to power.

Presence and the Presence of the Present

When children are born and during their early stages, the world is present to them. Piaget and Inhelder (1966) call this period "'sensorimotor' because the baby, lacking symbolic function and affectivity tied to representations that permit evoking persons or objects in their absence" (p. 7). In the course of its development, the child develops, abstracting from its experiences, a system of schemes and representations that allow it to make the world present again, represent it, both in its presence and absence. As the child grows older, it undergoes major developmental stages that end with the capacity to formally represent and reason about the world. "In the course of the second year … appears … an ensemble of behaviors that imply the representative evocation of an absent object or event and that consequently supposes the construction or use of differentiated signifiers" (Piaget & Inhelder, 1966, p. 42). Subsequent forms of thinking are attributed no longer to the world as it presents itself but only how it appears through the representations that are taking the place of the appearances of the world in intuition.

The constructivist position considers human behavior only under the aspect of the capacity to make the absent or present world present again. In fact, actions can then be premeditated, based on the interpretations of preceding experience, and, once executed, the anticipated results may be compared to the actual results obtained. Actions that do not imply representations are of a lesser kind, such as the concrete operations characterizing children between 6 and 9 as compared to those formal operations that characterize individuals in their adult stage. In the research literature, this leads to the observable fact that participants in conversations are said to interpret what others say, as if they were representing the talk of others, operating upon it in their mind to extract and determine "meaning," and then constructing a reply in turn.[2] Thus, it is not surprising, for example, to see classroom events characterized in terms of representations and interpretations: "These symbolic representations involve students' actions, they are used as reference in students' discussion and the tasks lead students to interpret them at the conceptual level and also in relation to the material situation" (Tiberghien & Malcoun, 2009, p. 49).

The fundamental aspect of the constructivist position is that we perceive the world through our concepts, making it present again so that it can become the object of our thought. Thus, as Kant (1870) suggests, experience is possible only through the representation of a necessary connection of perceptions. This is so because experience is a form of empirical cognition, whereby an object is determined by means of perceptions. This synthesis is not itself contained in the perception but constitutes a synthetic unity of the manifold in consciousness; and it is this unity that "constitutes the essential of our cognition of objects of the senses, that is, of experience (not merely of intuition or sensation)" (p. 197). This conception will lead us directly into the cause–effect figure, for it explains necessary temporal relations between different otherwise independent, subjective perceptions. The problematic nature of this approach is apparent as soon as we think of phenomena that are in the making, which cannot be cognized as specific phenomena because they are inherently unfinished. This approach is inherently unable to capture events in the unfolding because it favors an "intellectual-centric" distance between acting subjects and their social-material worlds (Bourdieu, 1997).

---

2   On the problematic notion of "meaning," see Roth, 2013b.

Change and the Cause–Effect Figure

To understand events, we have to understand change. This is so because events, in their very nature, are unfolding happenings. The traditional approach is to understand change in terms of an aspect change that a self-identical object undergoes. A post-constructivist perspective allows events*-in-the-making to be indeterminate, that is, we do not know *what* kind of event we participate in and witness while we participate. That is, the very nature of the thing undergoing change is undetermined when we consider it from the perspective of pure mobility. In the constructivist perspective, however, change can be perceived only in the form of the changes in the attitudes or aspects of an otherwise constant and immutable substance. It is the approach that the natural sciences tend to take, as many observers have noted. Change, therefore,

> *cannot be perceived* except in substances, and becoming or disappearing, in an absolute sense, that does not concern merely a determination of the permanent, cannot be a possible perception, for it is this very notion of the permanent that renders possible the representation of a transition from one state into another, and from non-being to being, which, consequently, can be empirically cognized only as alternating determinations of that which is permanent. (Kant, 1870, p. 206, emphasis added)

For Kant, all changes are subject to the law of the connection of cause and effect. The very idea of change requires the same substance, with two opposite determinations, and, therefore, as constant. We can immediately see how this conception expresses itself in current (constructivist) theories of knowing and learning. Thus, knowledge is presupposed as the underlying substance, which has different determinations before and after the change (learning). Some even speak of specific *learning pathways* that can be selected beforehand so that students can follow them from their initial (mis-)conception to the target conception. The concept and phenomenon, thereby, are taken to be unproblematic, and learning becomes an expression of the change between two states of the underlying "thing." For constructivists, this underlying substance is the cognitive framework or the set of conceptual constructions, which are considered to remain constant as long as new experiences can be assimilated to them. The conception of change requires, in the constructivist formulation, constancy or permanence. Change is a way of existing that follows another way of existing. The emergence or creation of something new and the disappearance of something already existing are not changes.

In this approach, self-identity is postulated and taken as a measure for change, which manifests itself in the different way that the otherwise unchanging substance appears. But we may also change our supposition and take pure mobility and change as the fundamental unit. In this case, change – e.g., learning – is unproblematic because it is part of the supposition; and stability – manifesting itself, for example, in relatively stable cognitive frameworks and conceptions – comes to be problematic (Lave, 1993). This is so because the Heraclitean flux, difference in itself, cannot be captured by the methods of the objective sciences: It would be hopeless, in fact illusionary, trying to explain something in flux – like knowing, *learning*, consciousness, or the *living* curriculum that is of interest to the educator – under the "ideal presumption of a possible explication by means of identical elements that can be captured in stable concepts" (Husserl, 1973, p. 86).

In the metaphysical approach, the cause–effect figure is required because it alone allows the cognizing being to order the different states in time. Perception alone only leads to the consciousness that one state appears in imagination before the other, not that there is a necessary relation between the two states. To understand the relation between two states as a necessary one, "the relation between the two states must be so cogitated that it is thereby determined as necessary, which of them must be placed before and which after, and not conversely" (Kant, 1870, p. 208). This ordering is done by the conception of cause and effect: "[I]t is the conception of the *relation of cause and effect*, whereby the former determines the latter in time, as a sequence, and not as something, that merely antecedes in imagination (or which might in some cases not be perceived)" (p. 208). Experience itself, empirical cognition of phenomena, becomes possible only because of the law of causality. This has the consequence that phenomena "themselves, as objects of experience, are possible only by virtue of this law" (p. 209). The cause and effect figure is required, for, as Kant exhibits in an example, the changing manifold of our perceptual experiences when we look at a certain building does not mean that there is a causal relationship between these experiences. That is, the change from one experience to another derives from a succession of representations all belonging to the same phenomenon, the house, which is captured in the concept of a house. The experiences (appearances) of the different aspects will be the same independent of the movement of the eyes, which allows the mind to postulate a permanent thing the appearances of which depend on the perceptual process.

Kant contrasts this situation with another, very different one: a boat drifting on a river. It, too, will appear differently in our perception. But the sequence of the representations of this boat will always be a temporal one: the drifting boat will first appear upstream and then downstream, never the inverse. The ordering of the consecutive representations can be predicted based on the cause–effect relationship, because there is a necessary relation between the direction of the water flow and the consecutive positions of the boat. This allows Kant to distinguish a subjective sequence of phenomena, which is a function of the perceptual apparatus (apprehension) and independent of a logical necessity. The objective sequence between the two states of a phenomenon, which appear differently in empirical perception, can be attributed to the change in the thing only when there is a cause-effect relation.

The one science that differs from the classical approach of understanding change is quantum mechanics. For example, in Schrödinger's formulation, change is described by an equation. We do not, however, know anything about the state of the system until we look; but in looking, we disturb the unfolding event. But in looking, we find out about a state. The seminal example that has found its way into the popular literature is that of Schrödinger's cat. A live cat is placed in a box together with a vial of poisonous gas. The vial is broken when a radioactive atom decays at some unknown time. The box is then closed. The paradox is that we can say nothing determinate about the cat in the box – other than that it is alive or dead. But this does not help us understand the *process*. Schrödinger's wave equation describes the process, the changing likelihood of finding the cat alive or dead when we (dare to) look. As observer, the change only manifests itself when we compare our two observations, which are states. But the *process* of change is not described by the difference between two states. Whereas the classical approach has to assume our next observation to be random, either dead or alive, Schrödinger's equation, which describes the process of change, gives us information about the probability of finding the cat in one or the other state. This change in probabilities is a description of change itself.

The Bodily Origin of the Cause–Effect Figure of Reasoning

The problematic of cause and effect arises, as said, from the attribution of necessary temporal relations to the natural and cultural world that built on the idea that our actions bring about predictable changes in the world. Moreover, as evident in the constructivist conception of the action schemes, what the acting subject does is determined by these (mental) schemes, which are updated when the anticipated result does not match (fit) the actual result. The problem here is that a relation is made between thought and action without articulating how an abstract (ideal) thought can bring about any concrete change in the material world. That is, the cause–effect figure has been abstracted from an idealized relation between thought, intentions, actions, and their effects. The confusion derives from a conflation of different ways in which our bodies exist: there is not one body but there are three bodies (Henry, 2000). The first is the organic body, or rather, the flesh (*Leib, la chair*), which does not require any representation at all to function. It moves itself prior to the newly born having had the time to develop any conception, moving itself, for example, as the heart beats or the chest rises and falls to allow an oxygen flow through the lungs. "We have here 'a something' that gives itself only to the movement and in the absence of all representational intentionality, and in the absence of each of the traditional senses, which are vision, audition, touch, smell, and taste" (p. 210). "*It is a body before sensation, before the world. A body invisible to the same extent as our original corporeity*" (p. 211). But because this organic body exists prior to felt sensations, it remains invisible to our senses. Any movement of this flesh is capable to auto-affect such that from some first time the movement comes to regenerate itself even in the absence of mental representations – typical for the kind of relations athletes develop. This organic body is endowed with a primary "I can," which produces recurrent movements in the absence of any representation. The flesh excludes all theory, all a priori intuition of space that, as Henry points out, Kant develops in his transcendental ethics.

The second body is the felt body, that is, the body how it is experienced from the inside. That is, there is a doubling effect, whereby the organic body comes to be accompanied by the felt body. In this instance, some aspect/s come/s to stand out, to transcend the original body. Thus, as a result of movement, we come to feel sensations not only on the outer side of the skin (roughness, hardness) but also on the inside (e.g., when we scratch an itch). This second body is a represented body, though its experiences are inaccessible to others. My pain remains my pain, and nobody else will feel it; others can only empathize and sympathize with me. If there are action schemes, these exist at the level of the felt body, which already is a transcendent body, not the original flesh in which reside the powers of movement.

The third way in which our bodies appear is the material body, resembling all other material bodies, accessible to collective experience in the public domain. This body is objective, because it can be described in ways that are accessible and reproducible by all observers on the outside. It is the world of the objective phenomena. The second and third bodies have been referred to, in part based on Merleau-Ponty's (1964) investigations, as the constituting and constituted bodies. The difference between the two becomes apparent in a now classical investigation of a hand touching the other hand, the former being the (subjectively experienced) constituting body, the latter being the (objectively experienced) constituted body. Whereas another observer has access to the hand that is explored and can derive the same kinds of observations, or at least engage in negotiations about its appearances, the constituting hand, and its sensori-motor experiences, remain inaccessible to her.

The constructivist mistake consists in conflating the original, organic body, the flesh, with the felt body, the sensorimotor body of our transcendental experience. It then theorizes bodily action as *determined* by the mental schemes.[3] The problematic of this conflation comes to stand out particularly when athletes attempt to change their ways of moving by representing their own movements. In this case, as reported time and again in the media (e.g., when Tiger Woods changed his swing, or some tennis players change their ways of hitting the ball), the performance levels decrease: they exhibit lower competence levels than when they leave their movements to themselves. Intentions, which themselves are transcendental, the result of cognitions, are deemed capable of directly affecting the organic body. But how does a transcendental thought affect the material body? It does not:

> Our action is that of our originary corporeity and of its powers, it is the drive moving itself and bending the "organs" that give in to its power. Our action upon the world produces itself at the end of this organic deployment, there where, directly reached by it as its proper foundation, the world opposes to it its absolute resistance. Because the reality of its content is held there, not in its appearing but at the limit of my effort, given in this fashion to the movement of my life. (Henry, 2000, pp. 215–216, original emphasis)

There is an inherent and unbridgeable gap between our intentions that are representations and the movements of the organic body, which, by its very definition, remain inaccessible. It is perhaps not surprising that the some phenomenologically oriented psychologists and philosophers speak of kinetic

---

3   Piaget and Inhelder (1966) do in fact allow for a beginning that lies before the stimulus–response state but locates it in "the spontaneous and total activities of the organism … and in the reflex conceived as differentiations of these [activities], and which can, in certain cases … present a functional activity that entails the formation of assimilation schemes" (p. 9). Piaget does make reference to Maine de Biran to suggest the emergence of a "magical" causality scheme in the child, inappropriately suggesting that the philosopher postulated a conscious self that delimits itself from the world. Precisely the opposite is the case, because the world comes to be separate only when it has become independent of actions.

melodies that unfold on their own once triggered. There is not a causal connection between the two. As a result, it is not intentionality that constitutes the principle of our experience. There is an originary auto-revelation that precedes, orders, and determines the process of the insertion of movements in the body and their dispositions within it. From this perspective, intentions are not plans that describe actions with any precision. Rather, intentions are triggers that set the movement, which unfolds on its own like a melody from a player piano once the starter button has been pushed. Thus, when we consider learning by heart a text or series of words, what happens in fact is that this is facilitated when the person articulates the text aloud. In this case,

> By repeating several times the same exercise, the vocal instrument shows itself increasingly persistent. The attention or deployment of the in-principle necessary forces to execute each particular movement diminishes progressively; soon the animated spring plays by itself following the weakest of impulsions: The recall operates upon the first term, all the others will come to align themselves in their order, without being called, without the possibility to dismiss them. (Maine de Biran, 1841, p. 191)

The same kind of account is provided in a cultural-historical approach to speaking, which focuses on the serial organization of movements that are needed in pronunciation (Luria, 1973). Thus, to speak or write normally, the links between individual composites – i.e., written and spoken letters, phonemes – have to allow smooth transitions so that the written words and spoken sentence unfold without requiring representation. Even the faculty to understand sentences (sound sequences) is tied to the such kinetic melodies (Luria, 1970). That is, to understand in hearing, to produce sentences in speech and writing, we do not need to put them into representations prior to externalizing them by means of motor activity. The movement itself, produced in motor activity, constitutes the memory, comprehension, and competent action.

Plans and Action Schemes

In the preceding sub-section, I show how bodily movements, which first appear at the plane of the flesh and then, in transcendental form, on the level of sensorimotor actions, constitute the source of intelligent action. The idea for the cause-effect figure therefore derives from our action sequences that arise from habitual movements, kinetic melodies, which are attributed as essences to beings. Causes and effects are not inherent in nature, not even in the relation between our intentions and our situated actions, but they constitute a conception on the basis of which successive perceptual impressions can be ordered. But in Kant's constructivist approach, which is the target of Maine de Biran's critique, they constitute the schemes (plans) for action. Thus, "cause" is an idea that "comes to us, originally, from the exercise of our movements, from our own actions; it is only by modifying everything that surrounds us, by exercising our powers, that we can consider ourselves to be active causes" (Maine de Biran, 1841, p. 130). The idea of the force is then metaphorized, "first by means of our will, then abstracted from will" transporting it "to the bodies that move, we consider these in turn as *agents*, as endowed with *forces*, as *causes*" (p. 130, original emphasis).

In the constructivist position, actions that are determined by underlying schemes determine what an agent is doing. In scheme theory, the acting subject first puts together a plan of action, which is built from (a) the perceived situation, (b) through mental activity, (c) yielding a plan as the expected result of future action. This is so because "every implementation of an action scheme requires the acting subject to recognize a triggering situation" (von Glasersfeld, 2001, p. 146). The scheme is updated when there is a deviation between expected result and actual result so that in future actions, the scheme is more viable and leads to less discrepancy between expectation and actuality. But this fails to explain why we get better at something – playing tennis or soccer, speaking a language, speaking without an accent – without updating anything; simply participating in playing tennis or soccer or in speaking a language changes what we do and how (e.g., accent) we do it. Scheme theory, on the other hand, makes the assumption that recurrences in experiences are established only when the subject is capable of "remembering and retrieving (re-presenting) experiences and the ability to make comparisons and judgments of similarity and difference" (von Glasersfeld, 1989a, p. 128). When the results of actions do not match the actual outcomes, the problem is one of the scheme, which will then be accommodated so that it produces better action schemes than on the last attempt. The acting subject therefore does not directly deal with reality but only through its re-presentations, which mediate both access to the world and prepare for future action.

The usefulness of schemes, from the constructivist perspective, derives from the fact that they allow the acting subject to formulate explanations, make predictions, and "even manage to control certain events in the field of [his] experience" (von Glasersfeld, 1989b, p. 440). The constructivist mind is concerned with experiences, which derive from observations, themselves processes of assimilating to existing schemes. Even *"predictions*, again, regard experiences, not events in some 'real' world that lies beyond one's actual experience" (von Glasersfeld, 1989b, p. 440). It is quite evident that the vital activity of the acting subject occurs within the mind, which re-presents things and phenomena in the world, acts upon them, derives hypotheses, and then predicts "an event that has not yet been observed" (p. 440). The subject then acts in the world, has new experiences, the access to which requires re-presentations. The problem is not the relation between schemes and action but with the schemes themselves, which may or may not be viably predicting the outcomes of future actions.

"Only if we consider an experience to be the second instance of the self-same item we have experienced before, does the notion of permanence arise" (von Glasersfeld, 1989b, p. 442). The fundamental item of thought is self-same, and, because of this, stable across time unless subject to reconstruction when new experiences no longer fit. The structures of the mind are viable when they predict a relatively stable world. They do so by "creating individual identities of which we can believe that they recur in our experience" (p. 442).

Critiques of the Constructivist Fallacy

Constructivist theorizing has driven a wedge between thought and actions in the world in the form of representations. The present is not present itself but only through representations, which, by their very nature, have transcended the material world and stand above (Gr. *meta*) it. "Pure understanding distinguishes itself not merely from everything empirical, but also completely from all sensibility. It is a unity self-consistent, self-sufficient, not to be augmented by external additions" (Kant, 1870, p. 110). It is this aspect of the constructivist approach that cultural-historical activity theorists, generally following K. Marx and his diction that the point of the mind is to change the world, complained about and mounted an alternative epistemology and psychology. Thus, the problem of traditional psychology is that it considers thought as an "autonomous stream of thoughts thinking themselves, which isolates itself from the plenitude of real life, from the living motives, interests, needs of the thinking person" (Vygotskij, 2002, p. 54). As the result, thought becomes an epiphenomenon in life. Yet thought in itself, as theoretical understanding of the world, does not automatically lead to changing the world. The constructivist fallacy is that the world is present to us in and through our mental structures, that is, in mediated form. The author of the introductory quotation to this chapter, however, suggests that the uniqueness and singularity of actual life cannot be thought of but only experienced through participation and living through events the nature of which is not available to us until these have finished and have become graspable.

Taking up Hegel's approach and then expanding it to take account of the fact that mind is not just active in and for itself but because it is in the service of humans to control their environment leads to the dialectical materialist critique of the constructivist position: The god's eye totality on the world*-in-the-making is a product of the mind, which has only one manner of operating, that is, with the crutches of representation. But this manner "differs from the artistic-, religious-, practical-mental appropriation of this world. The real subject remains outside the mind in its independence – as long as the mind behaves only speculatively, only theoretically" (Marx/Engels, 1983, p. 36). The problem with constructivist theories of thinking is that these conceive of the movement of categories as arising from productive acts, a product of thought and comprehension, as a processing of intuition/envisagement and representation into concepts. What is required instead, to comprehend participative thinking, is a process of a "concept that thinks outside and above intuition/envisagement and representation and self-generates" (p. 36). The authors thereby contrast the agential mind that operates on its own with the process of a concept that self-generates and therefore is not the cause that effectuates thoughts, intuition/envisagement, and representations.

An aspect of the constructivist fallacy is that it rationalizes participants in conversations. Thus, in this approach the participants in the relation do not just hear and speak but also they are said to "interpret" the words of the interlocutor. Thus, "to understand what someone has said or written means no less but also no more than to have built up a conceptual structure that, in the given context, appears to be *compatible* with the structure the speaker had in mind" (von Glasersfeld, 1989a, p. 134). From a praxis-oriented perspective on life and consciousness interested in understanding real beings engaged in real-worldly pursuits, the constructivist position has reversed the relationship between thought and life. In this way, "not consciousness determines life, but life determines consciousness" (Marx/Engels, 1958, p. 27). Quite explicitly, this means that what we think of doing is not what *determines* (collective life). As the authors elaborate, "[i]n the first point of view we move from consciousness to the living individual, in the second, the one corresponding to real life, we move from real living individuals and consider consciousness only as *their* consciousness" (p. 27).

These authors critique the position that our actions first appear as representations (e.g., in the form of plans or intentions) and then bring about (determine) life. They contrast this position with their own, concerned as it is with understanding real living human being and life as movement, real life and living (not represented) individuals are the origin of consciousness, which always is the consciousness of the living individuals.

> The production of ideas, representations, consciousness initially is immediately bound up with material activity [Tätigkeit] and the material *relations* of man, *language of real life*. Representing, thinking, the mental relations of man still appear here as the direct result of their material behavior... .Consciousness [Bewußtsein] cannot ever be anything else but conscious being [bewußtes Sein], and the Being of humans is their real life process. (p. 26, emphasis added)

These authors also use the inversion of images in a camera obscura as an analogy for the inversion of life and thinking that constructivist theories produce. They orient us to real life, which is pure mobility in its sensuality: "The sensual world is the total, living, sensual *activity [Tätigkeit]* of the individuals that constitute it" (p. 45). The authors refer to the stoics and their interest in an "absolutely moving life, which emerges from its intuition of nature, which is Heraclitean, dynamical, developing, living" (p. 122).

Mikhail Bakhtin, across his work, shows us not only how to think about language specifically and culture and life more generally as something living but also how to do so through the lens of the unfinished and unfinalized "world-as-event." He refers to and grounds himself in the position that Marx/Engels worked out.

> Hence the profound dissatisfaction with modern philosophy on the part of those who think participatively, a dissatisfaction that compels some of them to have recourse to such a conception as historical materialism which, in spite of all its defects and faults, is attractive to participative consciousness because of its effort to build its world in such a way as to provide a place in it for the performance of determinate, concretely historical, actual deeds; a striving and action-performing consciousness can actually orient itself in the world of historical materialism. (Bakhtin, 1993, pp. 19–20)

In "theoretical cognition" there is an "essential and fundamental non-communication between the *subiectum* and his life as the *object* of aesthetic seeing, on the one hand, and the *subiectum* as the bearer of the act of aesthetic seeing, on the other" (p. 14). This is the same non-communication to which I already point above, which is brought about by the non-communication between representation and world – a fact that is explicitly recognized by constructivist theorists who suggest that constructions can only be tested for their viability, not for their truth, "if 'Truth' is to be understood as a *correspondence* to the ontologically real world" (e.g., von Glasersfeld, 1989b, p. 441). This is so because "cognition constructs a unitary and universally valid world, a world independent in every respect from that concrete and unique position which is occupied by this or that individual" (Bakhtin, 1990, p. 23). The theoretical world and the world of culture are actual and recognizable in the world: these are inner-worldly facts. But this theoretical world and the contents of cultural discourses *about* the world do not tend to be part of the world itself. Thus, "my participative and demanding consciousness" can see "that this world is not the once-occurrent world in which I live and in which I answerably perform my deeds. And these two worlds *do not intercommunicate*" (Bakhtin, 1993, p. 20), that is, theoretically cognized worlds – e.g., the weight, shape, and size of a hammer as objective facts – are not required in competent participation in the world, for example, in hammering a nail into the wall to suspend a picture.

The constructivist position takes an outside perspective on the individual, suggesting that what appears in the theoretical vision is what characterizes the way in which we go about our business in the world. The most immediate examples are the verbs "to construct" and "to interpret," which we can frequently find in this literature. Thus, individuals are said to interpret the world and to construct something thereof, including "meaning." However, this flies into the face of our actual experience, where we do not interpret our neighbor's greeting, "Hello, what a nice day today" but respond, for example, "Much warmer than yesterday" or "Spring is around the door." We do not think about placing our feet but walk, just as we do not have to cogitate to talk in a conversation with others. The difference between the two perspectives is due to the fact that "I experience myself in principle on a different plane than other actors in my life and dreams" (Bakhtine, 1984, p. 52).

Toward a Post-Constructivist Perspective

In education, the practice of writing curriculum plans that are subsequently to be realized in the classroom continues to be everyday common practice around the world. Evaluators of pre-service and in-service teachers alike assess the difference between the curriculum as planned (planned curriculum) and what actually happened in the classroom (enacted curriculum). This, however, does not take into account the gulf between plans and situated actions (Suchman, 1987), a gulf for which there is no remedy even when someone enacts his/her own plans. More importantly, this approach does not theorize the living curriculum as an event, for the "enacted curriculum" is something finished, which, only as object, can be compared to another object. But a living curriculum, understood as an event*-in-the-making – where the asterisk marks that the participants do not know what they witness (e.g., a successful lesson, teacher learning, an altercation or a relation that leads to learning, etc.) – leads to a very different appreciation of just what is happening in a classroom. In the remainder of this book, I use concrete lesson fragments and other materials to develop a post-constructivist perspective on curriculum that is grounded in a phenomenological approach concerned with understanding the never-ending movement of life. In this perspective, events* are understood as in the making so that we cannot know the precise nature of what we witness until after some completion has been achieved. Some gatherings become revolutionary social movements that uproot and change societies (May 1968, France), others become almost forgotten tidbits of history (Kent State shooting, 1970), and others uprisings squashed by brutal crackdowns by dictators and dictatorial states (e.g., Hungarian Uprising of 1956). While we witness, however, we do not know whether we ultimately understand the period as a revolution, as a tidbit of history, or a brutal crackdown. Similarly, looking at the curriculum through the lens of something in the making, where we know the *what* is happening only when the happening has come to an end. This leads to radically different forms of understanding of curriculum issues such as the subject, ethics, the role of possibility and passivity, the nature of the response, and the learning paradox.

In chapter 2, I develop a perspective on the curriculum as something living and, therefore, ever changing and, therefore, not as "some thing" at all. A living curriculum is an *event*-in-the-making* not captured by nouns but better denoted by infinitives – to learn, to teach, to event. In fact, to understand process we must not think in terms of categories (etymologically, things specified by predicates) but in terms of movement and mobility. The unfinished and inherently open-ended event*-in-the-making constitutes pure mobility, and this mobility manifests itself in a dialectic: When a possibility is realized (actualized), it disappears as possibility; but it simultaneously gives rise to new, unforeseeable and unforeseen possibilities. This movement is of the same kind as the mobility in Derrida's *writing* (on the magic slate), which erases (some of) the old at the same time it produces the new. An event*-in-the-making is characterized by its openness toward the future, unpredictability, and excess of intuition over intention. During the event*-in-the-making we do not even know what event, as the inner-worldly fact that we will be knowing, we are participatively witnessing (not looking at something from the outside). I use empirical classroom materials to exemplify (give a body to) pertinent issues and to ground my discussion. To understand the Heraclitean *flux* of a curriculum that is alive, we require ways of thinking that do not rely on stable concepts that are identical with themselves. The realization of possibilities is one such way of thinking, because it is a process that makes existing possibilities disappear while simultaneously giving rise to new possibilities. A second way in which the pure mobility of the living curriculum manifests itself is the movement from an unfinalized event*-in-the-making to the finalized, (al)ready-made event. There is mobility because we can grasp (prehend and comprehend) solely the latter, but only in the grasping of the (al)ready-made event can we think about the former. The event is a possibility, but as soon as it is realized as specific event, as an inner-worldly fact, it no longer is living.

Once we consider the living curriculum through the lens of the event*-in-the-making, we understand that the objects, subjects, goals, knowledge, learning, and lesson become graspable only once the Heraclitean flux is stopped in and through a process of completion. But such completion is required for understanding. Our understanding of curriculum and of all its aspects therefore arises from the (diastatic, dehiscent) relation between curriculum as event*-in-the-making (living curriculum) and curriculum as completed event (curriculum that participants have lived), the only way in which we may grasp it as something (i.e., some thing, phenomenon). It is in that movement from the living curriculum to the lived curriculum that our understanding of the "enacted curriculum" emerges to become the (finalized) object of our thinking. Learning tends to be theorized, in curriculum research and practice, from the perspective of the known and seen, as is apparent in the idea that learners *intentionally* "construct" knowledge. We need to ask, however, how students who do not know the learning object (what the teacher wants them to know) can orient towards this unknown, unseen, and therefore unforeseen knowledge. How can students be "metacognitive" when they cannot know whether what they do leads them any closer to the curriculum objective? The purpose of chapter 3 is to bring the problematic of this learning paradox into sharp relief by drawing on empirical examples from my research in a variety of settings. In this chapter, the movement characteristic of an event*-in-the-making generally and in *learning*-as-event specifically manifests itself in the dialectic of the unseen, which withdraws precisely at the moment that the newly seen ascends from the unseen to its own and, thereby, reveals itself in an unforeseen manner. Because this ascent is unforeseeable, the learner is *the gifted* (*adonné*). This ascent from the unseen – which affects learners prior to their comprehension – into the seen constitutes the mobility of learning. This ascent of the unseen into the seen constitutes the phenomenalization of the (learning) object, the very making (coming into being) of the object that accompanies the event*-in-the-making.

In chapter 4, I continue to work towards a curriculum theory that makes a radical commitment to the fact that learners (students or teachers) cannot see or comprehend what it is they are learning until *after* they have learned it. A fragment from a fourth-grade mathematics curriculum – intended for the learners to arrive at a generalization of the type $y = 3 \cdot n + 6$ to predict how much money a girl will have in her piggybank if she starts with $6 and saves $3 every week – is used to think and think about[4] learning given that the students cannot aim at this learning outcome precisely because they do not know (a) the generalization, (b) that they are supposed to generalize, or (c) from which aspects of their experience to generalize something. Because students do not know what they will know until *after* the learning event, this future knowledge may be better thought of as the (initially) *foreign/strange*, which affects students *before* they can grasp what is happening to them or what/that they have learned. What students learn – that which is really new in their knowledge and therefore cannot be derived from what they already know and see – is accessible to learners only a posteriori. Learners, however, do not directly encounter the foreign/strange, because it withdraws as what emerges becomes part of the familiar. Learning is constituted by the double movement of withdrawing and becoming familiar. Because this foreign *affects* students before they know what is happening to them, this notion of the living curriculum as event*-in-the-making has affect and emotion inherently built in. Passibility, pathos, affect, and emotion do not have to be introduced as factors external to cognition, as this occurs in constructivist theories. Instead, learning is an experiential manifestation of events*-in-the-making, whereby we know what we learned only after the fact.

---

4   The choice of the verb "to think" as transitive verb with direct object (i.e., "learning") and intransitive verb combined with "about," is deliberate.

Once we look at the living curriculum through the lens of the event*-in-the-making, we can no longer think of the subject in the way current theories tend to do it, as a monad with an identity that may be agentially asserted or reconstructed and which remain constant – as Kant suggested – and only its (outer) aspects change. In chapter 5, I re/write the subject from a post-constructivist perspective, that is, through the lens of the event*-in-the-making: It is a subject*-in-the-making. From this perspective, the subject as inner-worldly fact (i.e., without the asterisk) is a *product* of the living event*, so that the empirical subject (i.e., the *who* that is participating in and witnessing the event*-in-the-making) is available only after the same closure is achieved that also gives us access to the event, object, enacted curriculum, or tools as inner-worldly facts. Things advene (happen) to the participant in an event*-in-the-making. It is therefore more advantageous to think of the subject*-in-the-making in terms of the figures of the *advenant, interloqué, patient, gifted* (*adonné*), and *witness* in addition to thinking of it as an agent. The gifted is given simultaneously with the gift, as in the course of the ascent of the unseen into the visible; and the movement of this ascent constitutes the change inherent in the subject*-in-the-making. It is precisely because the advent and gift – which arrive at and are given to someone – that the subject*-in-the-making is given. But the subject*, being directly affected by the action, is given in the accusative form rather than in the nominative form, the (grammatical, constructivist) subject of the action. Because we cannot know the enacted curriculum until the (living) curriculum*-in-the-making has come to an end, the participants are witnesses who do not and cannot know what they are participating in as inner-worldly fact that could be the *object* of our knowing. Concrete classroom episodes are used to exemplify this different perspective on the participant subject, who not only acts but equally important is subject to and subjected to the living curriculum and thereby appears as the *advenant*, patient, and gifted. Identity as the inner-worldly fact discussed in current curriculum theory is an effect that arises in the movement from the living subject* to the momentarily finalized and graspable subject once some closure is achieved.

It is common practice in curriculum theorizing to think of the teacher–student relation in an asymmetric way: The knowing teacher somehow facilitates the learning of those who know less. Those educators committed to a socio-cultural perspective often draw on the work of Lev Vygotsky and his concept of the *zone of proximal development*, whereby a learner can act at a higher developmental level when scaffolded by a more competent teacher or peer. In chapter 6, I use empirical materials to exemplify how the perspective of the event*-in-the-making requires us to rethink that "relation" as relation*-in-the-making, which then opens new opportunities for understanding precisely what is happening in a *meeting* of students and teacher. Rather than having an asymmetrical relation where the developmentally more advanced person somehow enables understanding*-in-the-making: students may become more knowledgeable in mathematics and teachers may become more knowledgeable in general pedagogy, mathematics specific pedagogy, or mathematics. This is so because from the perspective of the event*-in-the-making, "teachers" and "students" are *advenants, interloqués*, patients, gifted (*adonnés*), and witnesses. The learning of teachers occurs precisely when some initial move to assist a student fails because the former cannot ever predict (with absolute certainty) the responses of the latter. Student understanding*-in-the-making is the movement from the unseen into the seen, a movement in which the unseen inherently withdraws. Through the lens of the living curriculum we can then observe how the institutionally designated students assist institutionally designated teachers in their learning as much as the reverse. Any "higher psychological function" – teacher pedagogical knowledge, student mathematical knowledge – *is* and appears in a societal relation first, which does not exist other than in the perpetual coming and going at the borderlines, marked by the vertical bar " | ," of speaking | hearing/understanding, hearing/understanding | answering. That relation cannot be reduced to individuals, as this happens in (radical, social) constructivist theories, which ground events in the actions of individuals who are said to construct alone or together. The relation*-in-the-making embodies an inner contradiction – which manifests itself in the different roles, perspectives, and understandings – because relation simultaneously means diachrony (it is spread across time) and diastasis (spread simultaneously across people and setting). The relation*-in-the-making, then, is a sign of pure mobility consistent with the framework of the event*-in-the-making.

The purpose of chapter 7 is to re/think ethical issues that arise once we view the living curriculum through the lens of the event*in-the-making. The constructivist epistemology focus on ethics as a constructed system of values in the mind – even when previously co-constructed in a social context – against which social agents compare the actions that they mentally plan before performing them. This approach is problematic, as it forces a wedge between thought and action, body and mind, universal and practical ethics, and thought and affect. Drawing on a fragment of a concrete classroom episode as an exemplary case, I develop and exemplify a post-constructivist discourse on ethics that centers on the dialogical relation of participants in conversation. This approach overcomes the problems of the constructivist approach because of the same perpetual coming and going at the borderlines of speaking | hearing/understanding, hearing/understanding | answering. Responsibility emerges from the fact that human beings are *able* to provide a *response*: their Response-ability. Responding embodies a movement, as it refers us to a process that begins with orienting to and listening to another and ends with providing an answer to this other. The concept of responding, therefore, embodies an inner contradiction because it is diastatic, covering listening and answering, and diachronic, because the two processes are spread out in time. Responding, therefore, constitutes pure mobility. This same process manifests itself in different ways. The first part of the response thereby means opening up oneself to being affected by the other (i.e., passivity and passibility) before speaking and, in turn, affecting the other. Opening up means making oneself vulnerable to the unforeseen and unforeseeable that is to come. Vulnerability, however, also arises on the part of the speaker, who, the exposition of the saying – in French phenomenology, there is a nice play on words where exposition is *ex-peau-sition* (positing something outside the skin) – exposes him/herself. The second manifestation of responding consists in the answer, which, in turn, affects the original speaker. The concept of responding harbors a dialogical relation of affecting and being affected, where we are exposed both in speaking and listening, leads us to a practical ethics that is at work with the living curriculum seen as event*-in-the-making. This practical ethics is consistent with Bakhtin's dialectical (dialogical) conception of the world-as-event and with Buber's understanding of life as event and its reflection in the Self–Other relation. I conclude by suggesting that the Saying constitutes a dialectical/dialogical paradigm of a post-constructivist ethics.

In curriculum theorizing, teaching and learning are thought of as inner-worldly things that can be planned ahead of the living curriculum. If what actually will have happened, as captured in the concept of the *enacted curriculum*, differs from what had been anticipated in the *planned curriculum*, teachers tend to be chided, held accountable, and even blamed. Teachers and their plans come to be treated as causes that bring about lessons as their effects, further inner-worldly facts. From the perspective of the event*-in-the-making, however, the living curriculum has an open horizon: there are no discernable causes and effects until after everything is said and done, at which time causes *may be attributed* based on known, finalized effects. It is only after the fact that what has happened is attributed to "poor" or "exemplary" teaching, students, curriculum materials, and so forth. In chapter 8, I use lesson fragments to exemplify the relation between planned curriculum and enacted (lived) curriculum as inner-worldly facts and contrast these with the living curriculum as unfinished event*-in-the-making. The dialectical relationship between living curriculum and enacted (lived) curriculum embodies the movement of witnessing understanding*-in-the-making: The living curriculum is graspable only as enacted, lived, and finalized curriculum – at which point the curriculum no longer is living. Therefore, this movement from the living and unfinalized to the enacted and finalized curriculum itself is understanding. This movement and our understanding are co-extensive. This movement can be understood in terms of the verb *to interpret*, whereby practical (unthematized) understanding begins, accompanies, and concludes description and explication develops understanding. *To interpret* therefore implies understanding*-in-the-making in the unfolding of the explication*-in-the-making, which itself is changing because of changing understanding. To interpret means (partially) erasing old (al)ready-made understanding as new understanding*-in-the-making unfolds.

When we rethink curriculum from the perspective of the event*-in-the-making, our research strategies and policies have to change because we may no longer take "curriculum plans," "curriculum objectives," "teachers," "students," "tasks," or "materials" as inner-worldly social and material facts that are used to attribute causes and effects, "impacts," or "mediations." Such attributions may be made only after the fact, leading to a form of Whig history of curriculum; and these attributions need to be understood as such. The purpose of chapter 9 is to refocus curriculum researchers on the living work involved in the event*-in-the-making that exhibits the orderliness of any inner-worldly social and material to the participants themselves. That is, the orderliness of the world is taken as condensation (effect) of the living work of the members to a setting. Looking at the living curriculum through the lens of pure mobility requires a different method than the qualitative and quantitative methods common in educational research, which some scholars refer to as the *Formal Analytic* technology. A constructivist curriculum researcher may say that a student is "classifying objects according to their geometrical properties," a statement possible only once the event*-in-the-making has come to an end and the object has found its intended place. In the proposed approach, which affiliates itself with phenomenology and ethnomethodology, the living work is made thematic in the formula "doing [classifying an object according to its geometrical property]," where the first part ("doing") refers to the living work and the second, bracketed part ("[…]") refers us to what is after the fact reported as the finalized social fact. The bracketed part is an after-the-fact account of the finalized event and what it has effectuated. In this irreducible pair of the doing and the eventual account of what has been done – e.g., the pairing of the unfinalized Saying and the finalized Said – there is an inner contradiction co-extensive with the double mobility arising within the event*-in-the-making and in the movement to the finalized event. The competencies required for this work are the same required for seeing (on the part of onlookers, e.g., researchers, evaluators, and supervisors), after the fact, a lesson as "failed," a teacher as "qualified" or as "struggling," students as "eager," "involved," or "resisting instruction." These are the same competencies required for identifying as teachers those institutionally nominated to be "teachers" and for seeing as students those institutionally nominated to be "students." The diachronic nature of this living work and diachronic nature of the movement from work to account (descriptions, artifacts) is a manifestation of the mobility embodied in the category of event*-in-the-making.

Difficulties of Re/Writing the Living Curriculum

The project of re/writing the curriculum through the lens of the event*-in-the-making is made difficult because the very grammatical structures of our language, as those of most languages, embody an epistemology that the present effort attempts to overcome. Thus, for example, a curriculum researcher might write a classroom observation in this way: "The teacher asks Connor a question." Here, the teacher is in the subject position (nominative or subjective case), who is the origin (cause) of the action. The student is in the accusative (objective) case; grammatically, he is the transitive object of the verb asking because the asking is affecting *him* (the accusative inflection of "he"). The question asked is the second object, constituting the effect that the action has brought. This grammatical structure directly maps onto the cause–effect figure, in fact, is co-extensive with the cause–effect figure in our thinking:

The subject is the cause or causing agent, the verb expresses what is happening, the first object (Connor) is affected by the action and the second object (question) specifies what the action produced. In fact, the very nature of the action as an act of asking is available only when the speaking has come to an end. Moreover, when such a sentence is written, it attributes a particular nature to the micro-event*-in-the-making, where we do not even know whether from within that there has been a question at all. If we may legitimately say that there has been a question, then this is but a gloss of an unfolding collective action (i.e., micro-event*-in-the-making), and there are aspects in this unfolding that allow us to delimit *something* in flux of life that we then denote by the term "question." The problem lies in our (Western) languages that nominalize what inherently are events*-in-the-making.

That we should be critical about accepting such statements as "the teacher asks Connor a question" without taking an from-within-the-event*-in-the-making perspective can be seen from the following example, which is of a kind that we find frequently in our lives. A wife may say to her husband, "Did you sweep the bedroom floor?" We may all too rapidly suggest that she is asking a question. For if the husband were to respond, "Why are you always on my case?," from within the event, this is not the response to a question but an instance of "being on the case of...." From within the event*-in-the-making, the participants now have to come to grips with this new historical situation. What will unfold from here will be different than if the husband had said, "Yeah, I finished" or "I started but will finish when we return from shopping." From within the event*-in-the-making, we do not even know what will have been said once the saying has ended. To write from within the event*-in-the-making, where nothing is finished, runs counter to the noun-centered way in which our language functions.

It may therefore appear cumbersome to work with expressions such as event*-in-the-making, which is to highlight that the nature of what is happening once we are in a position to grasp it remains open. But when we grasp something, it already is a completed form. The *future perfect* tense is one grammatical construction that allows us to keep the future open by referring that what will have happened in the past tense that provides a retrospective on the finalized event that can be grasped as such only in the future. The *future perfect continuous* tense allows us to take a future retrospective on what someone will have been doing up to that point. Throughout this book, readers should keep in mind that if we want to look at the living curriculum in its very aliveness, then we need to keep the world inherently open, in the form of "world-as-event," "being-as-event," or "object-as-event," where the "event" in these Bakhtinian expressions should be understood as event*-in-the-making, which Bakhtin writes about as the eventness (sobytijnost') of the event (sobytie). Three noun forms are distinguished: A noun without an asterisk (e.g., event, question) is something finished and treated in the situation as such; a noun with an asterisk (e.g., event*, question*) is something finished without yet knowing what it is; and a noun with asterisk and the collocated "in-the-making" (e.g., event*-in-the-making, question*-in-the-making") marks something in the process of unfolding that we do not know yet what will have been done and what the achievement will be after finalization (i.e., event, question).

· 2 ·

EVENT*-IN-THE-MAKING

There are neither causes nor effects. Linguistically we cannot get away from this. But this does not change matters. When I think the *muscle* separately from its "effects," then I have negated it… *In summa: an <u>event</u> is neither caused nor causing. Causa* is a potential to bring something about, invented and added to <u>events</u>… (Nietzsche, 1954c, p. 768, original emphasis, underline added)

To recognize an <u>event</u> implies admitting its irreducibly originary spontaneity, sovereignty in short. (Marion, 2010a, p. 281, underline added)

Educators are interested in *learning*, that is, a process of increasing students' knowledgeability and control over specific, age-appropriate tasks generally outlined in the official curriculum. According to the currently dominant paradigm/s – or dogma, ideology – learning is theorized in terms of individual and social construction. That is, what students know after undergoing some lesson or unit of lesson is theorized in terms of the outcomes of actions, which the agential subject of learning brings forth. Knowledge – in the form of cognitive structure, conceptions, or (declarative, procedural) information – is theorized as the outcome of actions that are the consequences (effects) of the learning intentions (causes) of agents. Learning is theorized in terms of nouns – often the difference between two states of knowledge – rather than verbs. But this is precisely the picture that the first introductory quotation asks us to abandon because there are no causes and effects, not if we look at events-in-the-making through the lens of the old English verb "to event" (to come to pass) – even though we may find it difficult to dissociate from the cause–event figure in/of our explanations. Just as the muscle brings about effects, the subject of learning is said to bring about (i.e., cause) its individual knowledge or contributes to bringing about collective knowledge. Nietzsche suggests, however, that this *negates* the posited origin of the action. To recognize the living curriculum *as* an event*-in-the-making – i.e., the event in its eventness, or, perhaps better, in its eventing – implies, as the second introductory quotation notes, admitting "its *irreducibly originary* spontaneity." That is, as an originary spontaneity the event *cannot be* reduced to a cause (e.g., the subject), which would take away the sovereignty of the former. In Nietzsche's view – taken up and transformed in post- and anti-Kantian philosophy including post-structuralism and phenomenology – an event is neither caused nor causing.

Event*-in-the-Making and (Al)ready-Made Event

In my re/theorizing of the living curriculum, I distinguish the *event*-in-in-the-making* from the (al)ready-made *event*. As long as it is in the making, I refer to it as event*, using an asterisk to denote the provisional nature of what is happening, as we do not know with any precision what we conceive of as having happened once some form of closure has been achieved. The (al)ready-made event, without an asterisk, is an inner-worldly fact, is something "unitary and self-equivalent … that could be read *post factum* by a detached, <u>non-participating</u>) consciousness that is not interested in the event" (Bakhtin, 1993, p. 46, original emphasis, underline added). But to this consciousness, which does not actually live and participate in the unfolding happening the nature of which is yet to be known, the very quality of being a witness in the event*-in-the-making, the event-ness of the event, is lost. Anyone who has ever participated in a competitive game will know that from within we relate to what is happening very differently then when we are mere spectators or Monday morning quarterbacks.

The very idea of a cause (we should really bar it: ~~cause~~) that brings about an effect has been invented and added on to events – it is an invention (of metaphysics) – to create a predictive model. That is to say, it has been added to a view of events *as* events, which "are pure 'mobility' – without *anything* that moves [itself]" (Romano, 1998, p. 1, original emphasis). Nietzsche further elaborates in a way that has implications for thinking not only the event – to be thought as event rather than thing – but also the subject. Thus, he suggests that the statement "'to every change belongs a cause/causator'" (Nietzsche, 1954c, p. 502) constitutes a mythology, which "*separates* that which is causing *and* the (act of) causing" (p. 502). He uses the example of lightning to suggest that the expression "the lightning bolt flashes" posits lightning as an action (flashing) and as a subject (i.e., the lightning bolt). However, this subject "is not one with the event, but rather *remains, is,* and no longer '*becomes*'" (p. 502). He then concludes: "To postulate events as an effecting [*Wirken*]: and effect [*Wirkung*] as Being: this is the *double* error, or *interpretation*, of which we are guilty" (p. 502). In his analysis, Nietzsche clearly distinguishes the classical approach, which is concerned with things that are stable ("remain") and are ("is"), and opposes this to "becoming." In curriculum research, knowledge similarly tends to be thought as something that is, can be identified and measured; learning (a form of becoming) is the difference between states, that is, knowledge before and after some curriculum event. Understanding an event*-in-the-making precisely means coming to grips with its continued becoming, its coming to be. This distinction is what we find in post-structuralist philosophy, where it is recognized that "[b]ecoming is not being" (Deleuze & Guattari, 1991/2005, p. 64), which can be read as "becoming *is not* being" or as "becoming *is* not-being." A similar critique shifts from the metaphysical "is," which is to be barred or crossed (i.e., "i̶s̶"), and replaced by theorizing process, such as in the concept of *writing* (*écriture*) on a magic slate, which, in creating the new also erases (part of) the old (e.g., Derrida, 1967; Heidegger, 1997).

Once we consider curriculum under the perspective of the event*-in-the-making – which can exist as a finalized entity only after what is happening has come to a conclusion and thereby brought closure to the process subsequently known as "the event" – we have to change our ways of thinking (about) the living curriculum. This approach especially shifts, as I show in chapter 5, what we conceive of as the subject of activity (teachers, students), and therefore the notion of identity towards the different and "*diverse modes of subjectivization* by means and through which an 'I' can come about [*advenir*], responding to what happens to him starting from the kernels of sense that are to him events" (Romano, 1998, p. 2). The curriculum as an event*-in-the-making tends to carry us – teachers, students – away, where "to carry away" should be heard as being moved by something that is in excess of our reason or judgment, something that we cannot fully grasp until it is all done and over. This also means that no individual or group "is in [total] control" of the unfolding curriculum, and the possibility that the unforeseen can happen unavoidably exists. The expression "to be carried away by" is used to indicate that something stronger than the will or intention moves the person or group of persons. It allows us to understand that a lesson that unfolds and concludes *as planned* is an accident rather than a necessity.

To think the curriculum as an event*-in-the-making requires us to understand it as the same and different simultaneously: the same because there is a mobility that we designate as "the event" and different because the happening is unfolding and therefore changing without ever being self-identical. The point is not to merely think *about* a lesson but to think the lesson as event or the lesson as "pure 'mobility'." The purpose of this chapter is to articulate the thinking of difference as difference and to think identity of the self-same event out (on the basis) of difference. This has repercussions for how we have to think (about) any object or (human) subject, for "insofar as I am actually experiencing an object, even if I do so by thinking of it, it becomes a changing moment in the ongoing event of my experiencing (thinking) it, i.e., it assumes the character of something-yet-to-be-achieved" (Bakhtin, 1993, p. 32).[1] Because it is an irreducible moment of the event*-in-the-making, the object, as I show in chapter 3, cannot be understood independently of it. Like the encompassing event*-in-the-making, in the happening there are objects*-in-the-making that are constituted by the changing whole as much as they contribute to constituting it (whole–part relation). With the curriculum as pure mobility, the object is not something constant and self-same but an ever-changing moment of that event*-in-the-making with an ending and outcome yet-to-be-achieved but inherently uncertain and unpredictable (unforeseeable).

The Living Curriculum as Event*-in-the-Making

Understanding lessons as events-in-the-making means that we understand their openness, for example, the gap between a lesson plan (planned curriculum) and the happenings from which the lesson as lesson emerges (enacted

---

1   In this book, I use the term "moment" in the dialectical sense of a constitutive part in its relation to the constituted whole and reserve the term "instant" to denote a period of time.

curriculum). Before and during a lesson, we, teachers, cannot ever know whether what is happening subsequently is denoted as "a successful lesson," "an unsuccessful lesson," or something else – that is, which kind of event they have been participating in – even though the likelihood of successful lessons tends to increase with professional experience (Tobin & Roth, 2006). In this sense, the living mathematics curriculum as event*-in-the-making is a draft *in* draft (flux) rather than a finished sketch that specifies the work to be executed. To understand the mathematics curriculum as event*-in-the-making, as something unfolding and never being self-same, that is, to grasp its eventness, requires situating oneself in the middle of the action. For "[i]f I abstract myself from the center that constitutes the starting point of my once-occurrent participation in Being.... then the concrete uniqueness and compellent actuality of the world will inevitably begin to decompose" (Bakhtin, 1993, p. 58). Methodically speaking, this implies that we have to take a first-time-through perspective of a happening, an attitude typical of ethnomethodology (e.g., Garfinkel, 1996), a point I develop in chapter 9. The following analysis takes us step by step through a lesson fragment by using forms of description that emphasize the unfinished and yet unknowable *what*, which we might say after the fact that *it* has happened. That is, I analyze the living curriculum from the perspective of the participating witness and through the theoretical lens of the event*-in-the-making – that is, without reducing what is happening to one of the moments of an (al)ready-made event accomplished and namable only after the fact. The entire Fragment 8.7 of an account concerning the incarnate nature of mathematical knowing (Roth, 2011a, p. 220) is taken up here.

The Invocation

> But the Saying extended toward the Said receives this tension from the Other, of Others, who wrenches words from me before appearing to me. (Levinas, 1978, p. 124)

The fragment derives from the first lesson of a unit on the geometry of three-dimensional objects in a second-grade class. The children have been asked to pull a mystery object from a black plastic bag and to group it with a set of existing objects or to begin a new set. At the instant when the fragment begins, Connor already has placed, after doing a reclassification that followed the teacher's request for an explanation, his mystery object. He squats next to the sheet of pink construction paper on which he has placed his object

Figure 2.1.   This artistic rendering of the classroom shows the physical relations at the instant of the conversation analyzed in the text. Mrs. Winter is seated to the right and points toward Connor on the left and the group of (cubical) objects at his feet.

and opposite from Mrs. Winter who is pointing in the course of much of the fragment towards the boy and "that group" of objects (Figure 2.1). Mrs. Winter is bodily oriented and points towards Connor and begins to speak. She begins with an interjection ("em"), followed by a sound "an" that we may hear as the connective "and" as soon as the interrogative "what" is forthcoming (turn 46).[2] As the words unfurl from her lips, her locution takes the grammatical structure of a (completed and understood) question even though the intonation is falling, typical for a constative statement, as Mrs. Winter arrives at what comes to be the end of her speaking. Her orientation and the fact that it is Connor's mystery object make it more likely that Connor is the intended addressee. But viewed from within the event*-in-the-making, we cannot know whether he or someone else is going to speak next and therefore will have contributed to constituting what exactly she has done with her words. (Transcription conventions can be found in Appendix A.)

---

2   A locution is one sided, it pertains to the physical production of sound, whereas an utterance is two sided, involving an articulation and its social evaluation on the part of the listener (Bakhtine [Volochinov], 1977).

46   W: em an   [↑what did we say that group was about.
                     [((begins to point to the group of cubes))
                     [((Connor gazes at her))

I stop the analysis here to ask what Mrs. Winter has done. Rather than assuming that she has asked a question – which already will have brought our cultural competence into play without marking it as such – we have to take our analytic position within the unfolding and unfinalized event*-in-the-making and see how the addressee is hearing what she will have said when the act of saying comes to an end. To understand speaking as micro-event*-in-the-making (rather than already-made-event), we need to look at its *internal* forces and relations, that is, we need to see and hear how and what the relevant members to the setting see and hear. But we cannot know what *Connor* (or any other participant) is hearing and seeing until he makes it available in his turn at talk. What will be the next thing that is going to happen? If Mrs. Winter could know with any degree of certainty what is forthcoming, then she would have been saying *exactly* what was required to allow Connor to reply so that he would learn a little more about proper geometric classification. At this stage, however, the reification of her locution as a question (rather than an insult, a solitary locution, or a way of re-orienting a student who is off-task) is only one possibility, and the very possibility of these different possibilities to hear a locution needs to be understood.

The possibility of possibilities denotes openness similar to that which we associate with a draft-in-the-making. A *realized* possibility, on the other hand, already has annihilated not only the possibility realized but also all the other possibilities that existed. However, this destruction of possibilities opens up and gives birth to new possibilities. That is, "the *realization of potential* is an *event* of neutralization" (Levinas, 1978, p. 69, emphasis added). The eventness of the lived curriculum is captured in this phase shift, that is, by the fact that at the instant that the possibility is realized it actually disappears as possibility and becomes actuality. The concept of the *realization of possibility* therefore captures the movement of the event*-in-the-making because it designates the destruction of a space of possibilities in the actualization of a particular one. But it is also a birth of new possibilities. That is, the eventness of the event, its very mobility, is characterized by the simultaneous disappearance (death) and appearance (birth) of possibilities in and through the actualization of possibilities. One way of thinking this movement that we call "the living curriculum" is to think of the realization of possibility, which is a process that annihilates and creates at the same time. Without the process, there is only possibility, and with the process, the possibility is destroyed. In this way, we capture precisely what the notion of écriture (writing) was designed to capture (Derrida, 1967), as a process of creation of new understandings and the erasure of what we have known before, spatializing and temporalizing the eventness of the event. It is also the process by which dialogue develops new ideas all the while sublating (rescinding and keeping) the old ideas.

In speaking for Connor, in addressing him, Mrs. Winter enacts a concern, a form of solicitude, an orientation toward the realization of possibilities, solicitude and anguish. Solicitude is oriented forward, toward possibilities and uncertainty; anguish is directed backwards, defining the person who this anguish is anguished about. "The project-in-draft and dereliction, 'Being-ahead-of-oneself' [l'être-au-devant-de-soi], and 'being-always-already in' [être d'ores et déjà dans] are concretely reunited in solicitude understood by anguish" (Levinas, 1996, p. 31). The very act of speaking, the invocation of another, constitutes and expresses this concern. That is, to understand what Mrs. Winter is doing as she is doing it, which is but a moment in and of the once-occurrent event*-in-the-making that is called the lived curriculum, we also need to understand its ethico-moral dimension, because "the ought is a distinctive category of the ongoing performance of acts or deeds [postuplenie] or of the actually performed act (and everything is an act or deed that I perform – even thought and feeling)" (Bakhtin, 1993, p. 6).

Because we do not know yet how the utterance has affected the one invoked and called upon, Connor or whoever will speak next, we cannot comprehend, from within the event*-in-the-making, the nature of what is happening. From within the event*-in-the-making, Mrs. Winter is an advenant[3], "which is the term for the human being [l'homme] insofar as something happens to him and insofar as by his ad-venture, he is open to the event" (Romano, 1998, p. 34). In fact, comprehension is not already comprised, because it can happen only when some part of the past can be captured as a whole. The event*-in-the-making – which is "coming at" Mrs. Winter and therefore is an ad-venture – precisely because of its horizon that is open to the future, exceeds Connor's intentionality (quite literally). It is only in and through what Connor or someone else will do or say – i.e., the articulated part of the response – that Mrs. Winter and every other witness[4] present in the situation will find out just what she has said/done

---

3   The concept of the advenant is developed further in chapter 5.
4   The concept of the witness is more fully developed in chapter 5.

and how it has affected him, cognitively and affectively. That is, *what* she has actually done will be available only after Connor will have finished a reply (if he replies at all), that is, through the effect that her speaking has brought about. But at the same time, if it turns out from within the event*-in-the-making that he has been the selected one, this answer was destined to be wrenched from his lips as the introductory quotation to this section suggests. This from-within perspective, therefore, explodes the general tendency to attribute cause, for in this situation there is no way anyone can say what Mrs. Winter is doing *while* she is *doing* it.[5] Causa, here, is attributable only after the fact – as Nietzsche suggests in the quotation opening this text; it is *added* to the event, an addition that attributes rationality to what has happened. Such addition leads us to a teleological account of events by means of cause–effect relations, a way of reasoning about events characteristic of metaphysical thinking (Heidegger, 1997) – which does not prevent it from being useful in the increasing levels of control humanity has had over its natural and social world.

In addressing another, Mrs. Winter also opens herself to what is coming – her locution becomes utterance only through the social evaluation that subsequently occurs. She does not yet know what the social evaluation will be that is going to be embedded in the subsequent locution, and to get to know it, she has to open up to be affected by whatever advenes. This introduces a dimension of passivity that makes the term *advenant* appropriate, for it is a "term for the human being [*l'homme*] as constitutively *open to* events" (Romano, 1998, p. 33, emphasis added). Openness means that we inherently cannot predict with certainty what is going to happen: As I work out further in chapter 8, an inescapable gap opens between the planned curriculum and the living curriculum. The very concept of the *advenant* changes the way in which we think (about) the subject of activity, as worked out in chapter 5, no longer solely in agential terms, but in terms of passibility and vulnerability, that is, the affectability by what is coming in the *ad-venture* of the event*-in-the-making and what is happening to the person. No curriculum plan can get Mrs. Winter ready for what is actually happening, what she is provoking in/ by invoking Connor.

---

5   Readers certainly are familiar with situations of this kind: A first speaker says something, the second says "You are hurting/insulting me!" and the first one says "I am sorry, I only meant to joke/say.…" Here, too, the hurt/insult is available only in and through the second locution, and the third locution now has to address the unintended but nevertheless actual effect.

The Response

To respond: to give a formal reply, to answer a summons to appear, from Lat. *re-*, back, again + *spondère*, to give a pledge or promise

From the perspective of Connor, towards whom Mrs. Winter has oriented herself and points (Figure 2.1), in listening to her he already has been exposing himself. This exposure is an integral part of his response. Without this exposure, he could not have been affected and replied (etymologically, to fold back [the topic]). Connor does not know what is coming at him as the words continue to unfurl from Mrs. Winter's lips: Is she making a statement, asking a question, speaking ironically? But to be able to reply at all, he first has to open up, to listen to what she has to say. In fact, this opening up by listening is the first part of his response, the being-affected by something that cannot be anticipated – not in the least because the current speaker, here Mrs. Winter, cannot know what she will have said in her saying until she has said it. Connor, too, is the *advenant* while Mrs. Winter is speaking. *What* is coming at Connor, which he cannot yet comprehend, for it does not yet exist as an object, he nevertheless witnesses, "but as a witness that does not *thematize* what it bears witness of" (Levinas, 1978, p. 229). As *advenant*, the subject is witness *in* and *of* rather than having knowledge about the event*-in-the-making. Not being able to thematize here means that he inherently cannot cognitively grasp what is being said – a moment of the event*-in-the-making – until the saying has finished and the said has become available.

When Connor will be answering, therefore, his reply has to be understood as the second part of the response. *To respond* – the irreducible {listening → replying} unit – therefore is diastatic, internally shifted with respect to itself (thus also dehiscent), and, therefore, constitutes a diachronic way of thinking about the living curriculum as event*-in-the-making. It cannot be explained in terms of cause and effect. What the preceding utterance is/was *becomes* something in and through the second moment of the response, which is as active as the first part during which the reply forms itself. That is, the reply forms itself before the respondent is in a position to *prehend* the content of the *saying* that is, the *said*-*in-the-making*, let alone comprehend it. The *what* that is affecting Connor becomes available to participants (Mrs. Winter, his peers, the researchers present) as such only in and through his reply, which is itself only a moment of the response, the other moments of which include active listening and being affected (pathos). From the perspective of the event*-in-the-making, Mrs. Winter, too, cannot know what she is doing while doing it. For example, that she is saying something unclear, incomprehensible, or non-intelligible – if Connor were to make such a suggestion – cannot be apparent to her while speaking. It becomes available to her only in and through Connor's reply. "Her" action, therefore, cannot be grounded in her own intentions (i.e., as cause) because from *within* the event*-in-the-making, the effect of her action is available only later. But to know any cause, we require knowledge of the effect. Her intentions therefore are exceeded by the pathic experience of being subject to something outside of her, literally by something that advenes to her from the outside, something that eventuated.

Let us pursue the analysis of the living curriculum*-in-the-making. Subsequent to Mrs. Winter's locution reported above, there is pausing, which provides Connor, Mrs. Winter, or anyone else in the room with an opportunity to speak. In fact, the expression "there is pausing" has a grammatical structure that explodes the cause–effect figure of reasoning because the process of pausing also is the subject. At the instant Connor does begin to speak, the pause-in-the-making has ended and its effect, the pause, has been 1.00 second (turn 47), which is longer than what teachers normally allow for students to answer. Here, with a speech intensity (volume) much less than normal, Connor articulates what culturally competent individuals tend to hear as a question*-in-the-making, because of the (a) interrogative at the beginning ("what"), (b) the interrogative grammatical structure of the utterance as a whole, and (c) the rising intonation towards the end (which turns out to be the end as Mrs. Winter is already beginning to take another turn while Connor is still speaking): "What do you mean like?" (turn 48). But right at the instance of the overlap (turns 48, 49), *while* their mutual speaking is still unfolding, we do not know what will be happening next. It is possible that Connor will continue to speak, elaborating on what he has said or providing some instruction. But it is also possible – a possibility realized in this situation – that Mrs. Winter continues to speak. At the instance of the overlap, neither participant can know what will come next, "who will cede" the speaking floor, and what will come thereafter.

47   [(1.00)
        [((Connor looks down at the group of objects))
48   C: <<p>what do you mean li[ke?>   ]
                                    [((Connor looks up at Mrs. Winter))
49   W: [WHAt]
                                    [((Mrs. Winter is still pointing, as in Figure 2.1))

In this instance, Connor takes a turn at talk but does not provide the reply to a question. The turn pair does not actualize a question–answer pair. Connor's turn marks the preceding locution as something unintelligible, the "meaning" of which he interrogates – if he is heard as asking a question. His locution constitutes an offer of a question* about the preceding locution, the nature of which still is not settled. Although Mrs. Winter may have intended to address Connor for the purpose of bringing him to understand geometrical classification, Connor now indicates lack of understanding what Mrs. Winter wants from him or what she wants to tell him. In fact, the extended pausing already is an indication that there may be a problem and that time is required to reply or for an answer to form (which is why teachers have been exhorted to allow for more time between the question* and the first student reply).

Here, then, something new has advened. If Mrs. Winter (could have) had anticipated his question*-in-the-making, why would she have produced a locution that Connor does not understand? This has implications, for "when we did not know before, then we cannot claim in the pathic domain that one could have known, if one had known more" (von Weizsäcker, 1973, p. 270). This non-understanding of the question*-in-the-making directed to-ward Connor – which is not yet a question because marked as unintelligible and unanswerable – is unintended and, perhaps, surprising. Such surprise is precisely what we express while coming face to face with the unforeseen. We cannot *comprend* (= comprehend) an event*-in-the-making as a thing (ob-ject) denoted by a noun because it is unfinalized and only a possibility, and that is why they may *surprend* us when we are *prehended* (taken) by surprise.

As Connor before, for Mrs. Winter to be able to *reply* – etymologically, from Fr. *replier*, to fold (the conversation) back (toward the other) – she has to open up and listen/attend to Connor; her opening up and listening constitute the first part of the response. This first moment of the response, therefore, is itself diastatically stretched from the instance she has stopped talking in turn 46 to the instant she starts talking again in turn 49. When we position ourselves at that instant when Connor and Mrs. Winter speak simultaneously and from the perspective of the event*-in-the-making, we may wonder about what will happen next. Will we be able to say after the fact that Connor has continued and Mrs. Winter has abandoned her attempt at making it onto the speaking floor? Or will Mrs. Winter con-tinue, thereby, in a way, cutting him off from clearly designating his turn as accomplished? At this instant of the overlapping speech, neither of our participants nor anyone else witnessing the event*-in-the-making *can* know what will be happening and how this simultaneous speaking will be understood.

Typical for an event*-in-the-making is that something that we cannot anticipate is happening to us, advenes to us. Thus, any turn, as a second in the turn unit to a preceding turn is only one moment of the saying (i.e., said-in-the-making); its other moment "is pathos, a term denoting that we are or have been affected by something in a way such that the *what-by* cannot be grounded in an a priori (forgoing) *what* nor in an a posteriori achieved *what-for*" (Roth, 2010b, p. 84). To more accurately theorize the movement in and of the event*-in-the-making we require passivity as an integral moment to the experience of the living curriculum. That is, the person to whom something is happening in the event has no way of grounding the event in a cause that precedes the instant; s/he cannot know what s/he is affected by or what s/he has been affected for. This, again, explodes any cause–effect figure of thinking about the event of which the turn pair is but a moment – just as it is suggested by philosophers who approach an event from its unfinalized nature. This requires us to think the living curriculum as event*-in-the-making, that is, to think the realization and destruction of action possibilities as movement-in-progress.

Responsive (Responsible) Responding

In this particular instant, Mrs. Winter continues whereas Connor has stopped speaking. When she stops speaking, Mrs. Winter will have produced question* – because of the grammatical structure – even though the intonation decreases, as if she has been asserting something. After she has stopped speaking, there is pausing. Mrs. Winter still is pointing in the direction of Connor and the group of objects on the colored sheet at his feet (as in Figure 2.1). What will Connor say this time? Will he say anything at all? Will what he says reify Mrs. Winter's utterance as a question? The pause still is in the making. And then it is Mrs. Winter who takes the speaking floor again. Grammatically, her locution, once finalized, has the structure of a question ("What is …?") but is again intonated like an assertion (strongly falling pitch, as denoted by the period "."). If the subsequent locution will have been treated it as a question, it would be the third instance of a question (in addition to the one aborted ("WHAt was the (0.15) WHat …" [turn 49]).

49   W: [WHAt] was the (0.15) WHAt did we put
                                     [(((Mrs. Winter is still pointing, as in Figure 2.1))]
        for the name of that group. ((still pointing))
50   (1.51) ((still pointing, then pulls hand back))
51   whats written on the card.
52   (0.83)

The turns 46–48 have raised an issue. Rather than settling it, the reply calls for a reply in turn. Culturally competent witnesses tend to hear Connor's utterance as a counter-question*-in-the-making (the hired transcriber of the videotape did hear it in this way, indicated by her placement of a question mark). But we have to ask, from within this event*-in-the-making, is it treated as such or does the following turn "turn" it into something else? If there is anything like a decision to respond, it cannot be logically derived from the preceding event*-moments, and it cannot predict what will happen. Instead of providing an answer, Mrs. Winter says: "What was the … what did we put for the name of the group?" (turn 49). If there were cause–effect relations operating then, why would Mrs. Winter intend asking another question (to which an answer might have to remain outstanding)? In fact, there is a reply, but it ends up as a 1.51-second pause (turn 50), stopped by another turn (a continuation of a turn) on the part of Mrs. Winter: "What's written on the card?" (turn 51). Again, we may be tempted to say that she has asked a question, but to understand her saying from within the event*-in-the-making, we have to await the reply to know whether it will have treated the preceding locution as such. In taking another turn, Mrs. Winter thereby acts upon the unfolding pause as if it were an indication that the called-for answer could not be provided or remained to come forth (outstanding). The pausing, a form of active non-action, calls forth a reply: It calls upon Mrs. Winter. There now have been five questions in a sequence.

Throughout this event*-in-the-making (at this point, we still cannot know what will have happened once everything is said and done, that is, the finalized and namable event), Mrs. Winter is pointing into the same general direction and towards the cluster of objects at Connor's feet (Figure 2.1); the pointing is but another moment of the event*-in-the-making. We may therefore understand it as a way of orienting others or as designating what is the topic of the locutions. So far, the three (and a half) instantiations of Mrs. Winter's question*-in-the-making may thereby be heard as being about the "group." The question pertains to "what the group is about," "the name of that group," and "what is written on the card." What will be happening next? Will there be further pausing? Will there be another counter-question*? Will there be an answer that can be evaluated in terms of its in/correctness? Although I have posed these questions, there is actually no time out from the event*-in-the-making for the actors themselves to ask these questions – at least not within the temporality of the happening that we witness here (if the participant were to ask these questions, then it would be a different event*-in-the-making).

There is more pausing. At the instant that Connor begins to speak with a subdued voice, the pausing has been longer than the amount of time teachers normally tend to wait for students to answer. "Squares," Connor whispers (turn 53). Is it a reply* to her question*?

53 C: <<p>squares>
54 W: ˇsquare an::d?
55   (0.20) ((Cheyenne moves forward, repeatedly points to the word "cube"))
56 J: cube
57   (0.25)
58 W: cube.

In the next turn, which follows without a noticeable pause to have occurred, Mrs. Winter articulates with initially falling then rising intonation toward what comes to be the end of the locution, "Square and?" (turn 54). There are multiple reasons for the first part of this locution to be heard as positive evaluation* of the preceding locution and as the (partially) successful completion of the preceding sequentially ordered question–answer turn pair. First, the preceding locution of the other is repeated with falling intonation, as this is typical for constatives (affirmatives). Moreover, Mrs. Winter utters the conjunctive "and" spoken with rising intonation – which both attributes correctness to the preceding word "square" but also, in asking* for something else to stand side by side with the affirmed "squares" – designates it as insufficient. We observe precisely the same structure in the turn pair that follows, thereby completing the initiation–response–evaluation (I-R-E) structure of the sequence of turns 54 through 58.[6] Cheyenne moves forward and points repeatedly to the part of the label where we see "cube" (turn 55), and Jane says "cube" (turn 56). "Cube" (turn 58), Mrs. Winter repeats with falling intonation typical of a constative. We note in this instance that Cheyenne and Jane,

---

6   I-R-E or IRE is a sequentially ordered turn-taking typical of schooling, where a teacher initiates the sequence by asking a question, a student responds, and the teacher evaluates the student's performance. That is, the teacher takes the first and third positions in the exchange, and students take the second position. This sequence has cultural-historical significance, because it constitutes a corrective mechanism by means of which the reproduction of cultural practices is achieved.

rather than Connor, complete the sequentially ordered question–answer pair, even though one might have assumed that Mrs. Winter, based on her orientation and pointing, has designated Connor to speak. That is, although her intention *might have been* to call for *his* response, the event*-in-the-making takes a different turn as per what is actually happening. Now that Cheyenne and Jane have provided replies, the situation is different: There was a possibility for Connor to reply but he has not replied. Others, however, have done so.

Mrs. Winter, still oriented toward Connor, immediately continues producing yet another question*: "Does it meet the criteria of having the square or the cube?" (turn 58). She solicits* *him*, rather than anyone else, including the two peers, who, in their ways, have answered in the place of Connor. This increases the likelihood that the turn 54 was actually intended for him and because he has not replied, Mrs. Winter calls on him again. We may gloss this instant in this way: She "knows" that the other two students know, but she wants to find out whether Connor knows.

Following a very brief pause, someone on the floor whispers "no," followed by another pausing before Mrs. Winter, physically oriented toward Connor (again addressing *him* rather than someone else) is taking the speaking floor: "Do you think it does?" (turn 62). Again we might ask, what will be happening next? How will *Connor* reply if he replies at all? Here, someone else answered, but, as the repetition of the question* with a stern gaze and orientation toward Connor might surmise, *he* is asked to answer and not any answer – e.g., one provided by another student – therefore fills the bill.

58   W: cube. does it meet the criteria of having the square or the cube?
          ((looks at Connor sternly, nods while talking))
59   (0.25)
60   X: <<p>no>
61   (0.25)
62   W: do you think it does?
63   (0.84)

"Like what do you mean?" (turn 64), Connor says. We find here yet another form of repetition, where the student says the same words as the preceding speaker, something we have already seen as the second turn in a question–question sequence that opens this analysis. Here, the very nature of the question* as question is raised. Connor's locution is an acknowledgment of the address that has occurred, it realizes the address as an address, and it questions* this address designating it as not making clear what is meant. A longer turn follows. It begins with a segment structured like a question but intonated in the way of a constative. There is a constative statement about what has been said before, which is that "this group was square or cube." This is followed by another locution segment structured and intonated as a twice-uttered question*: "Does it match that?" (turn 66). Again, we can hear Mrs. Winter elaborating on her earlier question*, translating it for the benefit of the student who indicated that what she has said was insufficiently intelligible. At this point, we could ask the same questions that we asked before about Mrs. Winter not phrasing her questions in a way that Connor would understand.

```
64   C:   like what do you mean?
65        (1.10)
66   W:   <does it match. We said THAT this group ((points)) was <squa::re
          (0.31) or cube (0.49) ((looks at Connor, nods)) does it match that?
67        (0.41)
68   X:   <<pp>yes.>
69        (0.48)
70   X:   or::.
71   C:   ((gazes at teacher)) yes.
72        (0.70)
73   W:   <<p>o>kay. () ben you wanna add? ((nods in direction of Connor))
          () thanks connor.
```

There is a brief pausing brought to a close by someone saying "yes," followed by an "or," before Connor, gazing straight at the teacher, says "yes." There is another pausing, which Mrs. Winter brings to an end by saying "okay" (turn 73). She continues inviting* Ben to add. By nodding in the direction of Connor and saying "thanks Connor," she marks the completion of the exchange with Connor.

Rethinking the Living Curriculum as Event*-in-the-Making

Understood as a (micro-) event*-in-the-making, this fragment from a mathematics curriculum that real people have lived and lived through – a constitutive moment of a lesson, itself a moment of "life-as-event," "world-as-event," or "Being-as-event" which are the ultimate all-encompassing events* (Bakhtin, 1993) – has neither Mrs. Winter nor Connor as their causal agents. We cannot fully explain what is happening when we focus on the individual agencies of Mrs. Winter and Connor or the sum (seriation) of these agencies. There is a synergistic effect of their relation that is in excess of any agency that we can conceive of. They are (passive) *advenants* with respect to the unfolding event*-in-the-making, which they cannot yet comprehend as event because of its unfinished nature with an end result that unforeseeably emerges from the relation. Will Connor have learned? Will Mrs. Winter have succeeded in teaching (allowing Connor to learn)? While what will have been the event is in the making, there is no answer to these questions, for during the eventing, before we were able to name it this or that (kind of) event, it "does not have a cause and does not plead for any cause, especially not its own" (Marion, 2010a, p. 282). The event*-in-the-making has only itself to accomplish itself: *"it passes and comes to pass, therefore it renounces that which is not itself"* (p. 282, original emphasis).

There is eventing, unfolding, and advening that is in excess of anything that Mrs. Winter and Connor could have intended to happen. Because eventing exceeds intention and intentionality, because they do not cause the course the eventing takes, the event*-in-the-making is not homogeneous. If the event*-in-the-making were the sum or intersection of individual intentions, then we would not require meetings, such as those making decisions about research grants or tenure/promotion. We would not find pleasure in watching sports events if the outcome could be determined based on the abilities of each player. We would simply use an algorithm to compute the end result based on the combined individual evaluations or abilities of all participants. Events*-in-the-making are incalculable (non-computable), precisely because new possibilities continually arise in and with the realization of previous possibilities; and this trajectory brought about in the constant death and birth of possibilities cannot be anticipated. We can think of a decision point in terms of branching points (bifurcations) in chaos theory, where a system takes on new values that cannot be derived based on the values it has had prior to the bifurcation.

Of Causes and Effects – Critique of the Metaphysical Approach

> An event as unitary and self-equivalent is something that could be read post factum by a detached (non-participating) consciousness that is not interested in the event; yet even in this case there still would be something that remains inaccessible to it, namely, the very *event-ness of the event*. (Bakhtin, 1993, p. 16, emphasis added)

Classroom episodes such as the one presented in the preceding section tend to be analyzed in terms of causes and effects. For example, researchers might take individual lines, such as turn 46 or 49, and treat it as "asking a question," which then has as its effect a student response (or lack thereof). Or Connor might have been said to have "constructed" "meaning," where Connor would be the cause, who, through the intentional action of constructing, would have brought about "meaning" as an effect. Such cause–effect thinking is typical of metaphysics, the epitome of which is technology (Heidegger, 2006); the cause–effect figure of thinking "is the father of metaphysics" (Maine de Biran, 1852/1952, p. 129). The conclusion that there is an agent to each change is a "mythology" because it separates the act from acting (Nietzsche, 1954c). Thus, the event*-in-the-making is better captured by the verb "to event," which is turned with hindsight into a subject ("the event") that is distinct from has been happening. To learn is different from what has been learned (i.e., the difference in knowledge). As a result, the phenomenon no longer becomes: It has become a thing that does something. As pointed out in the introduction of this chapter, Nietzsche denotes this as the double error of theorizing. Thinking learning in terms of knowledge, an invariable substrate, and a variable accident, leads us to miss learning as a process of continual knowledge*-in-the-making. Thus, "Only through the seduction of language… which understands and misunderstands all effectuation as conditioned by a cause, by a 'subject,' may things look differently" (Nietzsche, 1954b, p. 789).

The analysis of practical action into a cause (e.g., the intention, the motive) and its effect is problematic because a "performed act or deed is split into an objective content/sense and a subjective process of performance" (Bakhtin, 1993, p. 12). That is, the sense or reason of the act (intent) is split from the actual performance, from which springs forth the outcome. In this way "an abyss has formed between the motive of the actually performed act or deed and its product" (p. 54), between the mind and the sensual practical action of the person, and between theory and praxis. As a consequence, the product of the act has been "severed from its ontological roots" (p. 54). The situation cannot be corrected by thinking the living curriculum from the perspective of the product (enacted curriculum), but rather we have to think it from within the unique eventing itself. This is so because "at the basis of an actual deed is a being-in-communication with the once-occurrent unity" (p. 56), which, viewed as a unity, cannot be understood in terms of the separated causation and effect.

In metaphysical approaches – to which since Karl Marx many philosophers have counted all forms of constructivism – processual phenomena, which are inherently non-self-identical, are thought in terms of concepts that focus on the identity of phenomena (concepts) with themselves. Thus, for example, learning is thought in terms of the difference between states of knowledge (before, after) rather than in terms of learning as knowledge*-in-the-making. Educators (reviewers of papers) may ask, "*What* has Connor learned?," and expect that the authors state some outcome. Thought in this manner, learning loses its eventual characteristics, and becomes subject to the cause–effect relationship. This is so whether learning is thought as the outcome (result) of teaching or whether it is thought in terms of the construction of knowledge, because in each case the subsequent knowledge state/structure is the result (effect) of an action mobilized by the intent to act (cause), whether this action is thought as external or internal to the person. It is in any case external to the phenomenon, in this situation, knowledge, which is *acted upon* in such a way that it changes to a new state. We may think here of Piaget's description of cognitive development in terms of the subject's (mental) actions upon its preceding (material, mental) actions.

The classical (metaphysical, constructivist) approach assumes that the curriculum*-in-the-making is present to us in the present, that is, that we comprehend what is happening at the moment that it is happening by means of representations (or re-presentations). In other words, this approach assumes the presence of the totality of the present in consciousness. But apart from the fact that even experienced scientists have been shown to find out *what* they have done *following* an entire day of work (Roth, 2009), the presence of the present is a logical impossibility, for it requires the curriculum to be present in its finalized form, *as* inner-worldly fact; it is also impossible because the representation would have to include itself as a moment of presence. But Kant (1956a, b, c) and Hegel (1807/1979) already knew that living thought and the object of thought cannot ever be the same. The said is not available until the speaker has finished his/her saying, which therefore requires us to await the end. Thus, amiable conversations among partners or friends sometimes turn into (unintended) arguments; a street gathering may turn into a riot (Vancouver Hockey Riot 2011); a protest march into an uprising (Arab Spring 2011); or expert think-aloud protocols may turn into tutoring sessions (Roth & Middleton, 2006). In the course of the conversation*-in-the-making we do not know what kind of conversation it will have been when all is said and done.

Thinking the Event*-in-the-Making

> The event arrives, or rather it happens to *me* [m'*arrive*], by surprising me, and by befalling me unexpectedly. (Marion, 2010a, p. 286, original emphasis)

Characteristic of the event*-in-the-making is that something-yet-unknown is arriving, happening to and overcoming us, thereby befalling and affecting

us. It is not even a *something*: it only will have been something when all
is said and done. Until then, we have but eventing. Moreover, the future
perfect tense suggests that something will have been. But from within the
event*-in-the-making, we cannot ever anticipate the arrivage: There is
always an excess of what we experience over what we anticipated – i.e.,
of intuition over intention. The description and analysis of the classroom
episode show that it is impossible to evaluate what a locution is doing independent of the effect (perlocution) associated with it. This is so because
if Connor had responded in turn 48 by saying, "Don't insult me. You are
treating me like a baby," then, for the purpose of understanding what is happening at the instant, we would have to take Mrs. Winter's locution as an
insult. The effects, thereby, come to be the origin of the attributed causes;
ultimately, then, effects are at the origin of the causes that are said to have
brought about the effect. This form of reasoning, the attribution of causes
once we know the effect, as per the introductory quotation to this chapter,
in fact negates the cause. To get us out of this theoretical quagmire, we need
to abandon the belief in cause–effect relations and accept the event*in-the-
making in its irreducible, originary sovereignty. The living curriculum is not
some complete entity but an unfinalized event*-in-the-making. We might
therefore use the now-obsolete verb *to event* to point us toward the eventing
of an event*-in-the-making.

Etymologically, the term Lat. *ēvent-us* means occurrence, issue, from
ēvenīre, to come out, happen, *ē-* out + *venīre*, to come. But events have
endings, they come to be understood as events in and through what they
have eventuated (product). Event*-in-the-making means *to event* and *to
eventuate* simultaneously and inseparably. To eventuate is used synony-
mously with to actuate, to realize, to make real. Yet we tend to understand
the living curriculum in terms of what it eventuated, that is, only after
the fact. That is, event*-in-the-making makes us think the process of
coming out (e-vent) and arrival (ad-vent) together, a process of coming
and becoming (*venīre*). Already-made events therefore will have arrived,
something will have arrived that is not knowable or foreseeable before
that as a *what*; it is unforeseen and undetermined, "i̶t̶" "i̶s̶" not. This view
invokes the passive side of human experience: "I consider everything
that is becoming or that arrives anew is generally called by philosophers
a passion on the part of the subject to whom it happens, and an action
in the eyes who makes it arrive" (Descartes, 1679, p. 2). But thinking
the living curriculum participatively, as a process, requires us to think

more than merely "to arrive" and "arrival." In the arrival, something arrives. Arrival therefore implies arrivage: that which happens to or befalls one. That which arrives, like the end result of a meeting, cannot be anticipated with certainty – though it may be considered before in terms of different possible outcomes.

The *event supervenes*: it comes on and occurs as something additional, as something that *cannot be* foreseen because it is unseen and therefore unforeseen. As the fragment unfolds, in fact constituting the ultimately enacted curriculum as such, Mrs. Winter *finds* a manner of asking the question in a way so that the called-for answer does *eventually* come forth – she does so not directly but what will have been the successful approach emerges after several attempts (a cognitive psychologist might use the concept of trial and error). Here, the verb "to find" implies something that is not readily available but something that is hidden or even unseen/unheard of; there is a degree of fortuity and something accidental about it. The manner of speaking so that a question will have arrived and will be calling for the response by calling on the respondent is not available beforehand, it cannot be anticipated with certainty. In this situation – as in others that have been described in the literature (e.g., Roth & Radford, 2011) – it involves seeking and *finding* a proper pedagogy. As our fragment shows, the seeking and finding are collective processes irreducibly involving Mrs. Winter and Connor.

For us to comprehend the already-made event means being able to apprehend it in the way we apprehend objects. To be an event*-in-the-making, the happening that will be denoted as the specific event has passed – otherwise we cannot *re*present it, make it present again – is subject to *eventual* closure: but then, it no longer is eventing. The living curriculum as event*-in-the-making cannot ever be an *ob-ject* (etymologically, something thrown [*jicere*] off thought that is standing over and against [*ob-*] the witnessing subject). An (already-made) event no longer is passing and unfolding but *has to have been* so that we can name it by some concept: "scaffolding," "an instance of the zone of proximal development," or "a teacher guiding a student to a realization." A happening can become a French Revolution or Arab Spring only when this revolution/spring is available as a whole, because prior to closure it is possible that what is in the process of happening will eventually turn out to be an unsuccessful uprising or a failed coup d'état. In 1956, what was happening in Hungary turned out to be an uprising that cemented the Soviet control over Central Europe rather than bringing about a change typical with a revolution. At the instant of the first writing of this paragraph, January 2012, we did not know whether what was happening in Syria would be a revolution or an uprising; at the moment of the editing of this paragraph, the media speak of a civil war where both sides have committed atrocities; what the event*-in-the-making will have been when everything has been said and done still lies unpredictably in the future. On the other hand, what we today know as the *French Revolution* now is considered a period, which the name denotes as a thing that comprised change and transformation.

Thinking the event*-in-the-making means participatively thinking an internally differentiated, non-self-identical unit, which, precisely because it encompasses everything, cannot be rendered in terms of cause–effect relations. Comprehending an eventing as event*-in-the-making requires not only historical thinking – which is impossible because we would not ever be able to achieve closure – but also unhistorical thinking. This is so because the "unhistorical is similar to an encompassing atmosphere in which life generates itself only to disappear with the destruction of this atmosphere" (Nietzsche, 1954a, p. 215); and it is also so because "pure givenness cannot be experienced actually" (Bakhtin, 1993, p. 32) requiring abstract categories instead. It is when we stop the happening – by partializing life, turning it into an object of thought by making it present again (i.e., *re*present it) – and make it the object of thinking that we in fact destroy the eventing and only have an (al)ready-made, finalized event: But in this destruction the event*-in-the-making becomes accessible to us vicariously in thought.

As a coming – in French we would say *à venir* (to come), which implies *avenir* (future) – we have to think the event*-in-the-making in its singularity, that is, also as a one (unit). It is singular because it never happens in this way ever again, it is "once-occurrent," and it is singular because it is a one. As a one, it also is a plurality, which manifests itself in the different ways that the event may appear. We can think these relations in terms of the realization of one of many possibilities, arrival and concretization of an eventing that is annihilated at the time. If there is only one possibility, there is certainty rather than possibility. When we speak about possibility, there is a plurality. This plurality collapses into a one, into certainty, with the concretization (arrival) of one possibility becoming certainty. But in this arrival, what have been possibilities no longer exist because these have been destroyed with the concretization of one of their own.

While the living curriculum is unfolding, for example, during Mrs. Winter's turn 46, we cannot say what *is* (the case, truth), because there is only becoming. In chapter 1, I describe the puzzle of Schrödinger's cat.

When the box is opened, we find the cat either dead or alive. But while the box is closed, there are only possibilities, one of which becomes certainty in and through the opening of the box and the observation that ensues. Just as we can only say that we will find the cat to be dead or alive (in terms of possibilities) without being able to say *what* the cat *is*, so we cannot ask about an *eventing what* it *is* until after the process has come to a close so that we can grasp it as a *thing*. While there is eventing, we have an irreducible plurality of possibilities (each with a probability of $0 < p < 1$), one of which is going to be realized, and, in this realization, this possibility is going to be destroyed because it has become actuality (with a probability $p = 1$, all others with a probability of $p = 0$). Thus, "*the event is nothing other than this impersonal reconfiguration of my possibilities and the world that advenes into a fact and by means of which it opens a fissure in my own adventure*" (Romano, 1998, p. 45, original emphasis). *Eventuation* is the name for the process of destruction of a possibility (all possibilities) as possibility in the event, which furthermore gives rise to a whole new set of possibilities. In quantum mechanics, observation is the process during which the eventing is destroyed to yield one manifestation; physicists call what is happening the "collapse of the wave function," the movement from possibilities to certainty.[7]

After Mrs. Winter stops speaking, even pausing opens and closes possibilities; the longer pausing lasts, the more likely is the probability that Connor cannot or does not want to reply. The pausing may give us access to thinking the event*-in-the-making because we cannot causally attribute it to Mrs. Winter or Connor or anyone else present. But in this pausing, we have a shift (change) in possibilities, and it is this shift itself that is constitutive of time. An event*-in-the-making is not *in* time – as Kant (1956a) thought, time as the a priori condition of experience – but is constitutive of time and experience. The displacement and dehiscence of event*-in-the-making and its comprehension in/as a finalized event – creating "room, place, space, or interval, *khôra [chōra]*" (Derrida, 2000, p. 13) – are constitutive of diachrony and time. Thus, to get us closer to the participative thinking of the event*-in-the-making, we need to insist on "self-inadequation, non-coincidence, dehiscence, fission, interruption, incompletion, and the visible body openly gaping, the hiatus, eclipse, and inaccessibility of this plenitude" (p. 239).

---

7   The wave function is not something that can be observed. It is a way of representing all the possibilities in which a quantum system may manifest itself once observed and the temporal evolution of these possibilities.

The Abyss in the Unity of the Event*-in-the-Making

> The name that doubles the *being* [*l'étant*] it names is necessary to its identity. (Levinas, 1971, p. 33)

An abyss is opened in the act of naming, an eventing comes to be treated as an event, a self-identical, namable thing (being, *Seiendes, étant*): this (happening) *as* that (category). The theoretical problem in thinking a living curriculum arises from the fact that on the one hand we have a dynamic, inherently open and unfinished eventing, and on the other hand we want to talk about this happening as a finished thing.[8] "Naming…constitutes identities" (Levinas, 1971, pp. 27–28), it "articulates the *ideality* of the same in diversity" (p. 28, emphasis added), and thereby loses the "modification without change, the phase shift of the identical" (p. 26). This loss leads to the difference between the (diachronic) Saying, as happening, and the (synchronic) Said, as what resulted from (of) the happening. There is an abyss, articulated at the end of the preceding subsection, which creates a tension, for the Saying only tends toward the Said, with which it is never identical. Because at the instant of the transcribed fragment, this moment of the living curriculum is still unfinished, the participants cannot grasp what is happening to them – other than that they are together in the same mathematics lessons, without, however, being able to anticipate its future course – until a finalization will have occurred. This finalizing closure is brought about in the conclusion of the relations concerning Connor's mystery object (his turn in the game). In the end, therefore, once the participants have concluded the episode, we can characterize (categorize) what has happened (it now is concluded) as some particular event. Mrs. Winter has asked questions and Connor, with some delay and helping, has answered.

Scholars using a Vygotskian framework might be tempted to say that we have observed an instance of the *zone of proximal development* (see chapter 6 for a development of this idea), a linguist might observe an *IRE*-type event, and a conversation analyst might characterize this as an instance of conversational repair to get a particular kind of answer realized.[9]

---

8   Using a simple (phenomenological) exercise, we can experience how eye movements *make* a "cube"; and without the eye movements, there is no cube but only indistinct grey (e.g., Roth, 2012).

9   Elsewhere I show with classroom examples that even grammar, the closing of classroom episodes, and other aspects of the living curriculum are *collective* achievements rather than things determined by this or that participant (Roth, 2010b).

It is only at this point that cause–effect relations may be attributed, for example, were we to say "Connor has had difficulties comprehending," which "required Mrs. Winter to spend an extra effort in helping him understand the question." In this case, Mrs. Winter's actions are determined to be the causal antecedents of Connor's comprehension. This is so even if we articulated the situation in more radical constructivist terms, for example, as "Mrs. Winter's making it possible for Connor to construct meaning." Here there are two agents, one bringing about an enabling situation, which is the causal antecedent of another cause, Connor's construction, from which "meaning" results as the effect. We cannot say that he is constructing "meaning" rather than doing something else until this "meaning" is available to us in some finalized form.

It is quite clear that we can make such causal claims only when some end result is objectively available (i.e., as object of thought), for in the course of the eventing (e.g., the construction of "meaning"), we do not know whether what we will have attributed after the fact to the actions has actually done what we claim it to do. This is so because the fact that two actions are aligned in a necessary sequence *does not mean* that they stand in a cause–effect relation; only metaphysical logicians are used to and accept the "presupposition that thoughts cause thoughts" (Nietzsche, 1954c, p. 728).[10] Will (intention) is *not* the cause of action, as I outline in chapter 1, so that it is only a (metaphysical) *belief* that the sequence of thought following another thought constitutes a causal relationship. Each thought in fact is only a one-sided reflection of the event as a whole.

There is therefore a gap between an open and unfinished happening and the things to which it gives rise (i.e., arrive), and there is a gap between the happening and the name attributed to it (the happening as finished that can be named). The gap is of the same kind as that which exists between the curriculum as plan – which also is the description of what has happened when everything has gone "according to plan" – and the curriculum as something living and lived through as witness (see chapter 8). When we think the curriculum as living, however, that is, when we participatively think the unfinalized *eventing* or event*-in-the-making rather than a completed already-made event, then we aim at the "verbality of the verb itself by ceasing to name actions and events" (Levinas, 1971, p. 26). That is, in curricular terms, we aim at *learning* rather than the change in knowledge

10   Nietzsche's own example is the natural number sequence 1, 2, 3, 4, 5.

brought about by constructions and teacher interventions. Only when the living curriculum ends, when it no longer exists, can we name *what* has happened and thereby arrive at an inner-worldly fact (Lat. *fact-um*, thing done, past participle of *facēre*, to do).

In the case of the event*-in-the-making, therefore, com*prehension* always arrives late. In fact, comprehension itself *constitutes* this delay, produces and provokes it. An abyss thereby is opened up for thinking the eventing of the living mathematics curriculum – between the happening and its outcome, which alone allows us to comprehend and name just *what* has happened in the now past. Only the event can be an object of reflection, because, qua *object* (i.e., *re*presentation), it can be placed before the mind's eye. This abyss is not a problem – the problem arises when we think the living curriculum only in terms of outcomes and add to the dead event causes. Such causes are not available to us during the event*-in-the-making because we *cannot* grasp in its (completed) entirety what is happening, and therefore cannot know what is causing what.

There are suggestions that events "can be described only participatively" (Bakhtin, 1993, p. 32). But describing a happening participatively, from the position of the participating witnesses, means no longer having a god's-eye-view that gives the event as a whole. The perspective guards us against doing Whig history by constructing teleological accounts of the living curriculum based on the cause–effect figure (scheme). Comprehension requires an object (flux cannot be *held*), which no longer is open as a happening with an uncertain outcome. We may then appropriate the event as such – and in this "ap-propriation resonates essence of that which speaks as language" (Heidegger, 2006, p. 48). Although it is the completion of the event*-in-the-making that leads us to the name, event*-in-the-making and already-made event belong together:

> "Identity"
> as event
> does not tolerate a proposition as that
> which properly is saying it –
> the saying of which
> belongs to it (the event). (p. 97)

Here the philosopher refers us to identity as an event*-in-the-making that does not tolerate, in fact is destroyed in the naming but requires the name to be comprehensible. But without the (al)ready-made event, we could not predict recurrences in the flow of life. This is so because "[t]he world which appears to you in this way is unreliable, for it takes on a continually new appearance; you cannot hold it to its word" (Buber, 1937, p. 32). But because we cannot hold to it by placing it in representations, the flow of life "has no density, for everything in it penetrates everything else; no duration, for it comes even when it is not summoned, and vanishes even when it is tightly held" (p. 32). The living object*-in-the-making can be finalized to become an object, "for yourself, to experience and use; you must continually do this – and as you do it you have no more present" (p. 33). That is, at the very moment that we have something to hold onto and prehend, the present has actually gone and we have nothing but the past made present again by means of representations.

There is both an abyss and a possibility, for when we conduct analyses from the perspective of the non-repeatable eventing, then we are confronted with objects*-, entities*, or world*-in-the-making (see chapter 3). This is so, for example, for the country of Italy in Bakhtin's (1993) analysis of a Pushkin poem: "The experiencing of Italy as event[*-in-the-making] includes, as a necessary constituent moment, the actual unity of Italy in unitary and once-occurrent Being" (p. 71). To participatively think the event*-in-the-making, "[w]e have to think the object from the phenomenon [i.e., event] and not the phenomenon from the object" (Marion, 2010a, p. 281).

Naming what is happening by means of a verb, however, does not get us out of the aporia yet, because we are naming again. Yet when used in a "predicative proposition," the verb "becomes the resonance itself of being heard as to be" (Levinas, 1971, p. 34). Thus, "Socrates socratizes, or Socrates is Socrates, is *the way* in which Socrates is" (p. 36, original emphasis). The equivalent in curriculum theory would be the statement that the learner learns, which points us to a process rather than to a state. There is therefore a "unitary two-sided reflexion" (Bakhtin, 1993, p. 14) between the content and living performance of the practical act, which binds them into a unitary whole. In other words, content and performance are but two moments of a single whole; and to understand the two, we have to approach them through the whole, itself an unfolding process. That is, the reason for an action and the practical action itself cannot be separated without losing the phenomenon (see chapter 9). But losing the phenomenon is what happens when we think about actions in terms of cause–effect relations.

· 3 ·

WORLD*-IN-THE-MAKING

Representation is a presence that is presented, exposed, or exhibited. It is not, therefore, presence pure and simple: it is precisely *not* the immediacy of the being-posed-
there but is rather that which draws presence out of this immediacy insofar as it puts
a value on presence *as* some presence or another. (Nancy, 2005, p. 36)

[T]he event of once-occurrent Being…cannot be determined in the categories of
non-participant theoretical consciousness – it can be determined only in the categories of actual communion, i.e., of an actually performed act, in the categories of participative-effective experiencing of the concrete uniqueness of the world. (Bakhtin,
1993, p. 13)

In the book's epigraph, Nietzsche (1954c) suggests that as soon as we grasp
cause–effect thinking as an artifice, the ideas of a thing in itself, its appearance, and their opposition crumble. When we attempt to understand the
world* as a whole and in its making, that is, as life, as becoming (in) continuous flux, then thinking in terms of self-same things does not help. The
things, to which causes are attributed and the things that have been affected,
in which the effects are noticeable as such, are but fictions. This does not
mean that these fictions – i.e., things made, from Lat. *fingēre*, to fashion, form
– are not useful. Rather, these fictions are the result of a "will" that allows
control and predictability: "Life is based on the supposition of the belief in the

durable and regularly-recurring; the mightier life, the broader has to be the divinable, simultaneously *manufactured* world. Logicalization, rationalization, systematization as expedients of life" (p. 541). Whereas this way of thinking gives us a considerable level of control over our environment, it does not assist us in our attempt of understanding the continuous becoming of the world, the Heraclitean flux of life.

In the first introductory quotation to this chapter, Nancy makes the difference between presentation and representation, which is a presentation of something not actually present by means of something other, a substitute. Without such a substitute, we would not be able to intentionally search for a thing that is hidden or out of view, because it is precisely the capacity to make it present again in our minds in the form of a sign (i.e., the *re*presentation) that we can have the intention to look for the thing that the sign stands in for. We are not born with this capacity to make present something that is absent. As I point out in chapter 1, Piaget's research showed that only around the age of 8 months something like "object permanence" is observable in infants' behaviors. Something that I do not know, and, therefore, something for which I do not have the means to *make present again*, cannot be the object of intention. There is therefore a learning paradox: how can we expect learners to orient toward learning some *thing* (concept, skill, generalization) if, precisely because learners cannot make the thing present by means of a substitute, they cannot *aim* at learning it, make it the *ob-ject* of their intention. There is no intention without object (Husserl, 1976); and there is no intentional learning without transitive, intended object.

In this chapter, I describe how the things that populate our world are the effects of knowing*-in-the-making that cannot be anticipated. Much like children, any person has to learn to see, a process that is not entirely and not even originarily in the hands (eyes) of the learner. Thus, it is said with "good reason ... that in infancy we had to anyhow learn to see things and that this had to genetically precede all other modes of consciousness of things" (Husserl, 1973, p. 112). Here, "genetically" refers to the developmentally prior situation. At this stage, in early infancy, when the child does not yet have the representations that adults use to make the world present in their consciousness, "the perceptual field *that gives beforehand* does not as yet contain anything that might be explicated as a physical thing in a mere look" (p. 112, emphasis added). It is only once we have seen, and formed the capacity to make this now visible present again when it is absent, that it can also be the object of our intentions. Importantly, there is a perceptual field that gives before it contains some thing. The ascent from the unseen into the visible, the invisible living work from which the thing arises, is the parallel of the ascent from the event*-in-the-making to the (al)ready-made event.

The Problematic of Intentional Learning

The world of aesthetic seeing, obtained in abstraction from the actual *subiectum* of seeing, is not the actual world in which I live, although its content-aspect is inserted into a living *subiectum*. … In the content of aesthetic seeing we shall not find the actually performed act of the one who sees. (Bakhtin, 1993, p. 14)

Learning means coming to know some*thing* new, something one does not already know. This something is the intentional object of learning – generally stated in the curriculum objectives. Learning refers us to the birth of objects and concepts that come to populate our world. But these things are themselves effects of perceptual processes, which come to event for a first time in the initial learning process. If these things do not yet exist for me, the learner, "how can I intentionally aim at learning something that I do not know?" To give this question a concrete context: How could Christopher Columbus intentionally sail to the *Americas* given that he did not know they existed? In fact, the very structure of the preceding sentence points us to a problem: the Americas are presupposed to exist and to be discovered when in fact there is nothing a priori that would allow us making a discovery. The question itself has come to be known under the name of *learning paradox* but has never been satisfactorily answered though some have tried (Roth, 2011b). To frame the question in perceptual terms, how can I intentionally look for some*thing* that I do not already know and therefore do not know what it looks like? This *thing*, as the Husserl quote states in the preceding section, is not yet contained in the perceptual field. How can I take aim at some*thing* – like hunters aiming at game they intend to kill – that I have never seen or heard about, and therefore do not know? How can learners, in a science demonstration, know *what* to look for and therefore learn what the teacher wants them to learn when precisely this *what* (thing, idea, concept) does not yet exist in the (eidetic, physical) field? Take the following episode from an Australian 12th-grade classroom, where the curriculum plan has specified what is to be learned about the physics of rotational motion.

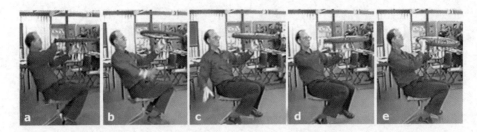

Figure 3.1. A teacher shows a demonstration and then asks, "Did you see it?"

In this episode, the teacher sits on a rotating stool holding a bicycle wheel in his left hand (Figure 3.1a). He pulls on it (Figure 3.1b) so hard that the hand continues to travel after having let go of the wheel (Figure 3.1c). He then grabs the wheel again (Figure 3.1d). Just after Figure 3.1e, he says, "Did you just see it?" The interrogative structure of the locution – which has the grammatical form auxiliary verb-subject-main verb – and the rising intonation in the locution toward the end both allow the culturally competent listener to hear a question. What were the students – who are presumed by the utterance to be culturally competent individuals – to have seen just prior to the utterance of the sentence? What is the *it*, the something (object, event), that they were to have seen? What can I see in the sequence of images when I do not already know what the demonstration is to exhibit? Was I to see that he pulled the wheel, the one he is gazing at intently during the event*in-the-making? Was I to see that his body moved a bit? Did the teacher want me to see that he leaned backwards? Was I to see that his foot touched the ground? As with any other manifestation of the Heraclitean flux, there is a potential ambiguity in the events can be taken from the fact that the teacher, when there was no answer, invites the students again, "Look again!" He continues, "Look at my my my body, main[ly]." This instruction – if I, as a student, actually hear the utterance as such – tells me to look mainly at the body. That is, from the multitude of things that I can see, the movement of the hands and feet, it is *mainly the body* I am to look at. But what is it in the body that I am to look at and see?

For the person competent in physics it appears to be self-evident that it is the body movement relative to the movement of the bicycle wheel that we are to see. Seen from the top – which the students do not do – the wheel spins counterclockwise whereas the body spins clockwise. When the teacher grabs the wheel (Figure 3.1d), his body moves counterclockwise back into its original position. That is, there are two complementary movements. *This* – the "two" "movements" that are "complementary" and in "opposite" "direction"

– is what I have to see to understand that the lesson will be about the conservation of the angular momentum. From the plenitudes of the happening, *this* ("it") has to settle out as the set of (al)ready-made facts. Seeing what has happened in the way described is required to understand the physics ideas: The momentum is zero to start with; because the system is closed (i.e., the teacher sits on the rotating stool) so that if a momentum is observed in the wheel an equal and opposite momentum has to be observable elsewhere in the system, here the body and seat of the stool.

Some readers may consider these questions to be academic. It turns out that these are not academic questions, but serious questions that we need to pose and answer through appropriate research. Thus, in the Australian classroom, I had wondered about what students were actually seeing while watching a demonstration like the one featured in Figure 3.1.[1] Several weeks after the students saw this one, we conducted a similar demonstration but asked them to write on a piece of paper what they *predict* they will have seen after the forthcoming demonstration. In the new demonstration, which the students had already seen before, the axle of the bicycle wheel was perpendicular to the axle of the rotating stool. Because the two axles were oriented perpendicularly with respect to each other, the person/stool should not rotate because there was no degree of freedom for the opposite movement so that the total angular momentum could be conserved. We then asked students to *observe* what they had seen and note the observation on their answer sheet. Finally, they were asked to provide an *explanation*. It turns out that out of the 23 students present, 18 clearly had seen movement and 5 clearly had not. When there are contradictory observations or explanations in the classroom, one popular teaching strategy among teachers is to count and "let the majority decide." In this situation, this would have been detrimental, for to be consistent with the theory of the conservation of angular momentum, no movement, as predicted by five students, should have been seen. It turns out that these five students used explanations more or less consistent with the scientific canon. The explanations of the 18 students, though all rooted in physics concepts, were inconsistent with the canon regarding this demonstration.

We now have to ask questions such as, "What sense did the students make of the original demonstration if they did not see what they were supposed to

---

1   We published a study in which we provide a response to the question why students often fail to learn from demonstrations: there is lots to see when we do not already know what to look for or why the monstration is a demonstration (Roth, McRobbie, Lucas, & Boutonné, 1997b).

see?" The teacher clearly had used it prior to talking about the conservation laws concerning the angular momentum, which were observed in the present case because the total angular momentum was *zero*, the situation after he spun the wheel also has to add up to zero: The angular momentums of the wheel and body/stool are equal and opposite, thereby cancelling each other. Thus, if students had not seen *that* movement required this relation between the two angular momentums then there would be serious problems, for they would have to somehow combine whatever they have seen and the equation that the teacher wrote on the chalkboard.[2] If we, researchers studying the living curriculum, want to be serious about understanding learning as a moment of the Heraclitean flux of life, then we have to have explicit formulations of this problem: How can we expect students to intentionally orient toward and look for the learning object – here learning the law of the conservation of angular momentum – when they do not know it, have never heard of it (in an understanding way), and have never seen it? Take the following analogy.

A host has gone to the airport or train station to pick up the guest whom s/he does not know. How can the host identify the person when everyone coming off the plane or train is unfamiliar to them? We often see many people standing there on the platforms or baggage collection exits with signs containing names. In this situation the host is letting himself be identified by the guest. The identification of the correct person then is the result of a donation, the guests giving themselves to be known, facilitated by the written name that serves as a mediating device. The notion of *donation* is deliberately borrowed from Marion (1998), because, as I outline below, learning something new is to a great extent something that *happens to* or *is given to us* as much as being the result of our intentional action. This passive dimension in learning is, as I show in *Passibility* (Roth, 2011b), both a challenge to constructivist approaches of all brands and a phenomenon generally not attended to by scientists studying student learning.

The case of the students in the physics classroom is worse than that of hosts looking for their unknown guests, for the former know at least to be looking for a person. (Sometimes the host has not arrived, which adds to the challenge.) As seen in the preceding episode from my research, the students,

---

2   For those with a knack for physics and mathematics, this equation is at work: $L_{TOTAL} = L_{STOOL} + L_{WHEEL}$, where L refers to the direction and magnitude of the angular momentum (it is a vector quantity). If $L_{TOTAL} = 0$ and the axles of stool and wheel are aligned, then the total momentum after spinning will also have to be 0, in which case the stool rotates in the opposite direction of the wheel.

not knowing physics, could not know what to look for and pick out from the micro-event*-in-the-making – and, as my descriptions and questions suggest, there was so much to see: a super-abundance of the seen. The teacher had done the demonstration twice, saying after the first time, "This wheel is not, this chair is not very good." So here, when he is finished with the saying, he will have said something about the wheel and the chair. In the course of my research I have come to the conclusion that we need to think about learning, teaching, and curriculum development in terms of the *invisible*, from which the *unseen* and, therefore, unforeseeable, makes its ascent to the seen. It is this process that constitutes the work of learning. If the students do not get to do *this* work, they literally will not be able to see and understand and may say, "I don't see it" or "I don't get it." They say this because what is currently invisible, this law of the conservation of momentum and the associated set of observations – cannot be aimed at, a fact that can be expressed in French with the neologism *invisable* (based on the verb *viser*, to aim at). This then allows me to pursue the learning paradox in terms of a problematic already treated in philosophical terms: how from the invisible, what initially is unseen rises to be seen in art (Henry, 1988; Marion, 2005) and the givenness as a fundamental dimension of human existence. Although I began to raise associated questions about 17 years ago, I have only recently developed the means to capture the problematic theoretically. I develop the dimension of pathos, and the associated dimensions of passivity, in chapter 4.

Learning Something New: An Experiment

> The sent happens this way or otherwise and always remains in coming. In this coming it can only be thought by taking it up and keeping it as the coming. Considered from the real [*vom Wirklichen*], that which is coming [*das Kommende*] is the not-yet-real, but is the already "operative" "unreal." (Heidegger, 1984, pp. 159–160)

During a stay in the section "Neurosciences and Cognitive Sciences" of the *Hanse Institute for Advanced Studies* (Delmenhorst, Germany) I took the stated problematic head on. While analyzing the videotapes collected during a 20-lesson tenth-grade high school physics course on static electricity, I also conducted an inquiry into the experience of learning and into the process of *coming to know*. I wanted to put myself into a situation similar to that of the physics students where I was learning something new that I could not aim at because I did not know the phenomenon before it revealed itself. I had been inspired by a series of publications concerning first- and third-person methods (e.g., Varela, 1996; Varela & Shear, 1999) and therefore kept daily notes not only about my learning while analyzing the video – my third-person perspective on learning – but also about things I noticed while riding the bicycle through the countryside for pleasure or while riding to the university. Most important for my research, I designed an experiment for the purpose of tracking knowing, learning, memory, noticing something for a first time, and so on. In this experiment, I would take the same tour for 20 days in a row. Preceding each trip, I would write down everything I anticipated seeing – an empty set on the first day, because I had never been where the trip would take me. Upon returning, I would note what I remembered having seen. The tour turned out to be about 25 km in length, taking me from the *Institute* outside the city, through valleys and fields, through an extended forest, and back (Figure 3.2).

Today I know that while I am riding, an event*-in-the-making is unfolding. There is a passing by of the world, and what I will have remembered are effects of processes, micro-events*-in-the-making that are part of the whole. From the perspective of what I know today, I would anticipate that the world of the trip is a world*in-the-making, as more and more things and phenomena come to stand out that initially did not exist for me. But let us turn to what happened then.

As the study unfolded, I noticed many interesting phenomena. One stood out in particular. Already on Day 5 of my experiment, I had noted, all of a sudden and completely unexpectedly, white posts on the side of the road. Then I realized that they came in what appeared to be regular intervals. Finally, I discovered that every now and then there was a number associated with the post, which I took – because they increased or decreased by 0.1 – to be distance markers. That is, once I had noticed the posts, a whole new set of actions became available and my agency expanded. Two days later, I was struck even more – as if someone had punched me hard squarely in the face. On the side of the road I saw twin silos. They are so big that they can easily be found on aerial photographs, sitting about 40 meters apart at a distance of 200 meters from the road (Figure 3.3).

These twin silos were part of the unseen and, in a process of phenomenalization too quick to be captured, had become visible and, thereby, had come among their own. Something had affected the retinas before I had come to see, and this affectation likely had occurred on the preceding days as well. But there was nothing like an active interpretation that led to the emergence of the twin silos: they are not the result of a construction. If anything, these had been totally unexpected and had been given to me as a gift in a process of

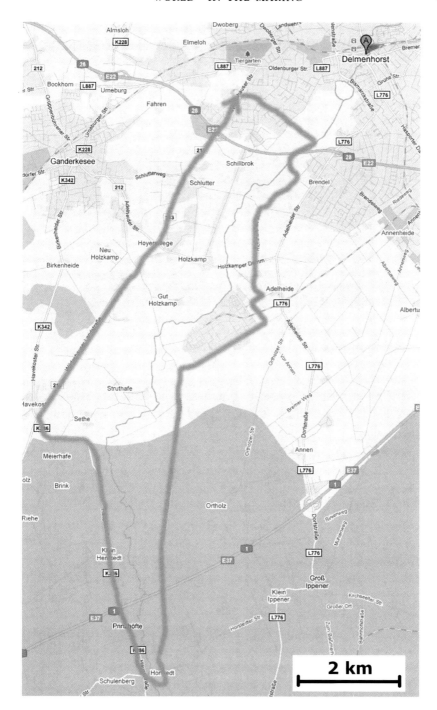

Figure 3.2. Map of the route taken for an experiment on learning and memory.

Figure 3.3. The areal photograph gives an idea of the size of twin silos that only revealed themselves during the sixths trip past them and their distance from the road (bottom right). (Map
data © 2012 Google)

donation. This donation, a process of phenomenalization, constitutes learning
or knowledge*-in-the-making. But now that I had come to see the twin silos,
I saw them every time I was passing on this country road, that is, on the 13 days
that followed this momentous seventh one. Whatever work is required to see,
was (invisibly and unnoticeably) happening with me. The twin silos had become an objective presence, and I could make them present again even when
I was in my apartment up to the present day.

A slew of what will have been questions began to arise and unfold in
my mind following the emergence of the twin silos in my perception. How
could I not have seen these twin silos on my first or at least second ride? The
realization emerged that I could not have answered questions about the twin
silos following my six earlier trips, and, during an examination, would have
failed *even though the examiners could have thought that I had had already* six *times
the experience*. At the time, I am in the process of coming to understand that
I could not have aimed at seeing these twin silos precisely because I had no
clue about their existence. I was in a situation not unlike that in which students find themselves when science teachers set up "inquiry learning." How
was I to know that from whatever was imaged in my retinas, these twin silos
were relevant and not something else? There is nothing that "construction"

of my experience would have allowed me to arrive at the twin silos, because nothing that *was given to me in my perception* would have lend itself as material to "construct" anything useful from it. From the Kantian and constructivist perspective, the image of the twin silos has to have stood out for the associated representation to operate so that I could see the twin silos as such.

An objection someone might raise is that a teacher could have told students to look for the twin silos. But in this case, the student would have had to know what a (twin) silo is. Such is the case when the 12th-grade physics students are to learn about angular momentum when they do not know what angular momentum is. The teacher could repeat the words many times over and write them on the chalkboard, and the students would still not be able to deliberately orient themselves towards angular momentum because they do not know the concept (the sound-word "angular momentum" is not the concept). Even when there is the possibility of a mediational term, such as in the case of the physics classroom above where the teacher said, "Look at my my body, main[ly]," there is no guarantee that student will have seen what the teacher intended them to see. As that research project in Australia showed, quite the contrary is the case.[3]

Another important question during my inquiry was, "How did these shapes come to stand out against everything else [in the landscape] as a ground?" Why *these* shapes and not some other shapes that could have become figure against ground in precisely the same setting, such as specific trees, the fields between me and the twin silos, or any other manifestation that could have arisen from the ground? I attend to answering these questions in the next section and return to the bicycle trip just after the twin silos emerged into my conscious awareness.

As the questions emerged into my consciousness and raced through my head, I experienced another shock: I realized that I had forgotten the world that existed for me before. Now I was thinking about a world populated with the twin silos, and I asked questions such as "How could I not have seen the twin silos?" My new world, in its coming, has erased the old world. In fact, because there were new entities and phenomena that I was becoming aware of every day, my world was not constant but a world*-in-the-making, a continuous birth and death of my road-trip world. This is why the concept of *writing [écriture]*

---

3   During a series of John Dewey lectures, I used the drawing of a cube (see Figure 3.6 below) and told the audience that there were two cubes that one could see and also described what had to be done to see them. Two days later, two audience members admitted not to have seen the second cube. That is, despite knowing that two cubes could be seen and despite the descriptions of what to do to see them, these audience members did not see the second cube, which they could intend given that they already knew what there was to be seen.

(on the magic tablet) is so powerful (Derrida, 1967), because it captures this disappearance of the old world with the arrival of the new one; but the old world is not totally forgotten but is giving our newly emerging worlds their historically contingent natures. *Writing* is *erasing* all the while it is creating. The questions that arose into my mind, however, presupposed the existence of the silos prior to my first actual experience of them. I was thinking in terms of a stable world. The thought emerged that if there had been a teacher with me, presupposing a world in which the silos existed, s/he would expect and anticipate me, the student, to see the twin silos, whereas I could not intentionally look for them.

Today I realize that this is precisely where Jean Piaget and his constructivism are wrong. He assumes that there are (mathematical) structures in the world, which children (he considered them to be little scientists) can discover. Thus, he assumed children to look at and interact[4] with a balance beam and then, depending on their developmental stage, *abstract* a more or less mathematical pattern (Inhelder & Piaget, 1958). But to do so, one has to see the weights *as* weights and distances *as* distances, which is absolutely not the case even among older students who might orient, for example, toward *locations* and number of objects suspended (e.g., Roth, 1998). Even mature scientists may see one aspect, such as the slope of a curve, when the relevant values required in solving a problem with the graphs they are looking at are the absolute values of the curve (Roth, Pozzer-Ardenghi, & Han, 2005). There is nothing, I realized, that children can inherently abstract from the balance beam much in the same way that there was nothing for me to abstract the twin silos from the perceptual experience. *These things did not exist for me.* I lived in a world *without* twin silos. The twin silos came into existence for me in a process of phenomenalization, rising to the seen from the unseen.

For teachers, *therein* lies the quandary. Having forgotten about the world without the twin silos, they can no longer *empathize* with the children and students, who inhabit a world that they have forgotten. They inhabit a world that they must forget unless they are to drown in the co-presence of all the worlds that they have lived in before. As I was able to experience, this world is in continuous flux because there is an excess of intuition over intention: with every bicycle ride, there was a super-abundance of new features that had

---

4   The term *interaction* is highly problematic, for it reifies persons as self-sufficient subjects as if they could be identified individually and separate of context. A better term is *trans-action*, which emphasizes the mutual constitution of people and their social and material context (Dewey & Bentley, 1949/1999). Here, I retain the word interaction when it appears in quotations but avoid using it in my own voice.

come to stand out for me. Today, I know that learning is associated with a form of amnesia, a forgetting of the world in the ways we know it: learning is like writing that is erasing at the same time, without time out and continuous precisely like the Heraclitean flux. To be an effective science teacher, therefore, I have to engage in a process of anamnesis, a process of recalling things (worlds) past. I then understood an aspect of my own teaching: Because I had failed, and therefore had to repeat fifth grade, I could later understand what it means not to see what the teacher wants a student to see.

In all of this I was a learner on two planes: My road-trip world has expanded, become populated with an increasing number of features that stood out. Simultaneously, I was learning about learning, questions were arising into my consciousness, of which I was not the agential causator. In the same way that the twin silos were given to me without my intention having played any role in it, the subsequent thinking was coming to me, and thoughts and questions resulted in a continuous process of generation of new possibilities of thinking when a new thought or question had advened.

Learning and Intentionality

The verb "to construct" is a transitive verb, which means that there is something that passes from the subject of action to the *object* of action. This same object constitutes the force that orients *intention*. It therefore does not come as a surprise that in the constructivist paradigm, claims are made about learning as the result of intentional engagement with the tasks that teachers pose to them. Thus, students are said to construct their knowledge (structures) to make it increasingly viable for navigating the world. In the absence of the (an) object, I cannot intend orienting towards it, as all intention requires an object. The constructivist theory therefore begins with phenomena and associated concepts that any learning theory has to endeavor to explain: "the ability to establish recurrences in the flow of experience," "remembering and retrieving (re-presenting) experiences," and "the ability to make comparisons and judgments of similarity and difference" (von Glasersfeld, 1989a, p. 128). I show below how the perspective I develop explains the origin of remembering and representations that allow the establishment of recurrences. However, for many years, as science teacher and as researcher, I had also thought in the constructivist manner – until I became increasingly dissatisfied with the blind spots of the theory. Thus, the experience of the twin silos and what I learned from it have changed the ways in which I think about learning generally and about its relation to intentionality specifically. This change has not come once and for all but is a continuing process that reveals new aspects every time I revisit the experience. But there is still a long way to go from this understanding to the point of having good examples and developing a good theoretical description. Both of these *came* or *were given to me* – perhaps because I was sensitized to a particular kind of need – in the way of (a) a familiar kind of image and (b) the phenomenology of perceptual learning.

First, in the course of our lives (at least in Western cultures), we encounter pictorial puzzles where we have to find something already known to their designers. Children are asked to find a certain (familiar) figure in a complex picture – as in the well-known children's book series "Where Is Wally?" – and adults may be asked to find some thing hidden in a field of splotches (Figure 3.4). How can you look for something specific in such a field when you do not know what it is? You may look and look, perhaps rotate the page to look from another side. But if you do not know what to look for, if you do not already know how Wally looks like, then there is little you can do until some *thing* is given to you in your perception. There is an extended unseen, and you cannot know what it might reveal. As soon as some*thing* appears as some thing, it is seen, just as something appeared to me that I came to know as the twin silos. This seen, as my experience has shown, after the fact is interpreted as having been unseen before, no longer invisible but precisely unseen. When you look at Figure 3.4, the unseen that you are looking for

remains, up to the point of its final appearance, unforeseen – unseen thus unforeseen. The unseen, or the unforeseen par excellence. Like death, which (in principle) is not here so long as I am here, the unseen remains inapparent as long as it is, and disappears the moment that it appears as visible. The unseen appears only in order to disappear as such. Further, one is not able in any way to foresee the new visible in terms of its unseen, which is by definition invisible. (Marion, 2004, p. 28)

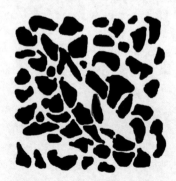

Figure 3.4. A perceptual puzzle.

How can something inherently part of the invisible or unseen be seen if I cannot intend seeing it? By means of which process does what will have been seen – i.e., the now visible – arise from the currently unseen? It is that which I cannot see that must be part of its own emergence into my perception and consciousness. That is, it is what has become visible after the fact that has to provoke its own aim/intention, which alone renders it accessible. Thus, that which will have become visible precedes its aim. The now visible, "[c]oming among its own, it had to note that its own did not foresee it and therefore rendered itself [surrendered itself to being] visible by them" (p. 33). Here we are confronted with an apparent contradiction, which only resolves itself in a perspective of the event*-in-the-making. The now visible must provoke the intention that makes it visible; this happens when the now visible is not yet visible at all but, in retrospective, while it is still unseen. That which is seen precedes its aim. The unseen already affects the learner in what comes to be the first moment of learning, the ascent from the unseen to the seen. In other words, that which is seen cannot be anticipated because it does not exist for us. But together with the visible comes the associated intention to see: I have no trouble seeing the twin silos from the country road or finding the hidden image in Figure 3.4. Readers will be familiar with such perceptual puzzles where, after gazing a while or after someone shows (describes) what there is to be seen, one comes to see this thing. Now that we have seen this thing for a first time, we can easily make it present again and therefore represent it as often as we wish.

The now visible has come among its own, exists, qua visible thing, among other visible things. But these other visible things – in edu-talk, the "prior knowledge" – did not allow the newly visible to be foreseen, much in the way I could not foresee the twin silos from the other, preceding experiences along this country road. These twin silos *rendered themselves* (surrendered themselves) *visable*, something that can be aimed at, by everything visible to me at the moment. But without my riding along this road, these twin silos never would have been a possibility. That is, to understand the way in which the newly visible comes into existence, I cannot think in terms of what is already seen and subject to intention, precisely because the visible "did not foresee it."

By the time readers arrive at this paragraph, I hope they have tried to see what there is to be seen in Figure 3.4 (that which I want them to see, like the Australian physics teacher expected his students to see one among many possible things). I have drawn the splotches such that once you know how to look, once the unseen has revealed itself and has become visible, you see a killer whale. (If you have not seen what there is to see, Appendix B.1 outlines

the hidden figure.) If you have not seen it yet – or if by some chance you have
seen something else – you may want to return to find it. Now your search
will be facilitated, especially when you already know and have had perceptual
experiences with killer whales generally and with this kind of killer whale
specifically. If I had said that there is an *Orcinus orca*, the scientific name
for this species, it would not have helped you: There would have only been
a sound pattern that linguistics transcribe using the International Phonetics
Alphabet as /ˈɔrkinəs ˈɔrkə/ or /ˈɔrsˌʌɪnəs ˈɔrkə/ (or some regional variation of
the pronunciation). That is, if the Australian physics teacher above had told
his students to look for the "angular momentum," or had shown them arrows
pointing up and down, the students would still not have had enough to *see*
the phenomenon. They could not have seen it because, considered a future
perfect perspective, the angular momentum was still hidden in the foliage of
the ground (of the perceptual image) from which the students had to extract
it. That this was the case, as I further explain in the following paragraph, can
be gauged from the fact that these Australian students did not understand a
gesture by one of the researchers thought to be pun and therefore a joke.

　　The researcher in question had given the students a "thumbs up," by means of
a familiar gesture that tends to be used as an alternative, stand alone expression:
the hand being curled, thumbs sticking up (Figure 3.5a). Thumbs up is a sign of
approval, acceptance, or encouragement. Viewed in this way, the researcher was
providing the students with some form of positive feedback or he might have
thanked them for participating in the research project while they were completing the task, that is, as a living moment of the curriculum*-in-the-making. But
there is much more to it, only visible to the person already competent in physics. Unbeknownst to (most of) the students, the gesture is part of the answer to
what they were to see and learn from the demonstration. They could not see
this pun ("get" the point of the joke) precisely because they did not know angular momentum so that the point of the joke will have revealed itself to them
only after the learning object (angular momentum) also will have revealed itself
to them. The gesture is the answer, and in fact a mnemonic device for thinking
about angular momentum, where the "right hand rule" states that if an object
rotates in the direction of the fingers of the fist, then the angular momentum is
represented by a vector in the direction of the thumb (Figure 3.5b). The other
researchers saw (got) the joke and grinned, whereas the students, not yet knowing the concept of angular momentum and the representations thereof *could
not* see that the researcher had actually provided them with the correct answer
to the problem they were working on. This can happen only when they see in

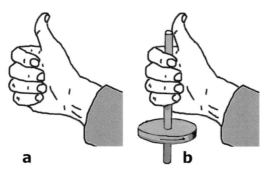

Figure 3.5. The "thumbs up" gesture (a) may in fact be a signifier of the "right-hand rule" (b), which relates the orientation of rotational motion and the vector of angular momentum (thumb) that represents it.

the events of Figure 3.1 something that can be modeled by a physical concept denoted in Figure 3.5b. This concept is signified by the curled hand, which presents the direction of the turning wheel again, and the thumb then points in the direction of the angular momentum (Figure 3.5a).

The Work of Seeing and the World as Independent Galilean Object

True beings are lived in the present, the life of objects is in the past. (Buber, 1937, p. 13)

In the introductory quotation to this section, Buber distinguishes between the way in which the world appears in the flux of life, on the one hand, and the life of objects, which, living their life through representations, inherently are present to us in the past. For Buber, then, "the object is not duration but cessation, suspension, a breaking off and cutting clear and hardening, absence of relation and of present being" (p. 13). But objects, representations, allow a certain stability precisely because the flux of life has ceased in them. Objects and representations, as stable entities, are sedimentations or condensations from the flux of live. They have to be *made* rather than existing as such.

In the previous section I note that the seen precedes its aim,[5] which may lead some readers to think that I am back to presupposing the physical world that exists

---

5   This structure is of the same kind as the one that Vygotsky (1989) describes for the emergence of pointing gestures in children. First there is a haphazard movement, which, in and

independent of the living being. But this is not so. What I attempt to understand and theorize is how some*thing* comes to be seen in a process evidently dependent on the perceiver – e.g., the process of the phenomenalization of the twin silos in my perceptual experience – and only then, by some process to be explained, takes on an existence independent of the person (in the way twin silos come to have existed all along). Although philosophers have worked on this problem for quite some time, neither their interests in it nor their findings have made it into the common knowledge or into scientific investigations of curriculum studies.

Object*-in-the-Making → Object* → Object

It is generally well known that the world is not independent of perception for most organisms, which tend to be living in the here and now. This independence of the observing process and the world itself is a historical achievement that was initiated by Galileo. A popular adage capturing this fact is "out of sight, out of mind," used frequently in the context of a dog that abandons a chase when the prey no longer is visible or when its scent is no longer present. Very young children, too, do not recognize the world as a stable context populated with permanent though temporarily invisible features. Thus, "if a 7- or 8-month-old child is reaching for an object that is interesting to him and we suddenly put a screen between the object and him, he will act as if the object not only has disappeared but also is no longer accessible" (Piaget, 1970, p. 43). In fact, Piaget could have formulated this statement much stronger, and thereby might have come closer to the truth. It is not so that the object has merely disappeared and is inaccessible. The object does not exist for him when it is not present; and, therefore, the child cannot intend reaching for it. This does not prevent the recognition of the object when it is itself present. That is, at this stage there is pure presence unmediated by representations that make the object (without asterisk!) present again. It is in fact an object*-in-the-making that is an integral aspect of the event*-in-the-making.

We, adults, do have experiences where objects are on the borderline between subjective experience and objective existence: they are objects*. For example, when we perceive a sound or shadows in the house and think someone is present, we might then walk about to check only to realize that the object*-in-the-making has been a figment of our imagination – unless

---

through interaction with a significant other, comes to be reified as a pointing gesture as the latter brings objects in the general direction of the movement closer to the child.

we actually find someone (e.g., a thief) present. Scientists, too, have to go through all sorts of work to make sure they have a fact rather than an artifact of the investigation (Garfinkel, Lynch, & Livingston, 1981). When a signal* in the laboratory recurs – in repeated trials under different, controlled conditions, i.e., as signal*-in-the-making – it becomes a signal detached from the process of investigation and from the instrumentation. But when the signal* does not recur or recurs only sporadically and without apparent reason, the scientists constitute it to be an artifact that belongs is attributed to some other moment of the event*-in-the-making. Scientific research is interesting because the process of coming to see, object*in-the-making → object* → object is slowed down so that one can actually observe the phenomenalization itself, whereas in situations such as the twin silos or the killer whale (Figure 3.4) it is so fast that we no longer notice the work that goes into phenomenalization.

If I had been a child of less than 8 months, then the twin silos would not only have disappeared but also would not have existed for me once these were out of sight. Their existence would have been a function of pure being*-in-the-making: these are present or not present but cannot be present in their absence. To exist independently of the present, the child has to become able to *make* the object* *present again* even in its absence – the child has to be able to *represent* the object. It is precisely then that the objects specifically and the entire world generally become independent of my world*-in-the-making. Without this capacity of making present another present, a phenomenon would no longer exist once it has stopped (Husserl, 1980). That is, a child becomes capable of stepping out of pure Being (*sein*, εἶναι) precisely at the point when the capacity emerges to think Being in terms of beings (*Seiendes*, τὰ ὄντα), stuff that points to other stuff and therefore serves to represent the latter (Heidegger, 1977b). *This* is what Nancy articulates in the quotation that opens this chapter – representation is not "presence pure and simple," "*not* the immediacy of the being-exposed there," but it is something that draws its own "presence out of this immediacy." For the adult, there already exists an independent world so that we experience a new object as something that was simply unseen prior to the instant where it is an object*-in-the-making. We update our representations of the world and forget the one that existed prior to the instant when the heretofore unseen begins to reveal itself, as object*-in-the-making, among other visible things. But, to reiterate the main point of the present investigation, this independence of the world, the permanence of objects in their absence, is not possible without representation.

Phenomenalization: Object*-in-the-Making

Up to this point, we have not yet considered the following questions: "How does the reduction occur whereby an object*-in-the-making that is an irreducible moment of the event*in-the-making becomes an object?" and "Why, once we have seen an object for a first time, do we remember it and can see it any time we so desire?" In the course of my inquiries into the learning paradox, the following exercise has turned out to be instructive. Take a look at Figure 3.6 before continuing to read. What do you see?

The figure is a well-known feature among perceptual scientists (psychologists) and goes under the name of Necker Cube. Although there are only black lines on a plain white surface, most people see one or both of two differently oriented cubes in three dimensions. (If you do not immediately see one or the other cube, it is even better, as you might experience the process of phenomenalization right here and now.) One cube is seen from the bottom and extends to the back and left; the other cube is seen from the top and extends to the back and right (see Appendix B.2). What is it that allows us to this or that cube? That is, what is it that allows us to see a three-dimensional figure where there are only lines on a flat surface? And, what is it that makes us see one versus the other cube? The answers reveal themselves when we try to quickly go from one cube to the other. Look at the lines (Figure 3.6) so that you see the cube from the bottom extending backwards to the left. Close your eyes. Open them again but with the intention to see the cube from the top extending backwards to the right.[6] Practice until you can quickly flicker your eyes and rapidly shift between the two perceptual experiences. What are your eyes doing during the closing of the lids and while intending the second cube? You may realize that when your focus falls near the bottom intersection within the figure and moves parallel to "the exposed side" (i.e., parallel to the line from the intersection diagonally "backward" and left), then you see a cube from the bottom. Doing the same but from the upper intersection on the inside of the perimeter moving toward the right and "backward," then you see a cube from the top.[7] That is, the object is an object*-in-the-making, because your eyes have to move to see: The three-dimensional cubes exist only in the making, in the movement! The eye movements bring either one or the other

---

6   Of course, you can have such an intention only when you already have seen this cube, which is precisely one of the main points of this chapter.

7   If these instructions provide you with trouble, Appendix B.2 shows where to focus and how to move your gaze; on the trouble. On the problem of following instructions, see chapter 8.

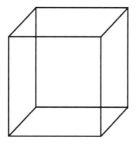

Figure 3.6. The Necker Cube.

cube to life. Without *this* movement, only lines will appear on the page. More-over, without any movement at all – which takes a lot of practice or a special device that psychologists use to fix an image to a constant location on the retina – not even the lines will be present and the perceptual field dissolves into an indistinct and indescript grey (e.g., Roth, 2012a).

Some readers might think that this makes perception entirely subjective. But this is not so: because I am able to instruct others what to do to experience in the way I have experienced it, the cubes are *instructably* present and there-fore objective. That is, the world is objective precisely because everyone can experience it in and through their subjective (eye) movements; and, as the neologism "instructably" makes thematic, the movement can be taught[8] and learned. Geometry is an objective science precisely because each individual human being can reproduce it – independent of location and historical time – in and through her actions, producing the same diagrams and proofs (Husserl, 1939). Each diagram and proof thereby serves as an instructional object, like a recipe, that makes it possible, though without providing a guarantee, that others will do precisely what it takes to reproduce the diagram and proof in and through their own subjective actions. It is in the living work that we find the geometrical object*-in-the-making. Without this living work, there sim-ply is no geometrical object. That is, the finalized object always already is the result of living work, always already is an object*-in-the-making and only as such can ascent to the finalized object.

We now have the first two moments required for understanding why some physics students saw the motion that the teacher intended them to see or for

---

8   The relation between "teaching" and learning is of the same order as that between a recipe in a cookbook and learning to make the dish: the novice cook learns to see in her action the relevance of the instruction. See chapter 8 for elaborations of these and associated ideas.

me to see the twin silos. To see anything at all, the eyes have to move *between* the thing that will have been seen – the teacher, twin silos, lines – and the ground against which the figure comes to stand out against and become salient (from Latin, *salīre*, to leap).[9] A second kind of movement is required *within* the object*-in-the-making so that it can become *that* finalized, structured object that it is. In the case of the twin silos, the eyes have to move so that the resulting object becomes a silo rather than something else (or remaining ground); in the case of the cube, the eyes have to focus on a particular location within the context of the figure and then move in a particular direction for this or that cube to appear as the finalized result of the movement. In the case of the killer whale (Figure 3.4), the eyes have to find the right beginning and then stabilize the internal field required to see the structures of the killer whale and then move away from it to stabilize that figure against everything else, which becomes indistinct ground. That is, the killer whale is *continuously in the making* rather than being made and remaining. Even when we make the killer whale present again, the movement or some mirror image thereof (see below) has to be made. The killer whale exists only in the perpetual making it present.

But, we might ask, *how* do your eyes know how to move so that from the patches emerges a killer whale and so that from the lines emerges a cube (or two cubes in alternation)? It is the thing itself that directs (affects) the eye even before the eyes voluntarily focus and follow certain features in a movement that makes the newly seen become visible. This movement lies entirely outside the realm of our intentions. We can provoke its coming by engaging for an extended amount of time with the image, by looking, for example, for a long time at the splotches (Figure 3.4), by rotating the page, by squinting – that is, by means of many of the practices that in the past have helped us to see a situation differently, "under a different light (angle)," so to speak. The movement of the eyes is guided by following lines, colors, and patches until a something *almost* instantly appears, the twin silos, the Dalmatian doggy, or one or the other cube. That is, *we are willing recipients, hosts, to this new thing that is* given to us *in our perception* rather than merely active constructors / interpreters of a pre-existing world an image of which made it onto our retina.

---

9   This is why I entitled chapter 1 "The Ground of the Image," that is, the figure of the event*-in-the-making.

The heretofore unseen reveals and thereby gives itself when the eyes are moving in a particular manner, and are *doing* so in recurrent ways. Much in the way we become better at riding a bicycle, eyes become better at finding a killer whale or a cube in a display when they have done it a few times before. Because the eyes can do these movements in the absence of the thing present, the repetition of *this* movement is the same as remembering the thing (Maine de Biran, 2006). That is, there is no representation as a thing, a signifier standing for something else, but a making present again of the thing by a repetition of the movement. The eyes do not require a special memory: their capacity to move in *this* way *is* their memory: an immanent and therefore immemorial memory. I have been able to show elsewhere that the hands might remember in and through the finger movement a telephone number that our minds have forgotten (Roth, 2011a). It is precisely this movement that hides behind the notion of representation – for, as soon as the movement unfolds, the thing presents itself to our eyes again. In fact, neuroscientists are now showing that the firing of the neurons responsible for the movement is accompanied by the firing of a set of mirror neurons. Whenever these neurons fire, we see/think of the thing, whether it is actually present or absent. When the eyes of Piaget's children are moving, they see the object; but because they do not yet have the mirror neurons, they cannot make the object present again in and through the firing of these neurons.

The Cultural Dimension of the Object*-in-the-Making

Up to here, it may have appeared as if objects are completely subjective – though I point above to the objective nature of geometry that arises because of the particular artifacts, drawings, proofs, and formulas that everyone can learn to see and work with. The movements that are responsible for the object*-in-the-making are the movements of the person, but these are not random. Particular ways of moving, doing, and seeing tend to be characteristic not of individuals but of groups of people who participate in the same cultural *field* (Bourdieu, 1997). Living in the same field, people develop a disposition for moving, doing, and seeing in very similar ways. This disposition has been attributed to the openness of the body to the world so that we come to comprehend (understand) the world because it comprehends (comprises) us. Thus, a child does not just point, it learns to point when an initially fortuitous movement comes to be "sanctioned" in social relations and, therefore, acquires socio-cultural and cultural-historical signification.

To understand why we come to see something heretofore unseen – i.e., why and how we learn something – we need to understand this passive entrainment that the eyes experience when confronted with the world that their movements come to reflect and constitute. This passive entrainment, whereby a movement trajectory *is given to* the eyes, constitutes the above-mentioned *donation*. If the mind had to direct the eyes, that is, to "construct" *de novo* the particular movement required, then the person might have to wait a long time before finding it, much longer in any case than any curriculum guideline can make available for a particular inquiry. We come to see a thing because *it* entrains our eyes into movement trajectories[10] that are constitutive of seeing, and these movement trajectories are reinforced in cultural settings. Learning is both active – the eyes move – and passive – the eyes are entrained into the movement trajectory by the socio-cultural and cultural-historical setting. The following fragment from a meeting including the members of a world-class research laboratory shows how scientists are entrained into seeing features in a collection of data points.

Some readers might be tempted to suggest that scientists surely can see what there is to see. But this is not the case as my own studies among scientists have shown. Time and again the question was raised about precisely what there is to be seen when they were looking at some focal object*. Thus, in one instance, 6 (male) scientists sit around a table. One of them projects different kinds of plots. Just as one of these appears (turn 109a), the lead scientist Carl gets up, walks to the projection screen where the graph is displayed, and tells the other scientists "what *it* looks like" (turn 110). Moving his right hand through the image, he invites the eyes of the other scientists to follow. If they do so, then their eyes will move in the way Carl's eyes move, as shown again in the movement of his hand; and they (likely) will have seen what he already sees. But it is entirely possible that someone in the room might have said, "I don't see it," which would have meant that his eyes did not make the movement required for the "it" to appear.

Carl now uses his hands – the hand movements are marked as lines in the associated video offprint next to turn 110 – to entrain the eyes of the other into a movement that will allow them to see what he already sees.

---

10   The Russian psychologist Luria (1973) calls these movements "kinetic melodies."

They will see that "this here" is a line (a), and that the "sort of a component" is something that looks like an inverted parabola or Gaussian; finally
he proposes two features by means of hand movements, one leading to an
upward directed left-most part of the data, the other one a downward movement ("down again" [turn 111a]).

This episode shows us that Carl does not leave it up to chance that
the others see what he can see. In fact, if the listeners do not follow his
hand gesture, they might be forever looking for the "component," which
comes into being precisely at the same time that the listeners' eyes enact
"the component" that the gesturing hand invites them to do, thereby re-
producing the movement prefigured by the latter. But as soon as others
will have seen the component*-in-the-making and can themselves de-
monstrably follow it with their own hands, the component* has become
a component objectively present for everyone in this community. It is
objectively present precisely because each person, can reproduce the required eye movements and, thereby, realize the object as the outcome of
the object*-in-the-making.

Fragment 3.1

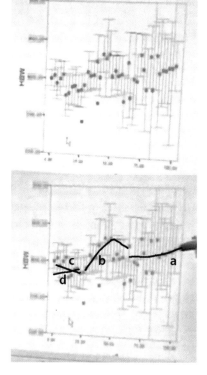

109a	(3.90) * ((*new graph appears*)) (6.00)
110 C:	so what it lOOKs like is ((*gets up and walks to the screen*)) that weve got thIS::: (1.00)
	HEre ((*draws imaginary straight line a on the rightmost of graph*)) and then weve got sort of a comPOnent in hERe ((*making arch gesture through middle of graph, b*)); and then it goes (0.68) ((*slightly upward movement, c*))
111 T:	ah (0.23)
111a C:	down again ((*gestures downwards at leftmost of graph, d*))

World*-in-the-Making

The world is the result of human relations. Beings (Wesenheiten) are lived in the present, entities (Gegenständlichkeiten) in the past, consistent with the present approach that takes world*-in-the-making and objects as the result of processes of object*-in-the-making available only *after* some form of finalization is achieved. He opposes what has come to rest and stays, the object over and against the person (Gegen*stand*) to the presence (Gegenwart), which he reads as that in waiting (Gegen*wartende*) and lasting (Gegen*während*e).

Curriculum and learning tend to be thought about and theorized in terms of (al)ready-made (visible, understandable) objects. The written curriculum (objectives) and the use of demonstrations in the sciences are but two examples of how the finalized object dominates our curricular thinking and theorizing. In English, as in other languages, saying "I see" is equivalent to saying "I understand." In this chapter I show that from the perspective of the learner, the yet-to-be-known does not only announce itself in the seen but also is unforeseen, precisely because it is unseen. For some*thing* to be seen, there has to be movement and work that constitutes the object*-in-the-making from which the tentative object* and the finalized object emerge. The point is that even when finalized, the movement is required for the object to become present. That is, there is an irreducible pair, the first of which points us to the work of movement, the object*-in-the-making, and the second to the (al)ready-made object. Without the doing denoted by the first term of the pair, without the object*-in-the-making, there is no second term. The same is the case for the objective world as a whole: it comes to be only in and through continuous processes of world*-in-the-making.

Prior to the first, fortuitous movement that is making some object* appear for a first time, there is no object. Our world*-in-the-making is different. But as soon as our eyes have moved to make the object, and can reproduce the movement over and over again, our world, too, has changed. But this new world*-in-the-making cannot be anticipated from the existing movements. The way in which I knew the world did not allow me to anticipate the emergence of the twin silos; looking at the splotches in Figure 3.4, readers could not know beforehand that there is a killer whale rather than a Holstein cow, Dalmatian, or something completely other that might reveal itself. Precisely because you did not know what you would eventually see, what will have been seen cannot be used to think about learning *from the perspective of the learner*. To know what learners can or have to do, we need to think about learning from within their world*-in-the-making and from within their range of move-ment capabilities. This means that we have to think about learning from the perspective of a world*-in-the-making that does not contain the movements required for the twin silos, killer whale, or different cubes to appear.

What already can be made to appear shapes our decisions. Because the twin silos did not exist for me, none of my decision-making processes could take them into account. From the outside, this might lead observers to think that I am irrational, when, in a situation where *they* would use the twin silos, I (student) do not and cannot use it because it is unseen. Readers might be in-terested in an analysis of fourth-grade students learning algebraic generaliza-tion, where the student is confronted with the task to do something without knowing what it will yield, and where the teacher herself does not know what the student does not know and therefore has to learn as much as the student does (Roth & Radford, 2011). That study allows us to understand that even in situations where there is teacher guidance, learning means confronting the unknown – i.e., the object/motive of the task – which reveals itself only when the student has come to make the movements from which what is to be seen emerges. The teacher could not reveal it *for him*, because, as I show in the chapter, he has to produce the required (mental, physical) movement for the learning object to emerge from the object*in-the-making.

Learning is like a situation in which I do not know where I will eventually end up – such as traveling in unfamiliar terrain without a map. I may do this for a while, but if it is in the wilderness, eventually fear might set in, especially with the sense of being lost without food supplies, without equipment to keep us warm, sheltered, and fed. Our well being in the best of scenarios and our life in the worst-case scenario comes to be at stake. If learning is anything like confronting the unknown, unheard-of, and unseen, then we might read-ily accept similar emotional qualities of the experience we have. *E*-motion already enters the picture with motion and movement, because it is the mech-anism that allows any living organism to "anticipate" possible outcomes of its movements and to assess the success or failure thereof (Leontyev, 1981). We can then understand learning something new as a continuous exposure to the unknown, uncertainty, and the emotional qualities that such situations entail for the individual. In fact, "I am lost" is a frequent comment students make in more traditional learning contexts; and it is a reaction to the understanding that something is expected of them but that they cannot see it, literally and metaphorically. Some students more easily than others cope with such situa-tions; others engage in engage in *defensive learning* that is, they learn anything that gets the task done without actually acquiring the competencies that the planned curriculum foresees (Roth & Lee, 2007). This dimension of learning, whereby pathos comes to be integral to cognition is developed in chapter 4.

Thinking about learning and the school curriculum in terms of the unknown, the invisible, the unseen, or the unheard-of orients us much better than other ways toward the problematic of learning captured in the learning paradox. Thinking in this manner forces us to theorize learning from the perspective of the learner, who, in and through his movement makes the ascent from the object*-in-the-making to the object. Because of the new forms of movements, the world as a whole has also changed. We therefore do not just have a world: my world is a world*-in-the-making. This research is only in its beginning. There is a lot more to be done to better understand the phenomenon of learning from the perspective of the learner who, in moving, makes the object present; and there is a lot more to be done to work out the practical implications of such a perspective for research, teaching, and curriculum development.

From the articulated perspective that seeks to think the event*-in-the-making, we have to research the structure of the world as in the course of being achieved. Above all, as an analyst to understand cognition of another person, I "must identify myself with the other and see the world through his system of values, as he sees it, put myself in his place" (Bakhtine, 1984, p. 46). For example, to understand how a person who suffers views the world, I must see this world from the inside, understand how his/her consciousness is shaped by this pain, and how this shapes how the person sees the objects that surround him/her. I have to project myself into this person and experience his/her life from within: "I have to experience – come to see and to know – what he feels, put myself in his place, coincide with him" (p. 46). But in this place, from within the horizon, there are facts that are inaccessible to this person, the facts accessible to the contemplative theoretician.

The architectonic of this world, seen from the perspective of this other person, "is something-*given* as well as something-*to-be-accomplished*, for it is the architectonic of an event" (Bakhtin, 1993, p. 75). But this event*-in-the-making "is not given as a finished and rigidified architectonic, into which I am placed passively. It is the yet-to-be-realized plane of my origination in Being-as-event or an architectonic that is incessantly and actively realized through my answerable deed" (p. 75). From within the event, *becoming* does not exist in some abstract way – as it does to the theoretician who after-the-fact gazes at what has happened, dissects the event whole into pieces to establish between them the cause–effect relation. Rather, to the participant-me, everything "is given to me within a certain event-unity, in which the moments of what-is-given and what-is-to-be achieved, of what-is and what-ought-to-be, of being and value, are inseparable" (p. 32). As a result, we come to understand abstract categories as "constituent moments of a certain living, concrete, and palpable (intuitable) once-occurrent whole – an event" (p. 32). This also allows us to understand life in the only way that it "can be consciously comprehended": "as an ongoing event [i.e., event*-in-the-making], and not as Being *qua* a given" (p. 56). It is only from within the event*-in-the-making that I can truly witness what is and what ought to be – just as it is only from within a game that the possibilities and constraints offer themselves (as to the player) but are hidden and non-understandable to the journalist, analyst, or spectator looking at the game from the outside and always with a delay.

· 4 ·

UNDERSTANDING*-IN-THE-MAKING

In painting, as elsewhere, the invisible *is received, but not produced*. (Marion, 1996, p. 46, emphasis added)

The purpose of this chapter is to work towards a theory of learning that makes a radical commitment to the fact that students cannot see or comprehend what is the knowledge they are to learn until *after* they have learned it. A fragment from a fourth-grade mathematics curriculum – intended for the students to arrive at a generalization of the type $y = 3·n + 6$ – is used to think and think about learning given that the students cannot aim at the future knowledge outcome precisely because they do not know (a) the generalization, (b) that they are supposed to generalize, or (c) from which aspects of their experience to generalize something. Because students do not know what they will know until *after* the learning event*-in-the-making has been finalized, I suggest that this future knowledge may be better thought of as the (initially) foreign/strange, which affects students *before* they can grasp what is happening to them or what/that they have learned. Before that we have to think understanding*-in-the-making, where we do not know what the nature of the (at least temporarily) finalized knowledge will be (which is why the term is marked by an asterisk).

In A *Cultural-historical Perspective on Mathematics Teaching and Learning* (Roth & Radford, 2011), the authors present an extended description and analysis of a student (Mario) confronted with a *learning paradox*: Because Mario does not know beforehand what he is going to know after having completed the learning task, he cannot know the *motive* of and for the learning activity. The authors suggest that this motive has to reveal itself in and as a result of the learning activity. Precisely because he does not know the motive, Mario cannot directly and intentionally aim at "constructing" the intended knowledge. He finds himself understanding rather than "constructing" this understanding or "the [associated] mental representations" in the way constructivist and enactivist educators tend to describe learning. Roth and Radford therefore note an inherent contradiction whereby mathematics students have to engage in activity without knowing its motive (unknown and yet-to-be-known outcome) and have to hope that this motive will somehow appear to them together with the (to the students) invisible knowledge to be acquired. That is, just as stated in the opening quotation, the invisible future understanding appears to be *received* rather than actively, intentionally *produced* (i.e., "constructed") on the part of the learner. The work characterized by the term understanding*-in-the-making becomes significant once the student has some form of socio-cultural and cultural-historical sanction his finalized understanding is (consistent with) the intended one. He can then do the living work again to reproduce the understanding when and where he wants.

It has been suggested that the enactivist tradition in mathematics education already has articulated the need to view knowing from the viewpoint of the knower. This, in fact, is the fundamental assumption of all constructivist approaches since Descartes and Kant. However, in recognizing that the learner does not grasp or interpret or construct what is *happening* (to them) out of which new understanding emerges, the phenomenological position espoused here radically differs, as far as I know, from all other approaches to curriculum theory. This is so because the things, processes, and phenomena that appear in currently used theories come into existence for the experiencing subject, in the phenomenological approach taken here, only after the unfolding understanding*-in-the-making has come to a closure (Romano, 1998; Waldenfels, 2006), that is, until after some "crisis" that has led to the emergence of something completely unseen, unforeseeable, and unforeseen from the perspective of the agential subject (see chapter 3). This approach differs from an enactivist position, summarized in the statement that it "is not the mere negation of representationalism –

namely, that the organism invents or constructs its own world at whim –
but, more interestingly, that animal and environment are two sides of the
same coin, knower and known are mutually specified" (Maturana & Varela,
1987/1992, p. 253). In the phenomenological approach, the distinction and
relation between knower and known is itself the result of a process that has
to be explained: in the absence of the distinction, it cannot but *be given* in
some originary event. Here, a term such as enaction "falsifies rather than aptly
captures – much less entails recognition or understanding of – the fundamental, everyday, *wholly spontaneous and natural* qualitative affective-kinetic
dynamics that ordinarily motivate and inform smiling and shaking hands"
(Sheets-Johnstone, 2011, p. 454). It also fails to capture the qualitative *kinetic*
dynamics that normally is created when we shake hands and smile.[1]

Fragments from an Episode of Algebra Learning in Fourth Grade

In the following, I analyze fragments from a lesson that the teachers had designed,
together with the researcher (L. Radford), to introduce fourth-grade students to
algebraic forms of thinking. Because it attempts to be consistent with the actors'
perspectives on activity, the form of analysis is grounded in conversation analysis
and ethnomethodology (see chapter 9), methods that render it illegitimate to
draw on information other than what the members of the setting make available
to each other.[2] The excerpts are taken from the complete French and English

---

1   This chapter is intended to present a perspective new to curriculum theory. It was not designed
     as a deconstruction of constructivism, embodiment theory, or enactivism. Readers are referred
     to the critical analysis by the philosopher of dance movements Maxine Sheets-Johnstone
     (2011), who already has done this work, summarized in a statement that lists all the major
     authors in the embodiment and enactivist literature (names are omitted for brevity's sake):
         The penchant to talk about and to explain ourselves and/or aspects of ourselves as
         embodied – as in "embodied connectionism" … and even as in "embodied mind" …
         "embodied schema" … "Embodied agents," "embodied actions" … and phenomenological
         embodiment … evokes not simply the possibility of a disembodied relationship and of
         near or outright tautologies as in "embodied agents," embodied actions, and "the embodied
         mind is part of the living body" … *but the spectre of Cartesianism.* (p. 215, emphasis added)
2   Some readers of an earlier version of this text requested "more information about Mario's
     interaction with the teacher." Because human beings in interaction always only have what
     others make available to them, the leading policy underlying the current analysis "is to re-
     fuse serious consideration to the prevailing proposal that efficiency, efficacy, effectiveness,

Number of week	1	2	3	4	5	6
Amount saved ($)	+ 6	+ 6				
Or	6	2x + 6	3x +6	x +6	x +6	x +

Figure 4.1. This table of values provided with the story about saving money in a piggy bank, is partially filled up to aid students in the process of arriving at the generalization of the type $y = 3 \cdot x + 6$.

transcripts that Roth and Radford (2011) provide in the appendix of their book. In the learning task that these authors describe, the students are provided with a worksheet that includes, as the problem statement, the description "For her birthday, Marianne receives a piggybank containing $6. She decides to save $3 each week. At the end of the first week she says to herself, 'I have $9!'." The first two questions are: (a) Model the problem until the sixth week using goblets and chips; and (b) Fill the following table of values (see Figure 4.1).

Radford and the teacher (Jeannie) had created the task because, consistent with the Ontario curriculum, they wanted students to arrive at a generalization of the kind "*amount in the piggybank = number of weeks · $3 + $6*." But, as shown in chapter 3, students inherently cannot aim at and intentionally construct this (al)ready-made generalization, precisely because it is unknown to them. Only after the generalization*-in-the-making has come to an end, when the generalization has *arrived*, in a moment of (sudden) insight that presupposes their practical comprehension of the situation, will they be able to make sense of what they have done and why. This is so because intuition (from Lat., *in-* + *tuērī*, to look), that which becomes visible in perception during the trajectory of understanding*-in-the-making, is *always* in excess of intention, current knowledge and action. In the process of understanding*-in-the-making, however, students do not and cannot know what this (al) ready-made understanding will be. In fact, what they come to understand and

---

intelligibility, consistency, planfulness, typicality, uniformity, reproducibility of activities – i.e., that rational properties of practical activities be assessed, recognized, categorized, described by using a rule or a standard *obtained outside actual settings within which such properties are recognized, used, produced, and talked about by settings' members*" (Garfinkel, 1967, p. 33, emphasis added). Good qualitative analysis makes use, as exemplified in Roth and Hsu (2012), only of what is given to and by members to the setting

grasp as their understanding may have little to do with what the teachers intended them to understand.

The Unseen and Unforseeable Understanding: Incomprehension and Negative Affect

The students begin with the first part of the task, as Mario counts out the red and yellow chips and places them into the goblets. Once all the goblets have received the chips corresponding to the consecutive weeks, the students begin filling up the cells in their worksheet. Soon after beginning with the worksheet, Aurélie throws herself against the back of her seat in apparent frustration (see the drawing that goes with the turn), which she verbally articulates about 1 minute later in what we can hear to be a plaintive voice: "I don't understand and I will never understand" (turn 029). A few seconds later, Aurélie pounds on the desk and Thérèse suggests, "Okay, we are all mixed up" (turn 038). But Thérèse then produces some interjections in what may be glossed as "being confident." Mario raises his hand and then takes it back again; Aurélie pounds on the desk (turn 042). Eventually, the teacher (Jeannie) arrives and asks what the question is. Mario clearly articulates, with frustration in his voice, "I don't understand" and he denotes "this" as "dumb," while pointing to the worksheet (turn 044, 046). Although he has already filled all his goblets with the correct number of colored chips, and although he has already filled up the first few cells in the table of value, Mario literally "does not see or get" the point of the task.

In this situation, Aurélie and Mario on state that they do not understand; and they produce unmistakable expressions of frustration. Not understanding*-in-the-making and frustration*-in-the-making are two sides of the same coin. They do not know what the task demands of them and cannot plan what to do next or whether what they have done so far is what they have been asked to do. Because they cannot know what they are supposed to understand until after they have learned the intended lesson, they are in no position to assess whether what they have done so far is what they are supposed to have done. This exposure to a task the intent of which they *cannot* know quite apparently *affects* them, giving rise to frustration, a form of negative emotion.

Mario does not grasp. He cannot grasp the understanding*in-the-making because it is not a finalized phenomenon but a process. But it is only through engagement, in a process of understanding*-in-the-making, that a possible finalized understanding* can emerge. The asterisk here marks that all sorts of finalized understanding are possibilities – and which of these (unlimited) possibilities is going to be actualized cannot be known beforehand with any degree of certainty.

Fragment 4.1

→ 029 A: <<plaintive>i dont understAND; and I will
           nEVer understand.> * ((*Stares at her hands
           placed on the worksheet.*)) (3:38)

      ---

  037 A: ((*Pounds on the table.*))
→ 038 T: <<p>kay we are all mi[::xed up>　　　　]
→ 039 A: 　　　　　　　　　[i dont understand]
           ((*Points to her page.*))
  040   (2.46)
→ 041 T: <<confidently>uh hu:::; uh huh. >
  042   (25.56) ((*Mario drops his hand.*)) ((*Aurélie pounds
           desk again, throws herself back against back of seat.*))

           ((*Mario gets back to the task, A leans back.*))
→ 043 J: <<f>yes.> (0.52) whAT is the ques[tion.]
  044 M: 　　　　　　　　　　　　　　　　[its　]
           ^this ::: (0.38) <f>um[::>　] * ((*Hands move
           downward, restrains not to pound on table, gazes
           at sheet*))
  045 T: 　　　　　　　　　　　[auré]lie sit
           properly (55:00)
→ 046 M: look this is (.) dUMb, <<p>i dont under-
           stAND.> ((487>217Hz))

His actions do not make sense; what he has to do is not intelligible. He is in
the position of the witness in a historical event*in-the-making, who cannot
know whether they will have participated in a revolution, an unsuccessful
uprising, or illegitimate coup-d'etat. Yet to have any hope of eventually understanding, he has to act and do something. If he does not act, he will never
know, as Aurélie states. To work towards understanding requires engagement
in a movement, understanding*-in-the-making, without knowing whether
there is any hope that he will end up with *the* intended understanding. Mario
has to transcend that which currently makes sense and is intelligible to him.
In a way, in acting he is therefore ahead of himself much like Christopher
Columbus was while on his way to discover the Americas. Without knowing, he was on the way of making a discovery, which, as a process, Columbus
could know only *after* realizing that he had discovered something new. There
is therefore a delay between witnessing a process (sailing, facing intemperies)
and knowing it as an inner-worldly event of a specific kind (i.e., discovery).
When Columbus was accosted, he responded to the sight of the foreign people
by calling them "Indians."

In our lesson, Mario responds to something that is unknown (therefore foreign) to him, neither different nor indifferent because invisible. The required action is in response to the foreign, which, qua foreign, does not make/have sense or is subject to an existing order/rule. In such a situation, "*what* I answer owes its sense to the challenge of that to *which* I answer" (Waldenfels, 2006, p. 58). Following the answer, however, the difference between how we answer and what we answer-to tends to be leveled in favor of an cause (intention)–effect relation. That is, after the fact we give reason to dimensions of actions that we did not have reasons for prior to acting because we could not anticipate the effects that were brought about. Columbus set out to sail to India, which is how he understood his voyage. It is only after understanding that he had discovered a new continent that his voyage became an aspect of an understanding*-in-the-making. But while he was sailing, he would not have been in the position to decide whether one rather than another action would help him in the discovery.

For students in situations like that in which Mario and Aurélie find themselves, there is no way that they can evaluate whether some specific action gets them toward the outcome intended by the curriculum, as they do not know which outcome is intended until that point when they have come to know that outcome that the teacher wanted them to learn. This requires that they can make the trajectory of the understanding*-in-the-making the object of their inquiries. Even those counted among the most intelligent and able of human beings, cannot know what they are making and what their understanding*-in-the-making is going to produce. Thus, "someone like Galileo, Yeats, or Hegel ... *is typically unable* to make clear exactly what it is that he wants to do before developing the language in which he succeeds doing it" (Rorty, 1989, p. 13, emphasis added). Taking a Wittgensteinian position, the author then takes language to be "a tool for doing something which *could not have been envisaged* prior to the development of a particular set of descriptions, those which it itself helps to provide" (p. 13).

To have any chance at understanding to arrive, a student *has to* act in the absence of a reason so that the intention (reason) for action becomes available together with the (by the teacher intended) learning outcome. I cannot say after the fact that I could have made a better decision if we had known more prior to it because it is precisely the decision alone that allowed me to know more. Mario is not in a position to say that this or that action is getting him closer to the intended understanding. It is only after the understanding will have arrived that Mario will be able to say, "Me, I now understand." The understanding *follows* and is irremediably tied to the process of understanding*-in-the-making, and therefore cannot be theorized as having had an intention (goal) that would have motivated it. In fact, the relevance of what he had been doing prior to its arrivage simultaneously arrives with understanding.

It is proposed here that we need to move toward understand learning as a dialectical process of stepping into the unknown in such a way that when we land, the unknown has withdrawn and things begin to look more like the familiar. Understanding*-in-the-making is a process at the boundary between order and the unknown yet-to-be subject(ed) to order (i.e., exceeds the categorization into order and disorder). This is so because the "radically foreign is precisely that which cannot be anticipated by subjective expectation or trans-subjective possibility conditions" (Waldenfels, 2006, p. 30). In the process, understanding*-in-the-making means stepping into the unknown where students are exposed and vulnerable, in any case affected "by *something* in such a way that the Whereby is founded neither in a preceding What nor in an a posteriori achieved What-for" (p. 43). Affectivity is precisely what Aurélie and Mario reveal through their engagement in (non-) understanding*-in-the-making reveals. *Pathos* names this originary affectivity that precedes, and is the condition of, any finalized understanding (Henry, 2000).[3] Pathos takes us back to the flesh, the originary body, which is the seat of the being affected.

Spreading of Affect

In the preceding section, Mario and Aurélie display what others (from the same culture) can see and feel to be tonalities of affect. Although Jeannie (the teacher) at first suggests to Mario to work with the others, she nevertheless stays with this group. Physically oriented toward Mario, she particularly works with and talks to him, but, in so doing, also speaks for the benefit of the others in the group. Despite the earlier admonishment to sit properly (which might also be heard as an attempt to orient her to the task), Aurélie does not

---

3   This approach to affect differs from Maturana's (e.g., 1988) concept of emotioning, which he describes as a flow of dispositions in the background such that when emotioning ends, "the process of language (the conversation) ends" (p. 49). That is, "in us human beings emotioning is mostly consensual, and follows a course braided with languaging in our history of interactions with other human beings" (p. 49). Pathos, on the other hand, is the very condition of the auto-affection of life, which occurs prior to any separation of animal and environment.

overtly display participation. Thérèse fills up her table of values apparently independently. We might think that working will get them on the right way in
their task. But, as Fragment 4.2 shows, this transaction, as the one intervening
between Fragments 1 and 2, does not get Mario back on track; and Jeannie,
too, begins to exhibit a negative emotional tone. Jeannie asks, oriented toward Mario and pointing to the table of values, why the three is in yellow
(turn 069). Mario produces some interjections and shrugs with his shoulders;
Thérèse says she does not know. Mario then says, "Because we are supposed
to write it?" He does so with rising intonation, which we can hear as both
offering a possible answer and asking whether the offered response is the one
the teacher is after (turn 074). Jeannie says, with rising intonation typical of
a question and emphasizing "where" and "three," "*Where* does the *three* come
from?" (turn 076). Thérèse says "donno," and Mario makes reference to some
"wedding thing" that has not appeared anywhere in the conversation or in
the task instruction. With apparent exasperation in her voice and comportment, Jeannie asks for the exact nature of the three dollars (turn 080). Mario
grimaces; he then brings his hands up to his face, burying it in the two open
palms (see drawing in turn 080).

Fragment 4.2

069 J: it EQuals to nine the first week. (0.78) wHY is the thrEE in yellow? whydyou
        think? ((*She points the index finger to the table of values.*))

070   (0.19)

071 M: um um, um ((*Shrugs shoulders, shakes head "no," features questioning look.*))

072   (0.20)

→ 073 T: <<all>i don[no]>

→ 074 M: [be]cause we are supposed to write it?

075   (0.44)

076 J: WHEREe does the thREE come from?

077 T: donno?

→ 078 M: <<f>a:=u:> (0.24) u:: (0.17) u: dududu:
          wedding thing there?

079   (0.76)

→ 080 J: <<exasperated>but ((turns head away from
          Mario and in the direction of the cam-
          era)) (0.14) the three dO:LLas? is wHAT
          exACtly?> * ((*Mario, who has looked at her,
          grimaces in desperation, brings his hands up
          and covers face*))

As this fragment shows, the societal relations with the teacher have not changed the tenor of the situation in the course of the event*-in-the-making. Mario continues to express what culturally competent witnesses see to be his frustration about apparently not knowing what Jeannie is asking of him. Not being in a position where he could know what to do or say, he cannot but act to see what this action yields: "because we are supposed to write it?" (turn 074) and "u: dududu: wedding thing there" (turn 078). That is, Mario has to act in the absence of a reason to *find* what the action yields, that is, to find an object that would give reason to the action a posteriori. Evidently, here, his action has not been appropriate, as Mario can take from Jeannie's apparent exasperation. He responds to this expression of exasperation by what we may gloss as grimacing and covering his face in a movement expressing despair. Thérèse, who continues filling up the table of values on her own, nevertheless says, in response to the teacher's questions, that she does not know. Jeannie in turn is showing exasperation, as she apparently does not know what or why the children do not know. That is, although she is engaging with the children – we do not know, at this instant, what type of micro-event*-in-the-making we will have been witnessing – she does not know what the children do not know and where the problem of lacking understanding originates.

It is not just that Jeannie is responding in despair, but her response actually begins by listening to what Mario has to say (see chapter 2). She is being affected by what he says, with apparent affective mediation: she is exasperated. Similarly, Mario does not just respond after Jeannie has offered up what can be heard as questions (turn 069): to be able to answer, he has had to listen to Jeannie and allow himself to be affected by what she is saying. By shrugging his shoulders, shaking his head, and making what we may gloss as a quizzical face, he is publicly making witnessable his cluelessness about how to answer. Everyone can observe the affective dimension of his response, which consists of grimacing in apparent desperation and in covering his face.

In this episode, the tone of affect has been spreading and contaminating others: exasperation now is observable in all participants. Maturana (1988) recognizes this consensual nature of affect, though he suggests that it "follows a course braided with languaging" (p. 49), whereas the phenomenological position underlying my proposal suggests that there is affect and affectability that necessarily *precedes* and makes possible languaging (Henry, 2000). The process may find a better analogy in the spreading of a virus (e.g., the HIV-AIDS virus prior to any discourse about HIV-AIDS), which affects us prior to any understanding of what is happening to us and prior to any language we may have in talking about it. The process is similar to the unseen affecting us in a first moment of the ascent of a figure from the unseen into the seen. How is such spreading possible? The answer is that we are affected in the initial part of responding that consists in opening up to be affected by something (e.g., the saying of another) that we do not yet know (i.e., we only know what has been said when the saying has finished). This is so because pathos – being affected by the utterances and actions of another – and answer are not two events: they are manifestations of one and the same event that is diastatically and diachronically shifted with respect to itself: Listening to another person (without knowing what s/he will have said when finished) and answering are but two sides of *responding*.

Arrivage of Understanding

Over the course of nearly 4 minutes, with further signs of frustration on both Jeannie's and Mario's part, neither of whom appears to know what is going on, the two are continuing to engage each other in filling one cell of the table of values after another. Following Mario's answer "three times three" in reply to the query about what is to be written in the lower cell of week 3, Jeannie says "Yes" with apparent excitement and relief in her intonation (turn 215). She then moves to week 4, asking Mario "How many three dollars do you have?" Mario produces an interjection, next says part of the number word "four," and then writes four times the number "3" into the first of the two cells below week number 4 (turns 220–221). Jeannie says with rising intonation, while pointing to the cell below the one Mario has just filled, "Instead of doing three plus three plus three plus three plus three, what are you going to write here?" (turn 222). Tentatively, Mario utters with rising intonation, as much asking as providing a reply: "Four times three?" (turn 224). Jeannie produces a hand gesture with palms facing upward as if saying, "you got it," which she follows up by saying a little while later, "I think you understand now, uh?" Both forms of action can be seen as an affirmation of the tentatively offered answer, which is intensified by Jeannie's leaving the group. Mario slightly nods and writes something onto his worksheet. About 26 seconds later, he leans over to look at Thérèse's worksheet, then continues. Another 24 seconds later we can hear him pronounce with apparent confidence, "Me, I understand now" (turn 229).

Fragment 4.3

→ 215 J: <<excited>yES::.> ((*Makes the same rH movement to right, opens palm toward ceiling.*)) (1.21) its just on the bottom its a [shortcut]

216 A: [madAMe:]

217   (0.42)

218 J: your fourth week; (.) how mANY three dollars do you have.

219   (1.00)

220 M: u:m::: (1.73) fo. ((*Fills up table, Therese makes noises.*))

221   (9.48) ((*Writes 4 '3s'*))

222 J: <<pp>kay> (0.97) instead of doing three plus three plus three plus thrEE whAT are you going to wrITE here? ((*Points to the row on the bottom of the table of values.*))

223   (0.66)

→ 224 M: <<tentative>uh:m:: (1.36) four times
             thrEE?>

→ 225 J: * ((*Two-handed gesture sideward,
             opening palm upward: "You got it."*))

226   (3.83)

→ 227   i=think you understand now. uh?

228   (50.93) ((*Mario slightly nods, writes, after 26 seconds looks at Therese's worksheet, back at his own.*))

→ 229 M: <<confident>ME i now understand.>

In this third and final fragment from the lesson episode, the emotional tide is turning – it is changing with the unfolding understanding*-in-the-making. Mario produces replies to Jeannie's questions that she evaluates positively both gesturally and intonationally, also expressing satisfaction on her part. She formulates explicitly to be thinking that Mario understands – i.e., that what has been understanding*-in-the-making now is (some form of) understanding*. Mario, with a comportment that we may gloss as newfound confidence and therefore positive affect, states some time later that he now understands – the statement and the affective expression merely being two aspects of the same utterance (action). From his tentative answers prior and right up to turn 224 to his confident statement that he now understands (turn 229), there is a change: the tentativeness of the replies suggests an emerging but not yet firm understanding*-in-the-making, whereas the confidence in the later utterance signals a true sense of understanding*. Because we do not yet know at this point whether his is the intended understanding, we mark the term with the asterisk (see chapter 1). He now witnesses the situation in a way that gives him confidence to have understood what he is to learn and why he is writing $4 \times 3 + 6$ in the column corresponding to week 4 and below the cell in which he has written $3 + 3 + 3 + 3 + 6$. As his subsequent cell entry shows (i.e., $5 \times 3 + 6$), he *appears* to have generalized – from the concrete instances of chips in goblets – the relationship between number of weeks and the number of chips in a goblet (or, equivalently, the amount saved in the piggybank).[4]

One only has to open the pages of any discipline-related research journal to anticipate that many (mathematics) educators and curriculum specialists might say that Mario "constructed" the generalization, and they might be tempted to write that he "constructed" "meaning," "understanding," "mental representations," "identity," and the like. But Mario's understanding – if Roth and Radford (2011) are right in suggesting that he had arrived at one – would be something radically new, previously unseen, and therefore unforeseen. It cannot have been then transitive *object* (i.e., goal) of his actions. He therefore could not have worked *towards* it and constructed the understanding intentionally – much like Columbus could not direct his ships towards *the Americas*. Because he did not know the Americas, he could not aim at sailing there. Even if Mario had done the mental equivalent of doodling (non-intentional construction), he would not have been confronted with something that not only is new but also is recognized as such. Even though he could not have foreseen what the (al)ready-made understanding will look and feel like, in saying "Me, I now understand," marks the recognition that it has arrived. That is, the understanding*-in-the-making has come to a temporary conclusion, its arrivage being marked only after it had already arrived and affected him.

As new, this ordered and orderly understanding prior to its arrivage is the Foreign: Mario offers up his answers with a questioning intonation that signals his uncertainty. Therefore, anything that appears *as* something to us in our perception, as seen, heard, felt, and understood cannot simply be described as "something that *receives or has its sense/signification* but as something that provokes sense without already having a sense, as something that we bump up against, that affects, irritates, surprises, and in a certain way hurts us" (Waldenfels, 2006, p. 73, emphasis added). That which eventually becomes visible, the (al)ready-made understanding, while it is still an undetermined and underdetermined understanding*-in-the-making, must "itself provoke the intention that will render it accessible and

---

4 After conducting a book-length analysis of the entire episode, we did conclude "that the entire multiplicative structure has been objectified at least in part from the societal relation and now is observable as a psychological function" (Roth & Radford, 2011, pp. 86–87).

bearable for the eyes previously half-closed. The visible precedes the aim: *It [visible] is what must render itself to be visable by us*, since we did not expect it" (Marion, 1996, p. 62). Mario's now (al)ready-made understanding* has emerged from a dark opening from which the unseen expels the unforeseen learning object – "in a debacle of the unseen as much as the foreseen" (p. 73).

Coming up Against the Unseen and Thus Unforeseen

Saturated Phenomena and the Excess of Intuition Over Intention

Much of educational psychology, constructivist epistemology, or enactivism has accepted the statement that we learn in terms of what we already know, which recognizes only one part of learning as understanding*-in-the-making, which requires a continuous coming and going across the borderline of the known and unknown. As a consequence, educators have theorized students as being aware, making deliberate choices, and co-evolving with the environment as "each living being begins with an initial structure...[that] conditions the course of its interactions and restricts the structural changes that the interaction may trigger in it" (Maturana & Varela, 1987/1992, p. 95).[5] It is out of existing conceptual elements and structures that learners are said to "construct" their mental models subsequently tested for viability. But how can those within a process of understanding*-in-the-making know *what* they are doing, that they are doing the right thing, and why it is the right thing? Roth and Radford (2011) already propose that this requires knowing the motive of activity, and this motive *inherently* is not available to the person who is a constitutive participant of the understanding*-in-the-making. In the present, the relationship between the new and the previously existing understanding is different. To be participating in understanding*-in-the-making means confronting the unknown, where we do not know what will affect us next; but once we land, following the arrivage of understanding*, we encounter

---

5   I point once again to the problematic nature of the term *inter*action, which is consistent with the general approach of the authors but inconsistent with an understanding of relations*-in-the-making and inconsistent with a symmetrical approach to the relation where subjects and subjectivity themselves are outcomes.

apparently familiar things. The newly seen has already been subjected to the colonization by the familiar and known. It is precisely because of this colonization that the new can be recognized *as* new, that is, that new understanding has actually arrived.

Paraphrasing Marion (1996) for the purpose of the present context, we might say that *coming among its own*, the new understanding had to note that its own [prior understanding] did not foresee it and therefore sur/rendered itself (to being) visable by it. That is, what Mario has come to see as (al) ready-made understanding exceeds everything and anything that he could intend prior to the task and in the course of his understanding*-in-the-making. His observable frustration is evidence that he did not forsee what will have been his (al)ready-made understanding. This is a characteristic dimension of *saturated phenomena*, that is, phenomena "where intuition gives more, indeed disproportionately more, than what intention could have ever aimed at or anticipated" (Marion, 2005, p. 54). Such phenomena are characterized by an excess of intuition, and, therefore, of donation (givenness) over intention, known concepts, and aims/motives.

What is unseen and that which Mario cannot aim at is the understanding that for any week n, the total amount of money in the piggybank y can be calculated as $y = n{\cdot}3 + 6$. That is, there are no apparent conceptual elements from which Mario could have constructed the understanding. Moreover, to understand does not mean merely knowing the formula. Rather, it means seeing the relevance of each action – counting out chips, going from chips to repeated addition $(3 + 3 + \ldots)$, going from repeated addition to multiplication – with respect to the story of saving $3 each week. If what was required for understanding had been present in his prior understanding, then Mario could have *derived* the new from what is already known. If he learned something new, it had to be invented *ex novo*. Ex novo translates to "from scratch," "from nothing": to invent ex novo is to produce a beginning of something rather than grounding it in a preceding order. As the etymology of the verb "to invent" suggests (Lat. *in-*, in, into, upon, against + *venīre*, to come) the process involves elements of unpredictability and surprise, essentially passive forms of experience, exposure. These all are characteristics of an event*-in-the-making, where the participants never know what will affect them next. Each newly arriving possibility, which could not have been foreseen because unseen, is a surprise. This surprise is, in fact, an indication of the excess of intuition over intention and action.

As suggested in the context of the riddle with the orca (chapter 3), the teacher could have given Mario something like the formula *amount in piggybank* = 3·

number of weeks + 6, but this would not have been the understanding that has emerged for him just prior to his announcement "Me, I now understand." Teachers know that telling formulas only leads to students' memorization and failure to use these in contexts where they would be appropriate. It is precisely in his doing that we find understanding*-in-the-making, much as we have to engage in doing a recipe to have any hope that the required knowing-how will emerge as ready-made fact. Not just the formula is important but its significance in the face of the goblets and the table of values. It – the equation and its sense – emerges as something new, totally unseen (invisible) and unforeseeable – as there is no concept to be seen by Mario but only the ways in which it realizes itself concretely in the materials he has at hand. The newly seen (al) ready-made understanding* is arising for him in the ascent from the unseen to the seen, traversing the ground (table of values, goblets) as a process of understanding*-in-the-making, all the while understanding remains invisible until it will have had arrived. Even if Jeannie had given him the formula, it would have been but another aspect of the ground from which the heretofore invisible understanding* would have had to arise before making the crossing via the ground, where it already affects the learner (see chapter 3), into the visible.

Some readers may want to suggest that the teacher is helping Mario out of the dilemma (contradiction) in which he currently finds himself. But the relation involving the teacher and Mario can be (and in fact needs to be) theorized in the same manner. Mario's response does not lie in his filling up a table (turn 221) or in answering "four times three" (turn 224) when the teacher says "What are you going to write here" (turn 222). Rather, his response begins with attending and listening to the teacher. As he cannot anticipate what she is going to say, he is inherently affected by the saying and how she is saying it even before he can understand what she will have said. That is, we cannot think Mario's reply to the challenge of the unknown other than in the tension with his exposure to the teacher's saying. Pathos is as much part of this understanding*-in-the-making as agency, deciding to expose himself to that which he cannot anticipate.

How Does a New Order Arise?

To date, there are no satisfactory responses to the learning paradox: How can the subject of learning know the new order (understanding) when the new *exceeds* the existing order (understanding)? (Roth, 2010a).[6] Inherently, the

---

6   Readers familiar with chaos and catastrophe theory know that system states following a branching point or a catastrophe *cannot be* predicted from prior states. Moreover, the

foundation of a new order of understanding is a critical and crisis-like event that exceeds and transcends any previously existing order, and it exceeds the order of the actions out of which new order *emerges*. Thus, an individual claiming to begin a new order of understanding within him/herself would only repeat what already is and would therefore *not* begin something new. The new understanding cannot be (entirely) grounded in the learner, who is as much subject(ed) to as the subject of understanding*-in-the-making – saturated phenomena are "irreducible to the I" (Marion, 2005, p. 70), who cannot see what is coming. This – by Mario non-anticipatable – historical understanding*-in-the-making "does not only happen to its witness without that he could understand (non-constituting *I*), but encompasses him in return (constituted *I*): the *I* is understood on the basis of the event that happens to him to the same extent that he does not understand it" (p. 74). This phenomenological approach to the arrivage of new understanding, cognitive development, and insight learning fundamentally and de facto adds a dimension of learning over and above all intentionalist (including the [radical] constructivist) adaptive (enactivist) approaches to learning.

Although Mario, Aurélie, and all the other fourth-grade children in the algebra class cannot anticipate what they will have come to understand, they nevertheless engage with the task environment, where they have to respond to arrive at something yet unknown. In fact, they *must* act to set off the process of understanding*-in-the-making to have any hope for understanding to arrive (think of the movements of the eyes that are required for us to see, as described in chapter 3). But the relevance of particular actions will be understood only with the arrivage of the newfound (al)ready-made understanding that is the outcome of the process. In this engagement, which requires them to act without knowing why and how, their "responsivity transcends intentionality, because the fact of entering into something that is happening to us goes beyond the sense, intelligibility, or truth of the response" (Waldenfels, 2006, p. 45). The present position, therefore, differs from the enactivism position, which focuses on the organism as the seat of the knowledge, which arises from its co-adaptive relations with the world. In fact, the system is the environment and the organism, each of which is irreducible to the other.[7] Much

---

transitions between two possible states cannot be predicted with certainty but are subject to infinitesimally small perturbations that trigger large-scale events (i.e., the "butterfly effect").

7 Here is insufficient space for articulating the (mathematical, ontological) difference between (a) systems of interacting elements that mutually affect each other (e.g.,

like a painting "does not offer any object to be seen" (Marion, 1996, p. 79), his objective activity does not show the learning object to Mario. Rather, much as the painting *"impresses our gaze with its own movement* as the imprescriptible condition to be able, precisely, to follow in the gaze the ascent to itself of the unseen into the visible" (p. 79, emphasis added), the objective life activity allows the understanding* *to reveal itself* to Mario.

An understanding* does not reveal itself to Aurélie, precisely because she has abandoned engaging with the task and therefore setting off and participating in understanding*-in-the-making. The task itself serves in the manner of the background in the painting, from which the newfound understanding* *extracts itself.* Much as we do not "learn to see the painting" but "that the painting, by having given itself, teaches us to see it" (p. 76), the objective life activity brings understanding* to life and makes the crossing from the unfamiliar into the familiar. In contrast to Maturana and Varela's (1987/1992) "observer," the learner in the phenomenological approach presented here is a *witness* – Columbus sailing across the Atlantic – who is not in a position to comprehend, because what is prehended (i.e., (al)ready-made understanding) does not yet exist (the discovery of the Americas). This observer never is affected by or encounters the unknown: the foreign, strange, and unfamiliar. This is so because the observer "receives the stranger by effacing his strangeness at the threshold, it would thus never have us receive him. But the stranger insists, and breaks in" (Nancy, 2000, p. 12).

In the end, Mario announces, "Me, I *now* understand." He discovers an (al)ready-made understanding* as the result of what his doing has given rise to, like the painter who, in stepping back, realizes after the fact what his brush strokes have allowed to emerge. And precisely this stepping back indicates that the person who has effected a stroke of the pen, placed a splotch of color onto the canvas, "did not know, at the moment of effecting it, what he did, since, in order to see its effect, he must detach himself from his work, in order to learn, afterward, what visible appears there" (Marion, 1996, p. 80). To see what an act has yielded (given rise to) is submitting oneself to donation, surrendering oneself to that which appears. Stepping back allows the new order, the new (al)ready-made understanding to arrive in/for the person who has been an integral part of the understanding*-in-the-making. This newfound

---

organism, environment), typical of cybernetic approaches, and (b) irreducible dynamical systems that cannot be decomposed in such a way, as treated in dynamical systems theory. Sheets-Johnstone (2011) does take a dynamical approach, which is why she is in disaccord with the enactivist and embodiment literatures (see Note 1).

understanding (i.e., the generalization $y = 3 \cdot n + 6$) is the stigmata of the unseen that arises from the understanding*-in-the-making itself rather than being imposed from the outside, the observer. This newly found (al)ready-made understanding stands out, is an *ectype*. Such ectypes, precisely because these are internal impressions that arise in the flux of understanding*-in-the-making, erupt from the background, a rising of the unseen from the unknown to the point at which they appear. "The ectypes triumph over the unseen by escaping from the background" (Marion, 1996, p. 71). Like an ectype, the (al)ready-made understanding "surges from the unseen into the visible but the unseen still shows through in the background" (p. 40).

Learning is often discussed in terms of situativity and context as ground against which concepts somehow take their signification (e.g., Kirshner & Whitson, 1997). In painting, the background is that against which the figure (type) comes to be. But the analysis of painting shows that "the background is not added to the ectypes, but the ectypes originate as from their most intimate unseen and, henceforth, the most foreign" (Marion, 1996, p. 71). The background itself shows nothing – this is why Aurélie and Mario are frustrated, they cannot see (al)ready-made understanding while understanding*-in-the-making is unfolding. But it is from and through the engagement in the process that the new types (forms) suddenly appear, "miraculous survivors of the unseen" (p. 71). Once we recognize in Mario's newfound understanding a true miracle rather than the mere result of constructive action, curriculum theorists will have evolved a new form of appreciation. The objective life activity in the classroom itself reveals what will have been seen and understood. That which is not understood or known also is not seen, and as "unseen remains inapparent as long as it is, and disappears the moment that it appears as visible" (p. 54). Future understanding, inherently invisible, therefore also is *invisable*, cannot be aimed at.

· 5 ·

SUBJECT*-IN-THE-MAKING

If I am myself a finalized Being and if the event is a finalized thing, I cannot live or act: To live, I have to be unfinalized, open to/for myself – at least that which makes the essential fact of my life – I have to be for myself a value still to come, I must not coincide with my own actuality. (Bakhtine, 1984, p. 35)

The *Thou* ... appears simultaneously as acting and as being acted upon – not, however, linked to a chain of causes, but in its relation of mutual action with the *I*, as the beginning and the end of the event. (Buber, 1937, p. 30, original emphasis)

In constructivist thinking, the subject relates to the world by means of the ensemble of its mental structures, the viability of which is continually updated to account for past experiences in anticipation of future, more appropriate (beneficial) relations in and with the world. Grounded in the Kantian analysis of cognition, constructivist approaches presuppose the presence of the world in terms of the categories (i.e., "constructions") of the mind. But we have seen in the preceding chapters that we cannot account for our participation in the once-occurrent event*-in-the-making through the lens of theoretical consciousness. Through the living event, the Other, Buber's *Thou*, is not linked to chains of causes but appears as a condensation, at the beginning and end of the event*-in-the-making. Rather, we need to think of our participation in terms of an actual communion, a "participative-effective experiencing of the concrete uniqueness of the world." That is, rather than considering our experience of the event*-in-the-making through the lens of categories ("constructions"), we are encouraged to consider participation through the lens of the eye witness (I-witness) who, without comprehending nevertheless witnesses in and through "actual communion."

The noun and verb *witness* has its etymological origins in the Proto-Indo-European root *u(e)id-*, to see, to know, referring us to the one who has seen, with her/his eyes something while it is happening. Thus, life reflected and refracted in terms of categories of mind ("constructions") is "in its very principle, *not* the self-reflexion of <u>life in motion</u>, of life in its actual aliveness: it presupposes another *subiectum*, a *subiectum* of empathizing, a *subiectum* situated outside the bounds of that life" (Bakhtin, 1993, p. 15, original emphasis, underline added).[1] The foregoing chapters already intimate the need for re/thinking and re/writing the subject, just as Nietzsche (1954c) anticipated it in the quotation that appears in the epigraph to the volume. But we are not mere witnesses, if this concept is thought of as being like a fly on the wall – like indifferent television spectators watching an event*-in-the-making featured on the evening news, such as at Tiananmen Square (Bejing) or Tarir Square (Cairo), without letting their appetites be spoiled. Rather, we require concepts in which affect is an integral part. As a result of this re/writing, the participant in an event*-in-the-making is not only the agential subject but also the *advenant* (see chapter 1), *interloqué*, patient, gifted (*l'adonné*), and participant (non-indifferent) witness.

Pathos and the *Advenant*

In the classroom fragments of chapter 4, Mario, Aurélie, and Thérèse – and their teacher Jeannie for that matter – are not entirely the subjects of their activity, pure agents who construct their knowledge to solve the problem at hand. They are subject to and subjected to the event*in-the-making, which they cannot comprehend because the (al)ready-made event does not yet exist to be grasped. They learn without knowing *that* and *what* they learn. That is, the approach to learning offered up here requires us to rethink the subject, which not only is agent but also patient. As a saturated phenomenon,

---

1   The Russian original does not use the Latin *subiectum*, but the Russian term *subiect* (субъект); the original does not italicize the term.

understanding*-in-the-making exceeds intention and therefore exceeds the agential subject that constructs its knowledge, understanding, and itself.

The description of the event*-in-the-making provided in chapter 4 allows us to see that all participants in the classroom are as much subjects of the events, bringing these about, as they are subject to and subjected to the event*-in-the-making. In this formulation, the different moments of the event*-in-the-making, the agential and the pathic, express themselves simultaneously. Because of our pathic nature, we can be affected, not only physically but also emotionally: "The subjectivity of the subject is vulnerability, exposure to affection, sensibility, passivity more passive than any passivity, an irrecuperable time, un-assemblable dia-chrony of patience, exposure always to be exposed, exposure to expressing, and thus to saying, thus to giving" (Levinas, 1978, p. 85). Levinas thematizes, in his typically hyperbolic style of writing, the vulnerability that comes from exposure to the unknown, the Foreign, and the unseen that comes with the unfinalized event*-in-the-making.

In chapter 2, I already suggest that the participants are confronted with the unforeseeable that is *coming at* them, that advenes, and that therefore we need to understand the participants as *advenants*. The concepts of *advenant* and pathos go together, because, as a phenomenological analysis shows, it is because of the passibility of life that we come to be exposed to and are affected by the unknown that arrives in unforeseeable fashion with and in the event*-in-the-making. The concept of the *advenant* already highlights the fact that we do not only appear in the subject position in accounts of experience but also in the accusative position of the direct object, who is affected by transitive actions and by the unknown that advenes.

Taking the perspective of the event*-in-the-making allows us to include the issues of affect, fear of the unknown, the feeling of insecurity and danger that comes when one is in an unknown situation, an indeterminate event*-in-the-making, without advance markers of possible success, left to one's own. Students and teacher cannot ever com*prehend* the unfolding event*-in-the-making precisely because it is unfinished and does not yet exist as inner-worldly fact (Romano, 1998). But they have to act (respond) by stepping into the unknown without knowing what will come of it and without the ability to have a clear intention oriented to the object of activity – they respond (letting themselves be affected and answer to/for), as we can see in the fragments of chapter 4, and thereby rise to the challenge. Here, responding means "answering to a non-thematizable provocation and thus non-vocation, traumatism responding, *before* any understanding, to a debt contracted before any freedom, before any consciousness, before any present" (Levinas, 1978, p. 26, added emphasis). Although Levinas did not write about the event-ness of the event or the event*-in-the-making – this was going to be part of the projects of phenomenological scholars that followed him (e.g., Marion, 1996; Romano, 1998) – he already distinguished the need to answer to/for the situation prior to the arrivage of understanding. He also described the effect that the unknown will have had on the participant, who must answer "as if the invisible that bypasses the present left a trace by the very fact that it bypasses the present" (Levinas, 1978, p. 26).

Re/thinking understanding*-in-the-making in terms of pathos – originary affectability that precedes comprehension but arises from being materially comprehended in the physical world – also requires us to think it in terms of affect, being affected by something alien (foreign) to ourselves. It means thinking about and theorizing learning in terms of exposure, vulnerability, which is an "exposure to outrage, to wounding, passivity more passive than all patience, passivity of the accusative form, trauma of accusation suffered by a hostage to the point of persecution" (Levinas, 1978, p. 31). This requires us to re/write the subject that we have become familiar with in constructivist theorizing of the (planned, enacted, (al)ready-made) curriculum so that we can move toward a post-constructivist way of understanding those who are participating in and integral parts of the curriculum*-in-the-making.

The Subject*-in-the-Making

Der Mensch wird am Du zum Ich [Man becomes I in contact with Thou]. (Buber, 1979, p. 37)

Buber realized that the person is not a self-identical thing, an "identity," but that the "I" *becomes* ("wird") in the relation with the Thou. The "I" is but a one-sided manifestation of the basic word "I-Thou." The subject*-in-the-making is a necessary correlate of the event*-in-the-making, which, for human life, is the relation to the Other. In chapter 2, I draw on a lesson fragment from a second-grade mathematics class, which is in the process of beginning a unit on three-dimensional geometry in and through a task that asks for the grouping of a set of mystery objects. The intended (planned) curriculum outcome is for the class as a whole to achieve a geometrical classification even though this is the first lesson ever that the children have had on the topic and, therefore, even though the children cannot anticipate the (al)ready-made understanding that will have arrived when the lesson or unit is finalized. But this event, in its unfolding, provides children with the opportunity to *eventually* understand the relevance of their collective actions with respect to three-dimensional geometry. It is in and through their actions as part of the understanding*-in-the-making that three-dimensional geometry accountably and relevantly emerges; and it is because of the nature of the understanding*-in-the-making that the participants are to be understood as subjects*-in-the-making. Seen through the lens of the event*-in-the-making, the specific categorical configuration of three-dimensional objects*-in-the-making that will have ultimately arrived is yet to be known; and so it is for the subjects*-in-the-making.

Here I return to that fragment to develop further aspects that come with the idea of the subject*-in-the-making: because the participant is confronted with the unforeseen, s/he not only is an agent but also a patient, who is subject to and subjected to the unforeseen and unforeseeable that arrives at the always changing horizon of the event*-in-the-making. In this confrontation, the unforeseen and unanticipated gives itself in a process of donation before it can show itself. Because the unforeseen is given to and then shows itself to someone, the subject/patient thereby also is given together with what gives and shows itself: it is the gifted (*l'adonné*).

Before the following fragment, Connor had placed his object on a sheet of objects next to which the second teacher in the room had placed a sheet containing the word "rectangular." Mrs. Winter had instructed Connor to take his object to each group to see whether it is similar to any other group or whether it is different. Connor has held his object next to those on all other sheets before placing it on the sheet next to which there is a sheet with the words "square, cube." The fragment picks up at the instant when Connor has placed his mystery object on the construction paper, saying that it "probably" goes with these, which he follows up, when asked, by stating "because they are all squares." We hear Mrs. Winter say, "Em an what did we say that group was about" (turn 46). When she begins to speak, Connor's gaze is directed downward toward the group of objects at his feet (Figure 5.1a), but by the time she has arrived at the "we," Connor's head has risen so that he is now gazing in the direction of Mrs. Winter's face (Figure 5.1b). Right after the word "about" can be heard, Connor's head moves downward again, his right hand, which has rested up to now on his shoe, comes forward to hover right over the red (his)

Figure 5.1. a. When Mrs. Winter begins to speak, Connor is looking at the objects. b. He then races his face until his gaze is directed towards her face. c. Just as he begins to speak, Connor's gaze has returned to the objects and his hand has moved forward, hovering over the red cube he had earlier placed.

cube when he begins to speak following a 1-second of pausing. "What do you mean like?," Connor says (turn 48).

Fragment 5.1

```
46  W:   [em ] an [↑what did [we ] say that group was about.
                [((Begins to point to the group of cubes))
         [5.1a]                [5.1b]
47       [(1.00) ((moves head and gaze downwards))
48  C:   <<p>[5.1c] what do you mean li[ke?>   ]
                            [((Connor looks up at Mrs. Winter))
49  W:                      [WHAt] was the (0.15) WHAt did we put
                            [((Mrs. Winter is still pointing.))
         for the name of that group. ((Mrs. Winter is still pointing.))
50       (1.51) ((Mrs. Winter is still pointing, then pulls hand back.))
51       whats written on the card.
52       (0.83)
```

Just prior to Mrs. Winter's beginning to speak, Connor has had a double turn at talk that produced completed question–answer turns, effectively producing a reply to the asked-for explanation for the grouping. Connor's gaze is directed towards the object when her voice is heard again. In the 1 second it has taken until we hear "we," Connor is facing her again. This movement exhibits his attention to her talking even though he cannot know what she will have said once her saying has come to an end. Her saying makes an appeal to an addressee, and the head movement exhibits the first moment of the response to this address; this response begins in and with his opening up to receive. But from his position, he cannot know what is coming. The what, that which is given in the offering that also serves as address, is unforeseeable and unforeseen. It is coming at Connor, advenes, and it is Connor who, from this perspective, is the advenant. He cannot know what it will be, so Connor cannot but wait for the said to arrive and be given to him. In taking the gift, he is the gifted (*l'adonné*).

From this we immediately arrive at the contingent nature of the subject, which is always a subject*-in-the-making. This is so because the word, as ideological sign, lives in the psyche. When Connor speaks, he exposes and exposes himself.[2] We may understand this as a movement from the inside to the outside. But his responding has been called for and is taken up in his reply, which means, the word as ideological sign already has penetrated him. This leads us to a re/writing of the subject, whose "psyche in the organism – exterritorial. This – a social penetrating the individual organism" (Vološinov, 1930, p. 43). There is therefore a continuous dialectical (dialogical) interplay: ideology becoming psyche and psyche becoming ideology. The subject, inherently a subject*-in-the-making, exists in and as the double movement. When the double movement ends, the subject will have been finalized and no longer lives to witness it. All of the following concepts – *interloqué*, patient, gifted (*adonné*), and witness only function in and through this double movement. This movement is the movement of the subject*-in-the-making.

Interloqué

From within the event*-in-the-making, Connor also is the one appealed to by the speaking, as shown in the movement of the gaze until the interlocutors face each other. In this way, he first appears in the accusative form, that is, he is, in grammatical terms, the direct object of the transitive verb "to appeal." He is the appellee – from Fr. *appeler*, to call, appeal – or, to stay on the discursive plane, he is the one designated as the interlocutor by another interlocutor. But as the one who is called upon by another interlocutor, Mario also is the *interloqué*[3] (Marion, 1988), a neological noun based on an adjective the semantics of which includes to be baffled, stupefied, bewildered, amazed, astonished, and taken aback. That is, although the etymological origin of the *interloqué* is Latin – from *inter-*, between, and *loqui*, to speak, say, talk – the word mobilizes passive forms. In fact, the Latin verb *loqui* is a deponent verb,

---

2   The French phonetic allows a play with words impossible in English: *ex-peau-sition* (homophone with exposition) is the placing (*situate*) outside (*ex-*) of the skin (*peau*). Exposition, therefore, always is *ex-peau-sition*.

3   The English text leaves this word untranslated.

that is, a verb that is active in use but takes its form from the passive (or middle) voice. In French, the verb is used in the passive form or in forms where the person appears in the accusative, as in the phrase "the gaze of his teacher bewildered him." Even in the reflexive use, *s'interloquer de* (*quelque chose*) (to forbid, to be astonished by) mobilizes active and passive voices.

This word choice has consequences, because the *interloqué* no longer is the autonomous constructivist subject constructing and "constituting in its atomic substantiality" (p. 179). As *interloqué*, Connor "finds himself the derivative pole of a relation in which he no longer has any of the (autonomous, autarkic) substantiality implied by even the least subjecti(vi)ty" (p. 179). Because he cannot know what is coming at him in the saying he now is attending to, he is also surprised – the verb to surprise in the senses of to implicate, capture, assail, to take hold of, to affect with. But surprise, in the same way as bewilderment, stupefaction, or astonishment, dispossesses the *interloqué*. We can understand the *interloqué* also in juridical terms, as the one subject to the interlocutor, an order of a court signed by the judge making or pronouncing an order. As such, the concept of the *interloqué* makes all questions "concerning his transcendental subjectivity, his powers, his limits and his figures" (pp. 179–180) questions that concern the *who?* It also makes the question of his rights subject to another question that precedes the former: *which fact?*

Patient

A patient is someone to whom something advenes. The word etymologically derives from Latin *patiēns*, an adjective denoting the capacity to endure, from the verb *patī*, to bear, undergo, suffer. When Connor is attending and listening to Mrs. Winter, he exhibits himself to the unknown, which endures as it is unfolding. That is, while he is the active subject, attending and listening to Mrs. Winter, he also exposes himself to what advenes. The unfolding understanding therefore is the two-directional movement of agentially attending/listening and patiently enduring. Grammatically, this situation can be captured by the middle voice, which has properties very distinct from the active voice that constructivist and enactivist theories use to describe the curriculum. Thus, "[i]n the active voice, verbs denote a process that is accomplished starting out from the subject and outside of it" (Benveniste, 1950/1966, p. 172). That is, in the active voice we have transitive verbs, where the "transitive" refers to a verb's passing over to an object. It is different from the "middle voice, which is the diathesis to be defined by opposition, the verb indicates a process where the subject is the seat; the subject is inside the process" (p. 172).

In Latin verb *pati* actually is one of those deponent verbs that was used in the middle (passive) voice. We therefore already have available the expressive capabilities to render this dimension of human experience that has come to be forgotten in constructivist, enactivist, and embodiment discourses about the curriculum. This "seat" that Benveniste writes about is what phenomenological philosophy makes thematic as the originary body, the flesh, where self- and other-affection first occur prior to their standing out as aspects of the second, transcendental, felt body (see chapter 1).

With the concept of the patient, we thereby achieve a dual movement across and constitutive of the boundary of the active and the passive. This dual movement is required, for attending and listening are insufficient for explaining how we can be affected by something that unforeseeably advenes. But passive reception does not account for the possibility of an intelligible *answer* that bears any relation to what preceded it (Bakhtine [Volochinov], 1977). Agency and passivity are but one-sided manfestations of the higher-order event*-in-the-making that transcends the opposition of the active and the passive. The constructivist approach is limited, because it makes thematic only the agential moment of dialoguing specifically and of participating in events*-in-the-making generally. The subject is not characterized appropriately if conceived in terms of agency. However, merely adding the passive dimension by collating the patient with the agential subject does not get us out of the quagmire, for there is passivity in agency as there is agency in passivity. The verb to listen for/to actually makes thematic this dual attention: listening for means actively orienting and attending and listening to means patiently receiving. But to receive the word, what is sonorous stimulus has to be transformed into the word that is heard; and to attend to means actively readying oneself to patiently receive.

The notion of the patient actually leads us back to the etymologically older sense of the notion of the *subject*, a term deriving from the Latin verb *subicēre*, to place under, to lay before, to put under the control of, and to expose. That is, the subject is not the pure agent in and of the event*-in-the-making but is subject to and subjected to all the contigencies that advene. Even the best among teachers – such as Mrs. Winter, who is recognized for her leadership, who has been called upon by the ministry of education to assist in developing the various curricula for this grade level, and who served as a vice-principal in the school at the time – never are in (total) control of what is happening. In fact, even when they can make things turn out as they intended, a lot of work tends to be involved until they do so. In the present fragment, there is a lot of collective work required until the intended description of the group of objects as being about squares and cubes has eventuated. This eventuation is not the result of Mrs. Winter's actions, though in the present case we do observe the description being articulated. But going to any classroom we will notice instances where a teacher's "question" does not lead to the anticipated response so that in the end teachers themselves provide the intended answers. The simultaneous possibility of a reply and non-reply is more general than the current achievement that has led to what was anticipated (at least implicitly) in the question "What did we say that group was about?"

In participating in an event*-in-the-making, students and teachers are subject of, subject to, and subjected to what is in and out of their hands simultaneously. The event*-in-the-making is in their hands because they are among its constitutive moments; it is out of their hands because of the advenant aspects inherently associated with the event*-in-the-making, which cannot be foreseen. In participating, they are subjected to statements*- and facts*-in-the-making over which they do not have control but to which they have made themselves subject to in and as of their willingness to participate (see also chapter 2). The subject therefore is a patient, to whom the unforeseen, which has arisen from the unseen, advenes. In this view, the perspective of the event*-in-the-making allows us to understand the participant in the simultaneous lights of agency and radical passivity.[4] As in the spectacle, where there are spotlights of different color, agency and passivity are different projections and therefore but manifestations of a higher-order phenomenon, the spectacle*-in-the-making. This spectacle*-in-the-making generally and the protagonist(s) particularly cannot be reconstructed by any composition of or relation between the projections.

L'Adonné, the Gifted

During the event*-in-the-making, the unforeseen gives itself; it is a gift. A rare English word for the gift is the *don*, the thing that is given in the process of donation. In the French of Marion (1998), who has developed a phenomenology of the gift and givenness, the verb *adonner* means to give in to, be/ turn favorable, or agree with and, in the reflexive use, to devote, consecrate, or dedicate oneself. *L'adonné*, as a neological noun, is the one to whom a gift has been given, "the gifted," the one given over, the receiver who also receives

---

4   Some scholars conflate (chosen) passivity (e.g., not contributing to a task), which, as a negation, still is a form of action and *radical passivity*, which is the result of passibility, which we are always subject and subjected to.

him-/herself at the same time as s/he receives and accepts the gift (Marion, 1998). As the translators of the work use either the French neologism or the English form "the gifted," both are used here synomymously.

Connor hears being appealed before being in a position of comprehending what the appeal is about. The appeal is an unavoidable fact from which there is no way out as soon as it is given before it reveals itself as an appeal. If Connor does not hear Mrs. Winter speak, there is ground to speak of appeal; but the hearing of the appeal precedes any understanding ("construction") of an "I" that precedes the appeal. But when the Saying appeals him, then there no longer is a choice: Connor can only accept or reject it. At this time, the appeal already has become fact that precedes the acceptance or refusal (e.g., if he did not answer). The appeal, which is appeal (fact) before the subjectivity of the subject, places the latter in the accusative position ("me" before "I"). The *adonné* "receives himself from what he receives" (Marion, 2001/2010b, p. 56). The *adonné* is "the one to whom that which gives itself from a first *Self* – any phenomenon – gives a second *me*, the one of the reception and the response" (p. 56). This gives rise to the post-constructivist subject, which is no longer the origin of its world but that is given to and arising from the unforeseeable emerging at the horizon of the event*-in-the-making.

Connor is attending and listening to the speaking. There is a said*-in-the-making of which he does not know whether it will be an offer or a question, a statement, or an evaluation. This attending and listening to constitute understanding*- and response*-in-the-making preceding any "I" who could say "I interpret," or "I am questioned," or "I am insulted," and so on. From a dialogical perspective, understanding itself is a form of dialogue, an unfinalized process of the kind that I am marking in this book by an asterisk and the modifier "-in-the-making": "it is to the locution what the reply is to the [preceding] reply in the dialogue" (Bakhtine [Volochinov], 1977, p. 146). We are therefore not dealing with (al)ready-made understanding but the unfolding understanding*-in-the-making, and its result, the understanding that will have arrived, cannot therefore be anticipated. "Understanding" is an open-ended understanding*-in-the-making, a moment of the event*-in-the-making. Understanding*-in-the-making develops (almost) despite of the agential subject, whose sense of Self evolves even before it can comprehend what will have been said when the Saying has come to an end. But because understanding* listening is already the first part of the response, it, too, exceeds the subjectivity of the subject.

The concept of the gifted (*l'adonné*) renders this dimension of the subject, who is not in control over itself, is not the result of a construction, but the by-product of an event*-in-the-making, and, as the latter, an unforeseeable result. But, in undermining and making illegitimate any claim to the subject as pure agent, the concept of the gifted does not make the subject a pure patient. "In fact, the *adonné* exceeds passivity as well as activity, because, in liberating itself of the royal transcendental status [*la pourpre transcendantalice*], it annuls the very distinction between the transcendental *I* and the empirical *me*" (Marion, 2001/2010b, p. 59). This approach then also allows us to understand the gifted as a project of the subject*-in-the-making. Because this work of understanding*-in-the-making consisting of attending to and listening to/ for is required each time the subject – here Connor – is appealed, "the adonné does not receive itself once and for all (at birth) but does not cease to receive itself anew in the event of each given" (p. 60). Although the given gives itself in a process that exceeds the subjectivity of the subject precisely because of its event-ness, there is an active role for the gifted: The operation by means of which the distance between the given and its appearance as a phenomenon is owed/attributed to the *adonné*. This is precisely what the dialogical approach frames as the active aspect of understanding, which is confronted with the unforeseen word, and which "finds a proper place for it in an adequate context" (Bakhtine [Volochinov], 1977, p. 146). In both instances, the work of understanding*-in-the-making increasingly comes to the fore with the difficulty involved in the transformation from the pure given to the phenomenalization of the given as gift (understanding). The more foreign a word is that a child or student encounters as part of the living curriculum, the more work is involved on the part the recipient to the point of the sound-word remaining an encapsulated and rejected intruder.

To the listener, a word arrives as sound before the listener can properly hear it as a word; the gifted becomes visible precisely at the instance when the sound that gives itself is heard as a word, because it is the understanding*-in-the-making of the word that defines the recipient-*adonné*. Thus, "the adonné phenomenalizes itself by the same operation that it phenomenalizes the given/gift" (Marion, 2001/2010b, p. 62). As a result, "the given/gift reveals itself to the adonné by revealing the adonné to itself" (p. 62). The philosopher uses the metaphor of the photographic developer, which gives rise to the latent image to reveal itself; in the case of the given/gift and the gifted, each serves as the developing agent allowing the other to reveal itself. The given/ gift becomes a moment of the event*-in-the-making, because its presence is the result of a revelatory process, leading to the fact that allows phenomenal moments of the event*-in-the-making, including the subject, to become processual in their turn.

Witness

The witness participates in an event*-in-the-making, "in the being-event of the world in its entirety" (Bakhtin, 1993, p. 49) and cannot therefore take a theoretical gaze: the witness can only think participatively rather than grasp. We comprehend the world because it always already comprehends us. This form of thinking is very different from the theoretical gaze, which constitutes a god's-eye-perspective on the world, rendering it in objective terms. The witness takes part, and therefore is partial, has a viewpoint and therefore a point of view. "The compellently actual 'face' of the event is determined for me myself from my own unique place" (p. 45).

The witness undermines the constructivist subject, which makes present to itself the situation in and through its representations (constructions, mental framework). From the constructivist perspective, Connor "interprets" what Mrs. Winter is saying; or, rather, the very notion of "interpreting" means that Connor *has to* have available what she is saying as an object, for interpreting requires, as its transitive object, some text. But what Mrs. Winter says is available, as inner-worldly fact, only once she has concluded. This would not force us to comprehend understanding that is forming in the very instance of the listening, when the unforeseeable words are still coming forth from Mrs. Winter's mouth.[5] The witness, on the other hand, is exposed to the event*-in-the-making without comprehending what is happening, whether a locution will have offered Connor a question, statement, or evaluation. Thus, "no witness, however educated, attentive, and documented s/he may be can describe, even after the fact, what is happening at the present instant" (Marion, 2001/2010b, p. 41). The witness, being caught up in the unfolding event*-in-the-making, not having a god's-eye perspective on it as completed inner-worldly fact, is constituted by what advenes and by the partiality that arrives with his/her position.

---

5 As Merleau-Ponty (1945) and Vygotskij (2002) suggest, even the speaker in everyday situations does not know in advance the precise words that s/he will use, and, furthermore, finds his/her thoughts in the words that have sprung forth from their lips.

Re/Thinking the Subject

When we think the living curriculum as an unfinished, yet-to-be-namable and yet-to-be-knowable and -known event*-in-the-making, we have to give up common notions of the "subject" as well as attendant terms such as "identity." The participant, as Bakhtin states in the opening quotation of this chapter, has to be open and unfinalized, just as the event itself. This is so because interpreted "in the light of the event," "man [*l'homme*]…is not man studied by anthropology, sociology, or psychoanalysis" (Romano, 1998, p. 2). Within the horizon of the event*-in-the-making, the "subject," just as the object or relation, is not simply given "as something totally on hand, but is always given in conjunction with another given that is connected with those objects and relations, namely, that which is yet-to-be-achieved or determined" (Bakhtin, 1993, p. 32). Thus, that which is in the process of happening necessarily escapes both Mrs. Winter and Connor. In this changed perspective, both are learners and teachers (see chapter 6), agential subjects and passive patients. They are witness in and to an event*-in-the-making that they cannot yet comprehend because it is not yet advened and concluded as some *this* event: It is not available as an entity in completed form.

The person becomes in the face of the other. But this other, consistent with the figure of the subject*-in-the-making, itself appears in time, but a time which is "that of the event which is fulfilled in itself: it is not lived as part of a continuous and organized sequence but is lived in a 'duration' whose purely intensive dimension is definably only in terms of itself" (Buber, 1937, p. 30). Within the event*-in-the-making and from the perspective of the subject*-in-the-making, the "other," too, has to be thought as other*-in-the-making. The finalized other is an objectified other, a thing among things that we do not meet because it exists in a representation and, therefore, is a thing of the past.

Constructivist theories focus on the agential subject. But we cannot understand the featured fragment or episode as an event*-in-the-making if we approach it through the intentions of the individuals or through the theoretical gaze of the analyst, who takes a complete, god's-eye-view of this episode as a particular kind of event. To understand this classroom episode*-in-the-making, we have to take a perspective situated in the situation without being able to anticipate its end other than in terms of possibilities. (A cop-out exists in framing these possibilities as so general that – as is the case with horoscopes – they always appear to come true.) From my viewpoint as a participant witness, the happening "is given to me within a certain event-unity, in which the moments of what-is-given and what-is-to-be-achieved, of what-is and what-ought-to-be, of being and value, are inseparable" (Bakhtin, 1993, p. 32). Thinking the living curriculum as event*-in-the-making forces us to change our thinking about the participant and participating subjects. As *advenants*, they are but moments of the event*-in-the-making, and therefore as much subject of as subject to and subjected to it – they make the event and are made by it. We can therefore assign the roles of teacher and learner (about teaching, about mathematics content) only after the fact. Mrs. Winter is teaching geometry as much as learning to teach geometry, and Connor is learning geometry as much as allowing Mrs. Winter to learn teaching geometry.

Bakhtin (1993) critiques Kant for his take on the subject, which is a purely theoretical subject engaged in "transcendent self-activity" but which, as "historically non-actual *subiectum*" (p. 6), fails to be the one actually witnessing life as event*-in-the-making. The subject is only an "epistemological *subiectum*," which is precisely the position taken in contemporary constructivism of the radical and social brands alike. But once we have detached the subject from the actual, living, historical situation from its actualization, "there *is* no way of getting out from within its content/sense aspect and into the ought and the actual once-occurrent event of Being" (p. 7). As a result, "[a]ll attempts to surmount – from within theoretical cognition – the dualism of cognition and life, the dualism of thought and once-occurrent concrete actuality, are utterly hopeless" (p. 7). In words that are strikingly similar to a complaint Vygotskij (2002) is making, Bakhtin (1993) suggests that the "detached content of the cognitional act comes to be governed by its own immanent laws, according to which it then develops as if it had a will of its own" (p. 7).[6]

Before their death, human individuals are unfinalized and unfinalizable, always in the making, always in transformation, never fixed and stable

---

6   Addressing the separation psychology traditionally makes between intellect and affect, Vygotskij (2002) suggests that the weakness of this approach derives from the fact that "it inevitably makes thinking appear as an autonomous flow of thoughts thinking themselves that isolates itself from the fullness of real life, from the living motives, interests, needs of the thinking human being" (p. 54). The author continues discussing how this makes thought an epiphenomenon detached from the everyday realities of life; and its connection with this life becomes a major problem, which cognitive scientists refer to as the "symbol grounding problem." The critique actually takes up the Marxist one, according to which it is an illusion to consider "the real as the result of thinking that gathers within itself, deepening itself, and moves itself" (Marx/Engels, 1983, p. 35).

(Bakhtin, 1984). In the traditional novel, this is the problem because the "ethical unfinalizablity of man before his death does not become the structural and artistic unfinalizablity of the hero" (p. 56). In the same way, the traditional approach to theorizing the subject does not conceive of it as an unfinalized project*- or by-product*-in-the-making. Thus, to understand the living curriculum we not only have to think it from the open horizon of the event*-in-the-making, but also we have to theorize the subject as subject*-in-the-making. This unfinalized subject*-in-the-making, characterized by "unfinalizable depths" (Bakhtin, 1984, p. 68), cannot be shown in theoretical approaches that abstract the finalized subject and any of its constitutive moments from the event*-in-the-making and the associated unfinished world*-in-the-making populated with equally unfinished objects*-in-the-making. Dostoyevsky is the one writer who actually populated his novels with unfinalized protagonists. These heroes are characterized by "the profound consciousness of their own unfinalizablity and indeterminancy," which "is realized in very complex ways, by ideological thought, crime, or heroic deed" (p. 59). Unfinalizablity of the subject also means "noncoincidence with himself" (p. 117).

The whole problem of thinking in terms of cause and effect, according to Nietzsche's position stated in the book's epigraph arises from the fact that the subject and its will or intention are taken as the model for understanding the world. Thinking the living curriculum as event*-in-the-making also questions – in fact, requires us to abandon – the whole idea (illusion, metaphysics) of the cause–effect composition of the (social) world. It requires us to do our research differently, if its purpose is to understand "the world *actually experienced*, and not the merely thinkable world" (Bakhtin, 1993, p. 54, emphasis added). How we might approach the problem of the unfinalized subject in research is one of the topics of chapter 9.

· 6 ·

RELATION*-IN-THE-MAKING

The life of dialogue is not limited to men's traffic with one another; it is, it has shown itself to be, a relation of men to one another that is only represented in their traffic. (Buber, 1947/2002, p. 9)

In the preceding chapters, we observe teachers and their students in dialogical relations. In the epigraph to this chapter, Buber explicitly links the life of dialogue and the dynamic nature of the relation*-in-the-making, observable as "traffic." Dialogue is not something that is dead, fixed, with specific content but is understood as a reflection of living life itself. The image of the relation is traffic, the very concept of people moving. A common way to think about teaching and learning has come to be the zone of proximal development, which has been defined as *"the distance between the actual developmental level as determined by independent problem solving and the level of potential development as determined through problem solving under adult guidance or in collaboration with more capable peers"* (Vygotsky, 1978, p. 86, original emphasis). Unfortunately, following a simplified reading of its original definition and primary sense in the quote that opens this text, the concept tends to be thought of in terms of the *opposition* of individuals. One of these individuals, a teacher or peer, is more capable than another individual, the learner. Somehow they engage on an "inter-mental" or "inter-psychological" plane from where the learner constructs knowledge from him-/herself on an "intra-mental" or "intra-psychological" plane. That is, such conceptualizations convey a substantialist approach that thinks learning as knowledge assimilation and relations in terms of ensembles of individual actors relating unproblematically. Their *interaction* is thematized through the dubious prism of the differences of what happens within the individual consciousness (within people) and what happens in collective consciousness (between people) – as if these could exist separately. Speaking is reduced to the individual, subjective intention of the speaker, who, in speaking, is considered to externalize ideas that have previously formed inside the mind. The approach is substantialist in that it takes some prior situation, including the institutional positions of the participants in a relation (i.e., teacher, student) and uses it to make causal attributions about what ensues. The approach also somehow postulates the individuals, subjects, as given in their difference as Selves, one of whom serves as the scaffold for the growth of the other.

Through the lens of the event*-in-the-making, a relation is alive only as a relation*-in-the-making, which takes place in the Bakhtinian chronotope of the "meeting." It is in the meeting, and by means of the dialogical development, that "that which confronts me is fulfilled, and enters the world of things, there to be <u>endlessly active</u>, <u>endlessly to become</u> It, but also endlessly to become *Thou* again" (Buber, 1937, p. 14, original emphasis, underline added). Here, Buber emphasizes the endlessly active nature of the relation, always in a process of *becoming*. The Other is alive in the meeting but also exists in embodied form: "its body emerges from the flow of the spaceless, timeless present" (p. 14) of the genuine meeting of people, including students and other students or students and their teachers.

Problematizing the Zone of Proximal Development

Traditional approaches to the zone of proximal development are unsatisfactory. There is too little attention given to the relational nature of subjective and collective consciousness, the former only constituting a concrete realization of the latter. Is it possible to think this concept in terms of the unicity and symmetry of a relation*-in-the-making in which any moments (individual subjects) are themselves in the making and *constitutive*, that is, cannot be thought independently?

In chapters 2 and 5, we see Mrs. Winter and Connor who are in engaged in a continuous process of understanding*-in-the-making in the exchange of what come to be questions. The "right" question, the one that Connor eventually will be able to answer, is itself the result of the unfolding curriculum*-in-the-making. In chapter 4 we see Jeannie and Mario in a relation with similar problems, having to engage with each other and the task to have any hope for mathematical understanding*-in-the-making to continue until the anticipated understanding has emerged. I note in the context of chapter 4 that Jeannie is learning as much as Mario does though the two types of learning outcomes differ. That is, there is a joint event*-in-the-making that effectuates different forms of understanding. But, as I elaborate in this chapter, this joint event*-in-the-making is possible only because there already is symmetry in the background understanding that allows the teacher–student relation to be produced: as the seat of the subsequent, objectified understanding, which is the result of the finalized understanding*-in-the-making.

In the work of Vygotsky, who created the concept, we do find starting points for thinking about the zone of proximal development *symmetrically*. The symmetric perspective is grounded in a common world of historical significations and ways of life that we come to share since our birth and that form the basis of common implicit or explicit reference, common knowledge, assumptions, etc. It is also grounded on the sharing of language. Thus, in a conversation – a word whose sense derives from the Latin *conversare* in the middle voice, that is, as I show in chapter 5, with active and passive aspects – speakers use words. But, any word spoken *for the purpose of* understanding*-in-the-making is symmetrical, belonging to both speaker and listener. Thus, "[t]he word is a thing in our consciousness, as Ludwig Feuerbach put it, that is absolutely impossible for one person, but that becomes a reality for two" (Vygotsky, 1986, p. 256). There is nothing like one person's word, just as there are always two hands involved in hand clapping. A *conversation* is when the word taken generally is a reality for two. That is, "each word has two sides. It is determined equally by the fact that it comes *from* someone as by the fact that it is directed *toward* someone. It constitutes precisely *the product of the interaction of speaker and listener*" (Bakhtine [Volochinov], 1977, p. 123, original emphasis). In terms of the theoretical approach developed here, the word is a word*-in-the-making, which, when it is finalized, will have been the "product of the interaction of speaker and listener." That is, the process of the relation*-in-the-making and the word*-in-the-making are co-extensive. The "word" becomes possible because of the relation, and the relation becomes possible because of the "word."

When we take the conversation*-in-the-making as the minimum possible unit, in which each "word" is understood as a sympractical word*-in-the-making and as a sympractical relation*-in-the-making, any asymmetry within the unit, that is, between moments of the unit, has to be thought of differently. This is especially so because in the happening, it is impossible to detach entities without destroying the unit, which is not only distended across and making the setting but also distended across time and making time. The very same Saying, which will have had as its Said a question directed toward the student that also contributes to constituting the teacher–student relation*-in-the-making; and the student reply that will have reified the preceding Said as a question also constitutes the relation*-in-the-making. As Foucault (1975) tells us, there are "power-knowledge relations," and these "are to be analysed, therefore, not on the basis of a subject of knowledge who is or is not free in relation to the power system" (p. 36). Instead and "on the contrary, the subject who knows, the objects to be known and the modalities of knowledge must be regarded as so many effects of these fundamental implications of power-knowledge and their historical transformations" (p. 36). It is precisely in the sense of Foucault's dictate that I implement a more symmetrical approach to the analysis of relations involving what comes to be constituted as students and teacher, a constitution that may run counter to the institutional positions that these subjects take as "students" and "teacher."

Symmetry in the Zone of Proximal Development

To understand curriculum as a form of life through the lens of the event*-in-the-making, we have to think about teaching/learning situations differently than from the asymmetry of institutional positions of teachers and students. In this section, I take another look at the exchange involving Mrs. Winter and Connor to lay the ground for a series of reflections on teacher–student relations in the context of a view that focuses on curriculum*-in-the-making.

As shown in chapters 2 and 4, the children in Mrs. Winter's second-grade class are in the process of classifying "mystery objects" that they are pulling from a black plastic bag. The 22 children sit in a circle on the floor. The center of the circle develops into space for a classification*-in-the-making where "mystery entities" become three-dimensional geometric objects as the result of the simultaneous process of object*-in-the-making (Figure 6.1). That is, with the becoming of each three-dimensional object we also have the becoming of the classification of three-dimensional objects: the two processes are manifestations of the living curriculum, which also constitutes understanding*-in-the-making. Each child gets a turn pulling an object and then either placing it on a colored paper with

Figure 6.1. Artistic rendering of the scene: Connor is in the center of a circle of second-grade students facing his "mystery object" and the teacher just off the left margin of the image (pointing finger can be seen in grey on left border).

other "like" objects or creating a new group. They are asked not to use color or size as a way of distinguishing objects, though most of the children continue to do so in this lesson. The two teachers teaching the unit – Mrs. Winter, the regular classroom teacher, here in the lead, and Mrs. Turner, a university professor of mathematics education – have stated previously (in their planning meeting preceding the lesson) their intent to allow the children to arrive at a classification system in which all objects are grouped according to their geometric properties, that is, as cubes, spheres, rectangular prisms, and so on. To achieve this end, Mrs. Winter engages in joint action with each child so that at the end of his/her turn, the object has found its place according to what we recognize – in the practice of Euclidean three-dimensional geometry – as its geometrical properties.

These joint actions may be thought of in terms of the zone of proximal development at two levels. First, at the whole-class level, the teachers allow a classification of the 22 mystery objects to emerge from the collective classification*-in-the-making. Second, the teachers work with each child, a process of a micro-classification*-in-the-making so that a classification of *this* object*-in-the-making emerges consistent with standard Euclidean geometry. The "mystery object" becomes a geometrical object as the result of the process that we denote by object*-in-the-making. Thus, as we see in chapter 4, Connor's mystery entity becomes a cube rather than a rectangular prism. Collectively, therefore, the "zone of proximal development" allows a category system to emerge as the result, and individually, each relation with a child contributes a proper grouping that is constitutive of the collectively achieved system. From the perspective of the living curriculum, the "zone of proximal development" has to be thought as zone-of-proximal-development*-in-the-making, for these things do not just exist somehow, with slots (roles) that people fill as if they were cultural dopes. The very doing and saying oriented towards and being about the "mystery objects" also is an aspect of the relation*-in-the-making. It is so because the relation is unfolding sympraxis (joint action) that teachers and students change and are changed, the former getting better at teaching the latter in the content area that the curriculum specifies. As part of this chapter, I bring out the idea of the institutionally designated student to be the teacher of the institutionally designated teacher, who thereby becomes the student.

The Lesson Fragment

Connor has pulled what we will come to call a cube but has classified it on its own rather than with the other cubes on the floor. Following the joint actions with Mrs. Winter, the mystery object finds its appropriate place. At this point, Mrs. Winter says, her intonation falling toward the end as if she were making a statement, "em an what did we say that group was about," while pointing from afar toward Connor (Figure 6.1). There is pausing, a process of a pause*-in-the-making that cannot be attributed to Mrs. Winter or Connor as the cause. Connor then takes a turn and says, with rising intonation characteristic of questions, "What do you mean like?" all the while touching his mystery object.

Fragment 6.1

→ 46 W: em an ↑what did [we say that [group was about.]
                          [((Points toward objects on the floor, maintained until turn 51.))
                                  [((Makes tiny circular movement with index finger.))
   47   (1.00)
   48 C: <<p>what do you [mean li[ke?>   ]
                          [((Touches "his" cube.))
                                  [((Looks up to Mrs. Winter))
   49 W: ^[WHAt] ↑was the (0.15) ^WHAt
           ↑did we put for the name of that group.

```
50      (1.51)
51      whats written on the] [card.
        ((still points))     ] [((Pulls hand back, no longer points.))
52      (0.26)
→ 53 C: <<pp>s:::::><<p>quares>·
54 W:   ˇsquare [ˇan::d
→ 54a C:            [(((Cheyenne has moved forward, jutting her index finger repeatedly to
        the card next to the cubes inscribed "square, cube."))
→ 55 J: cubes.
56      (0.25)
57 W:   cube. ˊdoes it meet the criteria of having the square or the cube?
```

At the end of this exchange, overlapping Connor, the teacher begins a new turn, "What was the…what did we put for the name of the group," her intonation falling toward the end of the utterance. Another pause develops, again much longer than the 0.8 seconds average wait time teachers tend to allow. After 1.51 seconds, Mrs. Winter takes another turn at talk, "what's written on the card" (turn 51), her intonation again falling toward the end as is typical for statements. Up to this point, her index finger has pointed toward the floor, and also has made a little circular movement while she was saying the words "group was about" (turn 46). After a very brief pause Connor says with a very subdued, almost inaudible, voice, while drawing out the initial "s" sound, "square" (turn 54). Mrs. Winter comes to have the next turn, "square and." But before Connor has the time to say something, in fact while Mrs. Winter says "and?" with rising intonation, Cheyenne has moved forward and points to a sign next to the colored paper on which Mrs. Turner had previously inscribed the words "square" and "cube" (turn 54a). Jane is next saying "cube" (turn 55). As before, Mrs. Winter can be heard to repeat the word and then begins what will have become, following the next turn, another question.

A "Socio-Cultural" Gloss

We might gloss this excerpt in a traditional way common among "socio-cultural" curriculum theorists and researchers saying that the teacher attempts to allow Connor to label his mystery object with the name of the group in which he has ended up placing it. She asks a question, which he does not understand, and then she facilitates the production of the answer. In traditional approaches, Mrs. Winter would be identified as the more knowledgeable individual who guides the six-year-old Connor to attribute the appropriate category name to his mystery object. The appropriate answers, "square" and "cube," are produced in a sequentially ordered turn-taking routine that has come to be known under the acronym of *I-R-E* – teacher initiation, student reply, and teacher evaluation. Here, the initiation occurs in turn 46, the student responses are produced in turns 53 (Connor's "square"), 54a (Cheyenne's pointing gesture), and 55 (Jane's "cube") (see arrows in the transcript). The teacher evaluation* comes in the form of the constative repetitions of the words "square" and "cube" and the open completion slot following "square and. ..." The evaluation will have been made but has to be thought, in the course of turns 54–57, as an evaluation*-in-the-making. As the subsequent turns show, the students do not revise the reply but provide, as per the offered request (turn 54), the remainder of the sought-for complete answer.

Turn 54 in particular may be thought of as a "scaffold," for here the teacher asserts a previous reply but also constitutes it as incomplete. This constitution is achieved by the production of the connective "and," which asks for something else, the asking further signaled by the rising intonation. In marking the incompletion and in offering an occasion for replying, Mrs. Winter thereby could be said to provide an opportunity for instantiating the correct response for a first time. That is, whereas we might think of the sequentially achieved *IRE* as a "technology" employed in the zone of proximal development that serves as the "scaffold" for getting children from where they are to producing the "correct" "replies" for a first time, we need to rethink this whole approach when we are interested in understanding the eventness of the living curriculum.

Sequences such as the one presented here are taken by curriculum researchers of the "socio-cultural" brand as evidence for the scaffolding that one party, the teacher or more knowledgeable peer, provides to another party. Within this overarching pattern there exists another one that specialists in the linguistic subspecialty of conversation analysis know as a *repair* sequence. Thus, everything that happens following the "question" (turn 46) and the appearance of the first, partial reply (turn 53) serves to "repair" the trouble of the intelligibility of the question. The student makes known that he does not understand (the question), and the conversational repair is oriented for him to understand the question before he can answer it.

A Second, Symmetric Return

In the preceding subsection, I provide a classical reading of the lesson fragment. Yet when we take an approach to the analysis in which each word said and presented again in the transcript is a thing in the consciousness of both, then the analytic situation changes. In fact, we may say that not only does Mrs. Winter guide Connor to the point of naming what his group was about, but Connor also guides Mrs. Winter towards what she needs to do to assist him. Connor, in fact, exhibits considerable cultural competence, which allows this to be a conversation*-in-the-making. Even though the intonation of Mrs. Winter has descended as is common in statements, Connor, in responding, designates himself as the addressee of the saying. By answering, Connor comes to inhabit the public space of the relation*-in-the-making and opens up possibilities for developing the topic as much as the relation itself. His return *question* renders what Mrs. Winter has said problematic: It is, at best, a question*-in-the-making reified as a question when the replies will have been accepted as such (turns 54, 57). In saying what he says, he allows her and every other witness present knowing more than that he has not arrived at finalizing understanding*-in-the-making: that the absence of a finalized understanding might have arisen from not listening or not hearing what she has said. But if he had not heard what has been said, he might have asked, "What did you say? I didn't (couldn't) hear you." He might have indicated that the problem is a failure to hear rather than a failure to comprehend. In asking Mrs. Winter what she means, Connor not only replies by stating a failure of finalizing understanding*-in-the-making about what she wants, but he in fact offers guidance to Mrs. Winter through what to do next: state what she really wanted to say by uttering "what did we say this group was about." That is, if we intend to use the verb "to scaffold," it actually works both ways. We not only observe Mrs. Winter scaffold Connor until the word "square" will have been said, but also we see how Connor scaffolds her to produce an intelligible question that will allow him to finalize an understanding concerning the nature of her question*.

Mrs. Winter is giving it a first try, which will have consisted in saying different words what she presumably already has said. That is, she is producing a within-English translation of the previous Said into another said with the same content. This will have been the way in which the participants will have treated what is panning out as one result of the relation*-in-the-making. (The other result is the relation itself.) In not taking another turn and allowing a long pause to develop, Connor lets Mrs. Winter know that her first attempt in telling him what she means has failed, and she promptly gives it another try. That is, in not taking a turn at talk, Connor also communicates to Mrs. Winter his evaluation that her first attempt at phrasing an appropriate question has failed. Yet, in and through our continuing participation in the relation*-in-the-making, they are decisively committed to make the relation work. This is so precisely because the Saying not only is about producing some finalized Said but also is making the relation* itself. It is in and as this relation*-in-the-making that other things come to live: a question*-in-the-making, reply*-in-the-making, subject*-in-the-making and so forth. As the reader can see, through the lens of the living curriculum, that is, through the lens of the event*-in-the-making, nothing is reified beforehand and is taken in finalized form only when the participants themselves are doing so (at least temporarily).

In the next turn falling to Connor, he says, "square." In repeating the word with falling (questioning) intonation, Mrs. Winter offers it as a constative, that is, an affirmation about a state of affair, which we may gloss as "square is indeed written on the card." In saying "square" with falling intonation, Mrs. Winter therefore ratifies the reply. This is put in relief if we consider a possible alternative course of the exchange in the following form.

Fragment 6.2 (Hypothetical)
```
01  W:   ´whats written on the card.
02  C:   <<len>square?>
03  W:   square.
04  C:   square.
```

In this alternative situation, we would hear Connor reply but, given the rising intonation in his voice, we would also hear a question. We might gloss the turn pair in this way: Connor is offering a reply but also raises the question about its appropriateness. That is, he also marks a certain degree of uncertainty about this reply being the one that constitutes a satisfactory second turn to turn 01. We then hear Mrs. Winter say exactly the same word, but her intonation is falling (turn 03). It is a constative that can be heard, as second turn to the offered question, as constituting an affirmation. Connor then says the same word again, but, in contrast to turn 02, he now does so with falling intonation just as Mrs. Winter has done (turn 04). We may therefore hear this as the "true" reply to the question* in turn 01. From anywhere within this fragment, in a first time through reading, we thereby observe what will have been a question–reply*-in-the-making, finalized only after Connor has ended turn 04 and, in its constative intonation, finalized what we now may denote as a sequentially ordered question and reply.

Eternal Return of the Same

Everything goes, everything returns; forever rolls the wheel of Being. Everything dies, everything blossoms, forever moves the year of Being. Everything breaks, everything is made anew; the same house of Being is forever rebuilt. Everything separates, everything greets again; the circle of Being remains forever loyal/true. (Nietzsche, 1954b, p. 463)

The volume epigraph shows us that Nietzsche is concerned with thinking life from the perspective of life.[1] In this quotation, the philosopher sees thematic constancy in the face of change. However, what remains the same is the eternal return, which is a continual dying and rebirth in which life manifests its presence and change. When Nietzsche talks about the "same house of Being," he does not suggest that life is self-same, which would be a contradiction. Rather, he modifies the house using the German adjective "gleiche" (same) as distinct from the adjective "selbe" (same). The former is used in the sense of "like," whereas the latter is used in the sense of "self-same." Capturing life and language in this way is the central concern of Bakhtin and other members of his circle (e.g., V. N. Vološinov and P. N. Medvedev), so that their way of understanding language fits the present project of the living curriculum.

Together, Mrs. Winter and Connor will have said the word "square" three times. Although the content of the sound-word is the same, specified by the different significations that we might find in a dictionary if we were to look up "square," there is a non-repeatable aspect to each saying of the word. This non-repeatable aspect has been denoted by the term *theme*, which is "*a dynamic and complex system of signs* that strives to adequately fit the *conditions of a given moment of the <u>Becoming</u>* (stanovlenie)" (Vološinov, 1930, p. 102, original emphasis, underline added). The author then defines the two concepts in a stenographic manner: "Theme – a *reaction of consciousness-in-becoming* [stanovjashchegosja soznanja] *to the becoming of life* [stanovlenie bitjia]. Signification [značhenie] – a *technical apparatus in the realization of the theme*" (p. 102, original emphasis).

The Vološinov text clearly focuses on the issue raised in and with this book: Taking a look at conversation specifically and at life more generally a perspective through the lens of the process of becoming. When Mrs. Winter and Connor engage (with each other) in conversation, they do repeat the word

---

1   This is the same type of move that will subsequently lead Heidegger to think language from the perspective of language and that will lead Derrida to think difference from the perspective of difference (i.e., as *différance*).

"square," and, with it, the signification. But the *theme**-is-in-the-making, always and already, much the same as other moments of the event*-in-the-making as a whole: consciousness*-in-the-making, understanding*-in-the-making, and so forth. In fact, we even have to take signification* to be in-the-making, for "square" might also be heard as "town square," "to be square (on equal terms)," the square of a number, the carpenter's tool, the "least squares" approach in statistics, a body of troops in formation, a parade ground (military slang), a city block, a measure used in roofing or building (1 square = 100 square feet), a "square party (of four)," "square (simple) rhythms," and so on. The theme*-in-the-making is constraining the ways in which "square" can be heard, without, however, eliminating multi-voicedness of any language-in-use.

Viewed in this way, sound transcribed in terms of the International Phonetics Alphabet as /skwɛə/ and rendered in the dictionary as "square," is but the technical apparatus of understanding*-in-the-making or, to use Vološinov's term, consciousness*-in-becoming, which is a reaction to the becoming of life: here the *becoming* of curriculum. This is why /skwɛə/ is in fact non-self-identical across the repetition. The irreducible sequences "square? – square" and "square. – square." harbor difference – or, rather, différance – which is the différance associated with understanding*-in-the-making. As stated in chapter 5, there are two levels on which we can consider understanding*-in-the-making: understanding *this* question*, which comes to be a question when its reply will have been confirmed to have arrived, and at the macro-level, where understanding*-in-the-making is the process the product of which we subsequently attribute to Connor, an understanding of three-dimensional geometry.

The process of becoming is irreducible to the individual: it is precisely the relation*-in-the-making that is expressed in the sequences "square? – square" and "square. – square." This relation*-in-the-making thereby also is the understanding*-in-the-making. "In this way, the theme absorbs and dissolves signification,[2] not leaving to it the possibility to stabilize and solidify itself" (Vološinov, 1930, p. 103). That is, unlike what constructivists tell us occurs in conversations, where participants are said to "make meaning," the dialogical perspective allows us to understand that signification ("meaning") never comes to be realized as it is continuously absorbed and dissolved in the theme.

---

2   The English translation uses the term "meaning." This is inappropriate, however, from a pragmatic perspective. For a table for consistently translating theoretical terms used by Bakhtin, Vološinov, and Vygotskij, see Roth, 2013a.

In uttering the connective "and" Mrs. Winter allows her listeners to come to understand that something else is required. Symmetrically, in producing at least the first part of what comes to be the sought-for reply, Connor lets Mrs. Winter know that she now has asked the appropriate question; the appropriateness of the reply thereby constitutes the evaluation of the appropriateness of her question. That is, Connor can be seen as a teacher allowing Mrs. Winter to find an appropriate manner to phrase her question at the very instant that she is attempting to allow him to articulate a proper response. In other words, Mrs. Winter and Connor are each other's teacher and student; and they are so simultaneously. These subjectivities arise from a power-knowledge relation that subjects and subjugates both to an event*-in-the-making that neither person controls.

Up to now, we have focused on Mrs. Winter and Connor. But the words that they have oriented toward each other also have been produced for everyone else present. The circular arrangement with the current speakers taking up a central position has the organization of a theater in which the audience is allowed to follow and understand. That is, each word not only is for the benefit of the two main protagonists but also for the benefit of the generalized other, the other children constituting this class, the researchers present, and all those who will vicariously come to know about the event through the researchers' writings. That is, the word itself invokes and implies the third, who is present in the face-to-face I-Thou that pre-exists all language (Buber, 1979). The active participation of the audience manifests itself in Cheyenne's pointing to the inscribed words that Connor and Jane pronounce for all to hear.

My analysis so far shows that far from exhibiting an asymmetry, the relation*-in-the-making that we denote by the term "zone of proximal development" is a continuous relational achievement. In Nietzschean terms, it is the relation that is "eternally" returning, but never in the self-same way only somehow in the way. It is in this returning that the participants become (as) teachers and learners. In this analysis, each locution has come to be paired dialogically with an evaluation. Not only does the participant with an institutional position of teacher evaluate, but so do the participants with designated institutional positions of student (learner). Each word, spread across the processes of speaking and hearing, is the finalized product of understanding*- and societal relation*-in-the-making. Each word (locution) is paired with a social evaluation; and it is the social evaluation that "defines all aspects of the utterance, totally permeates it, but finds its most pure and typical expression in expressive intonation" (Bakhtin [Medvedev], 1978, p. 122). It is precisely because each locution is taking up and commenting on the preceding locution that the teacher may have a developing sense that the student has or has not understood, and the student can know that he has or has not provided the appropriate response. In other words, it is the unfolding and unpredictable relation*-in-the-making that is allowed by the social evaluation of locutions that ties together, in a reciprocal manner, the participants in a symmetric space of the relation*-in-the-making.

Asymmetries are not only possible but inherent in the non-self-identity of each subject*-in-the-making: symmetry constitutes basis (ground) for asymmetrical teaching and learning roles to emerge from the relation*-in-the-making. In fact, asymmetries arise from the very fact of the word understood in a dialectical way. It is precisely because the word is not identical with itself that it is both one and many simultaneously. This is the linguist's case that is analogous to Marx's commodity, which, precisely because it is non-self-identical manifests itself as use-value and exchange-value (e.g., Roth, 2006). The different manifestations are not the result of different "interpretations," but different manifestations of one and the same phenomenon. But, as in dialectical materialism generally, these dialectical terms also express diachronicity, as the different values of a word – e.g., across the "square? square." unit, are realized in and make time. Just as a commodity that is exchange-value in the hands of the seller turns into use-value in the hands of the buyer, "square" is a question in the mouth of Connor and turns assertion in the mouth of Mrs. Winter. The changing themes in the course of understanding*-in-the-making are but expressions of the flux of life. "Language advances at the same time with this current and is inseparable from it. In fact, language is not transmitted, it lasts and perdures in the form of an uninterrupted process of evolution" (Bakhtine [Volochinov], 1977, p. 117).

This approach is based on the idea that a word never belongs to the speaker only because it "addresses itself to an interlocutor; it is a function of the person of this interlocutor" (Bakhtine [Volochinov], 1977, p. 123). The locution, therefore, "absolutely cannot be considered as individual in the narrow sense of the term; it cannot be explained in reference to the psychophysiological conditions of the speaking subject" (p. 119). The word *is* shared by speaker and listener – rather than "taken-as-shared" by their separate minds, as social-constructivist curriculum theorists like to express this – and is but a technology. The advantage of the symmetric approach to the relation*-in-the-making is that it allows the question of any "more capable subjectivity" to be the result of the relation*-in-the-making when part of it is finalized in a (gross) reduction of questions, answers, and evaluations to individuals.

Both Mrs. Winter and Connor take the role of teacher; and both take the role of learner. Each is a subject*-in-the-making, each a pole of the relation*-in-the-making. But as in ordinary magnetism, there are no monopoles, and the one hand clapping has yet to be heard. Who is in the know and who learns is falls out of the relation*-in-the-making after the fact is a condensation or sedimentation. In this fall-out, the diachronic and dehiscent relation*-in-the-making is collapsed into a a self-identical entity. The institutionally sanctified "teacher," a subject*-in-the-making (chapter 5), also is a "learner"; and the institutionally designated "student," a subject*-in-the-making, also is a teacher. In fact, the relational approach allows us to understand teachers as subjects*-in-the-making over the course of their professional experience: The higher psychological function and personality of the teacher exist in, as we see below, a societal relation before it can be ascribed to the person. This situation is in fact very common in the classroom. In my classroom research I have often followed teachers with a camera around the classroom, recording their relations*-in-the-making and finding traces from the relations* with some students in the relations* with others. As a result, the actions and discourses that we ascribe to them as persons continuously develop together with the living curriculum (e.g., as the teacher goes from one group of students to another). Far from constituting a sole opportunity for students to learn (e.g., subject matter), the relation*-in-the-making constitutes opportunities for all participants to change and develop.

The Zone of Proximal Development as Relation*-in-the-Making

To paraphrase Marx: the *psychological* nature of man is the totality of societal relations [obščestvennix otnošenij] *shifted to the inner sphere and having become functions of personality and forms of its structure.* (Vygotskij, 2005, p. 1023, original emphasis)

In general form: *the relation between higher psychological functions once was a real relation between people.* (p. 1021, original emphasis)

The reconceptualization of the zone of proximal development in terms of the open-ended and open-horizoned relation*-in-the-making rests in a common world*-in-the-making with historical significations and ways of life that we come to share since our birth. This is not some objectified zone out there in which people are slotted – somehow magically created when an institutionally designated "teacher" meets an institutionally designated student – but the name for a relation*-in-the-making that exists in, through, and because of the conversation*-in-the-making. As noted above, this always already common world forms the basis of common implicit or explicit reference, common knowledge, assumptions, etc. It is this common world of reference that makes intelligible for the teachers and the students the game of the "mystery objects" and all that this game entails. Any possible consciousness of and about the Self always already is *con*sciousness, knowing together (Lat. *con*-, with + *sciēre*, to know). But there is more: our shared complex language with its intricate forms of reference, auto-reference, and expression – accounts for the symmetrical role that participants necessarily come to play in conversations. This language, which never is that of one person, constitutes the technical apparatus for the continually developing form of life, which develops together with the language itself. Yet all this is not enough for learning to occur. What is still missing is what we observed in the second grade episode: the willingness to tune into the relation*-in-the-making, where the Other exists as non-objectified subject*-in-the-making, subject to and subjected to the same event*-in-the-making in which we, too, are caught up. Thus, in the conversation with Mrs. Winter, Connor could have given up the discussion. Mrs. Winter could have given up, too. She could have called on another student. But she did not. She kept adjusting to Connor, as Connor kept adjusting to Mrs. Winter, both oriented towards the respective other.

These considerations are tremendously important, for, as Vygotsky notes in the quotations on p. 35, all higher psychological functions arise in real, societal relations between people. These "relations," as I suggest here, and I am sure Vygotsky would have whole-heartedly agreed, are relations*-in-the-making. It is precisely because they develop that the participant "subject" also is a subject*-in-the-making, that is, as temporarily finalized subject, bears the marks of totality of societal relations that s/he has participated in before. The relation*-in-the-making gives this meeting its evolutionary aspect so that it is not a surprise to note that the meeting is characteristic of the eventness of life: "All real living is meeting" (Buber, 1937, p. 11). The meeting dissolves the hard boundaries around the constructivist subject caught up within itself and its constructions, for "[i]n the reality of this meeting no reduction of the *I* or of the *Thou*, to the experiencing subject and experienced object, is possible" (Smith, in Buber, 1937, p. vii). A fusion into the Heraclitean flux of life, that is, "into the whole being can never take place through my agency," because relation*-in-the-making means "being chosen and choosing, suffering and action in one" (Buber, 1937, p. 11). This mutuality is observable between Mrs. Winter and Connor, each of whom choses and is chosen, is subjected to the saying of the other and subjects the other to his/her saying.

Mrs. Winter and Connor did not come to participate as *tabulae rasae* in this relation*-in-the-making that was co-extensive with their learning and development. Both Mrs. Winter and Connor have come with their histories, the totality of all societal relations they have participated in. These histories and the totality of societal relations differ. Mrs. Winter knew beforehand some of the possible classifications of these mystery objects that would be consistent with classical geometry.[3] It is part of the historical and cultural knowledge that Mrs. Winter ubiquitously and continuously draws on to contribute to the curriculum*-in-the-making. This actual and presumed (on the part of the students) cultural knowledge of solids and their classification constitutes a resource to the making of the relation* that leads to asymmetries. It is this asymmetrical element to which Vygotsky referred in the definition of the zone of proximal development. Even Buber, who otherwise emphasizes the total symmetry of the meeting and dialogical relation ("relation is mutual," Buber, 1937, p. 8), postulates the necessity of an asymmetry in teacher–student, client–counselor, patient–psychoanalyst, and other such relations (Buber, 1979). To be effective, the teacher has to meet the student; it is only in the meeting, as relation*-in-the-making, that the teacher can enter and encompass the student's world*-in-the-making. The student, on the other hand, cannot in the same way encompass the teacher's world*-in-the-making.

But this asymmetry is not sufficient to understand learning; in fact, such asymmetries constitute lazy, commonsense ways of accounting for the diastatic and diachronic nature of any moment and category required to understand the eventness of the living curriculum. The teacher cannot make the object of knowledge merely appear in the student's consciousness – if Mrs. Winter had told Connor where to place his mystery object, he could not have "known" what grouping mystery objects according to geometrical properties is, for he would not have produced the required movements.

---

3   Classifications other than those that they ultimately arrived at are possible. For example, the cubes could have been grouped together with the rectangular prisms, of which the former constitute a special kind. The object could have been classified according to their symmetry properties, whereby cone, cylinder, and sphere all have at least one rotational axis where there is an infinite number of rotations that leave the object the same. From a topological perspective, all mystery objects belong to the same class and only cups, rings, or pretzels would have been in another class.

Thus, Vygotsky (1997) recognizes that "[i]t is impossible to exert a direct influence on, to produce changes in, another individual" (p. 47). He complains that "the old pedagogics...treated the student like a sponge which absorbs new knowledge" (p. 48). The primary asymmetry that results from any presumed social and societal distribution of presumed cultural knowledge becomes drowned in the unfolding relation*-in-the-making where participants' consciousnesses intersect. A relation*-in-the-making inherently changes, as "interrelationships with another person's discourse in a concrete living context are of a dynamic and not a static character" (Bakhtin, 1984, p. 199). The intersection of voices in the meeting requires the appearance of a form of intersubjectivity where the participants de-center themselves: The person becomes "I" in the meeting with the other (Buber, 1937). Their respective consciousness seeks the respective other through words and bodily actions and reactions, such as grasping, touching, and pointing. And it is only when the object of knowledge appears simultaneously in Mrs. Winter's and Connor's consciousness that learning occurs.

The notion of relation*-in-the-making, which describes the meeting between Self and Other ("I and Thou"), is consistent with the attempt to overcome cause–effect thinking that Nietzsche critiques in the quotations that begin this book. Thus, "[s]o long as the heaven of *Thou* is spread out over me the winds of causality cower at my heels, and the whirlpool of fate stays its course" (Buber, 1937, p. 9). In the meeting of teacher and student, therefore, neither is the causal origin of any presumed "knowledge"; their relation*-in-the-making is a moment of the encompassing life*-in-the-making. These also imply the subject*-in-the-making, so that inner difference and asymmetry characterize the living person.

To sum up, conceptualizing the zone of proximal development by means of the relation*-in-the-making rests on a non-transmissive form of knowing and on a non-individualistic conception of the participants. As to the former, knowing is theorized as process, knowledge*-in-the-making rather than as the reception of already-made pieces of cultural-historical knowledge. Knowledge*-in-the-making refers to the continuously disappearing and emerging possibilities that are available to the participants for thinking, reflecting, arguing, and acting in a certain historically contingent cultural practice – here the practice of Euclidean geometry. As to the latter, instead of conceiving of participants as self-contained agents having already pre-formed intentions and ideas, or as solipsistic actors that merely take knowledge and intentions as shared illusions of relations, each participant is thought of as subject*-in-the-making, continuously changed in meetings with others, relations*-in-the-making, which, as Vygotsky states in the quotation on p. 135, "become functions of personality and forms of its structure." It is in this meeting that the present comes to exist in a direct way rather than mediated by representations: "The present ... exists only insofar as actual presentness, meeting, and relation exist" (Buber, 1937, p. 12).

There are various theoretical and practical implications. From a theoretical viewpoint, the role of participants in a zone of proximal development entails a better understanding of language and joint social action. The perspective articulated here resorts to a conception of language and joint action that is at odds with classical ideas of information processing approaches and individualistic psychologies, including all forms of constructivism. Within this context, we need to better understand how participants draw from those resources in the course of and producing the relation*-in-the-making. We also need to better understand how participants deal with the various political forms of asymmetries (e.g., knowledge distribution, genre, and ethnicity) to orient to others in the symmetrical space of language. The iterable moments of language, its significations, tie us together but also constitute the technology of continuously evolving themes. A word, therefore, always exists for consciousness generally. But at the same time, a word is *ideological*; that is, a word always belongs to a system of ideas: "*The word is the ideological phenomenon par excellence*" (Bakhtine [Volochinov], 1977, p. 31). This is why Vygotsky's characterization of relations as *societal* [obščestvennix otnošenij] is important: it allows us to locate asymmetries and injustice in classroom relations that are not the same for all – precisely when conceived of as the "same" for all – because a girl is not the same as a boy, and a working-class child is not the same as a middle- or upper-class child. If the teacher, generally characterized by middle-class values and behaviors, works towards doing the same in relations with all children, she is disadvantaging some while advantaging others.

In the meeting of consciousness that the zone of proximal development as relation*-in-the-making brings together, there are also a change and exchange of perspectives. There is dialogue. However, the most important aspect of the zone of proximal development is not the mutual benefits that participants obtain in the actually achieved relation. To think along those lines is still to remain in the waters of individualism, a perspective that justifies relations in terms of the profits that each one of the participants collects. The most important aspect of the zone of proximal development is that it names the event of meeting that is co-extensive with "real living" and, therefore, denotes the eventness of the event. The motif of the *meeting*, one of the chronotopes mobilized in the novel, provides a unity in space and time where dialogical exchange and (developmental, evolutionary) change occurs (Bakhtin, 1981). The motif of the meeting, the dialogical nature of imagination, and the eventness of the event are co-extensive (Bakhtin explicitly refers to Buber and the role of the motif of meeting in his philosophy). In the meeting, ideas are no longer confined to the private mind, but rather, any "idea is a *live event*, played out at the point of dialogic meeting between two or several consciousnesses" (Bakhtin, 1984, p. 88). Thought in this way, "the idea is similar to the *word*, with which it is dialogically united" (p. 88). Meetings, dialogue, and discourse all are expressions of "language in its concrete living totality" (p. 181) and, therefore, co-extensive with the aliveness of life.

· 7 ·

FROM RESPONSE-ABILITY
TO RESPONSIBILITY

We call forth, and are ourselves summoned by, the words of others. (Holquist, 1990, p. xliv)

[T]he summons is understood only through the response and in it. (Chrétien, 2007, p. 39)

One cannot separate response from responsibility. (p. 3) Source also Chrétien

[T]he one has no sense other than the-one-for-the-other: the diachrony of responsibility constitutes the subjectivity of the subject. (Levinas, 1971, p. 45)

Constructivist epistemologies focus on ethics as a system of values in the mind – even when previously co-constructed in a social context – against which social agents compare the actions that they mentally plan before performing them. This approach is problematic, as it forces a wedge between thought and action, body and mind, universal and practical ethics, and thought and affect. I develop and exemplify in this chapter a post-constructivist discourse on ethics that centers on the dialogical relation of participants in conversation. This discourse overcomes the problems of the constructivist approach. The practical ethics emerge from this approach is consistent with the dialectical (dialogical) conception of the world-as-event. I conclude by suggesting that the *Saying* constitutes a dialectical/dialogical paradigm of a post-constructivist ethics. The Saying inherently is a micro-event*-in-the-making, and we will not know while listening what will have been said when the Saying has come to its end. The Saying therefore is an appropriate figure that goes with all other figures in this book that point to the unfinalized and continuously evolving curriculum*-in-the-making.

The Problematic

In education, ethics generally is considered through the lens of the agent – i.e., through the lens of (intentional) agency – even when authors recognize the mutual nature of the ethical commitment that participants in a relation *make* to a joint project (e.g., conversation). The position is common to constructivist and post-structuralist positions alike, such as when teachers are said to "have the sole responsibility for the well-being of their students" (Czarnocha, 2008, p. 80) or "primary school mathematics *is* what primary teachers make happen" (Brown & McNamara, 2011, p. 13). This approach of thinking ethics through the agency of individuals may be the case even for those who articulate a much more differentiated view, such as *caring*, a relational concept, in terms of agency (e.g., "[Women] define themselves in terms of caring and work their way through moral problems from the position of one-caring" [Noddings (e.g., 1984/2003, p. 8)]). Agency is problematic especially in the case of deontology, because ethics inherently pertains to relation*-in-the-making, a moment of the "whole being [that] can never take place through my agency" (Buber, 1937, p. 11).

Not only are ethical considerations conducted through the lens of agency, but also agents (students, teachers) are considered by and large in terms of their mental/conceptual frameworks and a pervasive regard for elusive "meanings" that exist only at a metaphysical level. Thus, the empathizing that comes with deliberate caring, that is, "aesthetic empathizing (i.e., not pure empathizing in which one loses oneself, but empathizing that objectifies) cannot provide knowledge of once-occurrent Being in its event-ness" (Bakhtin, 1993, p. 17). Bakhtin continues by stating that aesthetic empathizing "can provide only an aesthetic seeing of Being that is located outside the *subiectum* (and of the *subiectum* himself as located outside his self-activity, that is, in his passivity)" (p. 17).

The question of ethics is not just an issue of the (metaphysical) mind – which, Nietzsche (1954a) says, may be thorough and deep but is wrong nevertheless – but pertains to the whole person-in-situation. Thus, the question of ethics in curriculum theorizing is often quite abstract, such as when mathematics education is said to implement measures of mathematical knowledge; and this kind of implementation has consequences that allow a separation of good from bad actions. The problem with the metaphysical approach to ethics in education – which focuses on the agent who *takes* responsibility before he or she acts by implementing some abstract rule – has been pointed out in the context of mathematics education. Thus, for example, Walshaw and Brown (2012) "suggest that teachers who are invested in the common advantage of all" (p. 193), and thereby act according to the (Kantian) categorical imperative, "are developing ways of thinking and being in the classroom setting that may be perpetuating the marginalisation of (as in this example) an already disadvantaged class" (p. 193). This fact that teachers who aim at doing good actually worsen the situation derives from the fact that at their very bottom, all actions, practical or discursive, are illogical and unjust (Nietzsche, 1954a) because (explanatory) accounts of actions always follow situated actions (see chapter 8).

It is at this abstract level of the imperative that we can speak about obligations, such as the one that attributed to the curriculum means "to seek to transform classroom arrangements that impeded the production of knowledge" (Walshaw & Brown, 2012, p. 197). Ethics, thereby, first is an issue of the mind, which makes up plans of actions consistent with or against ethical standards that are subsequently implemented (on the relation between planned, living, and enacted curriculum, see chapter 8). Walshaw and Brown (2012) quite correctly note that there is a need to connect emotion to enactivism (embodiment), a move that can be completed through the manner in which participants in relations affect each other. But the relation of ethics to the practical classroom actions that they mobilize for their argument requires considerable levels of abstraction.

The four introductory quotations, which in fact outline a form of argument, direct us towards and guide us along the way towards an ethics that does not first exist in a metaphysical world to be subsequently grounded in and made relevant to practical action. Rather, in relations with others, we are summoned by the words of others, whereby we are already placed in an obligation to answer and answer for. Moreover, when we speak as part of a societal relation, the word is for the other, which places the speaker in an obligation to the listener, who, as shown in this volume, is also in a relation of obligation to the speaker. There is therefore a diachrony of responsibility, which makes for the very constitution of our subjectivity as the subjects in the relation.

In this chapter I show, on the one hand, how ethics is inherent in each and every act/deed precisely because it is a concrete act/deed with irreversible consequences in the world – thereby contrasting the reversibility of actions in the mind (pace J. Piaget) – and, on the other hand, the fact that there is a responsibility for the actions of the other. I ground this argument for a post-constructivist ethics in the work of three scholars in particular – Mikhail Bakhtin, Emmanuel Levinas, and Jean-Luis Chrétien – because they have laid a foundation for the active and passive nature of the question of ethics in the act of speaking. I begin, consistent with the praxis-situated nature of my argument, by presenting and analyzing an actual classroom event from a fourth-grade mathematics lesson and then proceed to making a more extended case for a post-constructivist approach to ethics in education.

The Ethics of Praxis Is the Praxis of Ethics

In this section, I present a fragment from a classroom episode that we already visited in chapter 4[1] to show that students and teachers do not just *take* responsibility but that they always already find themselves in a relation of responsibility and that each participant is answerable for the other. In analyzing the fragment, I am interested in getting the perspectives of the participants in and on the conversation. This requires me, as shown in the preceding chapters, to listen to the next speaker in whose locution we find reflected not only the understanding of the preceding speaker but also its social evaluation. In this sense, every act of speech is a response, even the solitary one, and therefore does not begin knowing and learning as constructivist scholars want to have it. Because we are interested here in ethics as it arises from the inner forces that move this dialogic conversation, we have to understand how the participants themselves hear each other rather than imposing our interpretation of what someone has said. Thus, for example, we may not say that one speaker asks a question unless the second speaker treats it as such in his/her turn.

---

1   The 229-line transcription of the entire 12-minute episode is available in the original French and in translation (Roth & Radford, 2011). Minor modifications had to be made, because errors in the original transcription became evident and it was necessary to appropriately bring into alignment actions and words.

This approach to method analytically implements the contention that *"the nervous center of any utterance, any expression, is not interior but exterior: it is situated in the social milieu that surrounds the individual"* (Bakhtine [Volochinov], 1977, p. 134). The recipient of a locution co-authors and countersigns it, and is thus as important as the speaker to the development of the *conversation* (Derrida, 1988). To understand the conversation as social situation in a specific societal setting, we therefore do not need to figure out what is in the minds of speakers hidden from view – e.g., their "meanings" – but we need to follow the social milieu that surrounds and comprises our speakers. In the meeting, ideas, as I suggest at the end of the preceding chapter, are right out in the open; and the developing idea is a live event that plays out in full view of the participants. That is, we have to hear a speaker as the listeners in the situation have heard him/her, which we do by attending to how these listeners make available their hearing to the speaker in their reply.

Saying Is Summoning and Questioning

The fragment derives from a classroom episode in which the fourth-grade students are asked to model a story in which a girl begins with $3 in her piggybank and adds to it $6 every week. (For more details see chapter 4.) The planned curriculum intends students to arrive at a generalized way for figuring out the total amount so that they can easily predict, without counting out, the amount of money in the piggybank when the number of weeks is very large (e.g., after 117 weeks). The video shows that Aurélie already has abandoned the task and, in apparent frustration, pounds her fist on the desk; and Mario signals that he has difficulties in understanding what he is to do. The fragment picks up after the teacher Jeannie completes an evaluation of an answer by repeating what Thérèse has said and by proffering the first turn to a possible question–answer sequence (turn 069). In this situation, the relation with and to the (generalized) Other, here the students at the group of desks, accomplishes itself in Jeannie's Saying, oriented toward and therefore addressing the children.[2]

Fragment 7.1a
→ 069 J: it EQuals to nine the first week. (0.78) wHY is the thrEE in yellow? whydyou think? ((*Index finger on number in first column.*))
    070   (0.19)

---

2   Instead of the capitalized *Other*, we could also use the capitalized *Thou* (Buber, 1937). In more recent phenomenological writing, the former or its equivalent (e.g., *l'Autre, autrui*) tends to be used.

071 M: um um, um ((*Mario shrugs his shoulders, shakes head "no," squinting eyes which may be seen a questioning look.*))
072   (0.20)
073 T: <<all>i don[no]>
074 M: [be]cause we are supposed to write it?
075   (0.44)

Jeannie's locution (turn 069) summons students to take the next turn, and in this turn to produce a reply to what she has said. She does not address the students in the way she would address the mathematics education professor in the room or some other adult. Rather, she addresses them at what is their understanding*-in-the-making – and thereby already has made an ethical commitment even though she might not have thought about her actions in this way. More importantly, the figure of question–response is subordinated to a more fundamental one of summons–response (Chrétien, 2007), this latter, as a fundamental form of the dialogical relation*-in-the-making, being more complex than the former (Bakhtine, 1984). The question of addressing the children is more primordial than the solicitation of a specific answer, for the second is impossible if the first condition is not met.

A summons is not a summons in and of itself. In praxis, it is a summons only if it is attended to and heard. There is a possibility for a summons – therefore a summons*-in-the-making. To hear this summons, the students actually need to be committed to the dialogical relation*-in-the-making: they need to be committed to listening without knowing "what is coming at them," which also could be an insult, a hurting remark, a slur. The children are vulnerable because, as stated in chapter 4, they cannot know what is coming at them in and with the Saying until it has arrived as the Said when the Saying has come to an end.

This next turn consists of interjections, which Mario accompanies by shaking his head as if signifying "no" (turn 071). Jeannie does not only produce a summons, in her saying she also exposes herself as Mrs. Winter is exposing herself in chapter 2. In producing the locution "why is the three in yellow?" as a candidate question for a question–answer turn, Jeannie in fact exposes herself to possible failure. She does not nor can she know what will come on the part of the students, that is, the social evaluation that completes her locution that transforms the turn pair into an utterance. Thérèse says "I donno," overlapped by Mario, who proffers a possible candidate for a question–answer sequence: "because we are supposed to write it?" (turn 074). That is, as intimated above, it is only through Mario's reply that we know the effect of Jeannie's locution. It is through his voice that we come to know what Mario has heard. In this situation, it is a candidate for an answer to a question. But whether it is a legitimate answer we cannot know until we hear Jeannie again, who makes available to us what she heard Mario say. That is, to reply is not only to provide an answer to but also to answer for, a responsibility for the other with regard to the particular hearing of the preceding locution, which completes a sequentially organized turn pair. It is a responsibility for an inherent and unavoidable irresponsibility that arises from the fact that there is an excess of consequences of the action over any intent (Nietzsche, 1954a).

The intonation is rising toward the end of Mario's locution (turn 74), which makes it possible to hear the locution also as a question. That is, the locution simultaneously is a constative – its grammatical structure makes a statement – and a question – its intonation moves in the way normally associated with questions. It may be heard as a question to Jeannie as much as to himself about the appropriateness of the constative as answer in the question–answer pair that Jeannie has begun. Intonation does not just mark the locution in specific ways, which written language transcribes in the form of punctuation (comma, semicolon, colon, period, question mark, or quotation mark). In living speech, intonation is an integral part and has important functions, as grammatical marker, as expression of social evaluation, and as expression of affect in living speech.[3] Thus, an *affective* evaluative tone colors the experience in this situation in addition to any cognitive experience that one might detect; the evaluative tone provides testimony of the event*-in-the-making. Such testimony is typical of the witness rather than of the detached and uninvolved theoretical spectator. As witnesses, the participants in this event*-in-the-making are affected in and by a situation even prior to comprehending cognitively the kind of event that we are involved in and what is happening to them.

Saying Is Responding, Evaluating, Exposure

As in the preceding situation, the locutions that Mario and Thérèse produce constitute summons to Jeannie, not in the least because Mario appears to offer a question (rising intonation) in addition to a statement ("because we are supposed to write it" [turn 074]). That is, if we take Mario's locution as the point of reference, then it constitutes a second turn with respect to Jeannie's earlier

---

3   Indeed, there are strong correlations between prosodic features and psychological states (Scherer, 1989). Intonation and other prosodic features that correlate with emotional states are not produced consciously and often despite the speakers' intentions (e.g., people blush when they talk about something embarrassing or tell a lie).

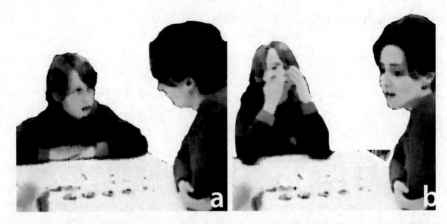

Figure 7.1. a. Mario gazes at Jeannie while proffering a possible second turn to complete the offered question–answer turn pair. b. Jeannie sighs, as in exasperation, turning her face away from Mario, who grimaces, as in desperation, and covers his face in his hands.

locution and a first turn to her subsequent locution. Each locution, therefore, has a double orientation, both backward, as social evaluation, and forward, as a candidate for another sequentially ordered turn pair of some kind. There is therefore a reciprocity, a double rather than a single *one-for-the other*, expressed in the locutions that Jeannie and Mario have produced. This reciprocity leads to the unitary nature of an unfolding and therefore non-self-identical conversation, which contrasts the constructivist perspective of a conversation as an additive phenomenon where individual subjects give and take.

Emphasizing the interrogative "where?," Jeannie proffers another candidate for a question about one of the two composites (3, 6) that add up to nine dollars in the piggybank and repeats the "three" from the preceding question (turn 076). In the repetition, she also emphasizes that the question is about the "three," co-articulates that the preceding answer candidates are not sufficient or insufficiently explained and, in this, provides an evaluation of the preceding locutions. Thérèse says "donno?" with rising intonation (turn 073); and Mario articulates, following several interjections, a candidate answer: "wedding thing there" (turn 078). (He actually mixes the two languages by saying "the wedding chose [thing] there.") Again, the intonation rises towards the end of the locution, which allows us to hear it as a question rather than a constative. At the same time, he also raises his gaze as if looking for Jeannie's reaction to (evaluation of) this answer (Figure 7.1a).

Fragment 7.1b

076 J: WHEREe it comes from the thREE?
077 T: donno?

078 M: <<f>a:=u:> (0.24) u:: (0.17) u: dududu: wedding thing there? ((*questioning look, gazing at Jeannie, Figure 7.1a*))

079 (0.76)

080 J: ˇbut=hh (([*mais=hh*] *exasperation, turns head away from Mario*)) (0.14) the three dO:LLas? is wHAT exACtly? ((*Mario, who has looked at her, grimaces in desperation, brings his hands up and covers face, Figure 7.1b*))

081 (1.61)

082 T: its its:: its [the three] do::llars there that s::he::.

083 M: [u::h:]

084 (0.48)

085 M: she takes [each] week.

086 T: [ss:]

087 (0.38)

088 T: aves ((*Jeanne moves head to side over shoulder, gives him "a look," Figure 7.2a.*))

089 (0.45)

090 M: like i dont understa:nd. ((*Eyes downward, erects, throws hands upward, Figure 7.2b, 460>229 Hz*))

This second turn in the pair not only is social evaluation and a marking of the effect (i.e., what has been heard, the Said), but also, again, exposure to the other. In producing the locution "dududu wedding thing there?" (turn 078), Mario not only proffers a possible completion of a question–answer turn sequence, a confirmation (evaluation) of the first turn as a legitimate question, but also exposes himself to a subsequent evaluation of what he has said (available after his Saying is completed). This evaluation comes in the form of a literally exasperated "buthh" (turn 080). There appears to be an incomprehension on her part about why there is not understanding*-in-the-making, which would be an incomprehension preceding the express comprehension of a finalized event.

Figure 7.2. a. Mario has proffered a candidate answer and Jeannie "gives him a look." b. Mario throws his hands palms upward while saying, "I don't understand."

Many educational researchers have been critical about the forms class-room discourse often take, where the teacher initiates, a student replies, and the teacher evaluates: an ordered and orderly turn-taking sequence that is often better known under the acronym IRE. Such a sequentially ordered turn sequence never can be ascribed to one person, as it always takes the contributions of several speakers who, in this way, co-produce it. Here, however, more is at stake. An IRE is only after the fact, that is, something that will have condensed from a collective event*-in-the-mak-ing. Mario not only contributes to the event*-in-the-making such that it can be seen after the fact as contribution to the sequentially organized IRE routine but also appears to *seek* rather than avoid the social evalua-tion on the part of the teacher. Thus, his intonation rises, as it would in a question, which might be glossed as saying, in a constative form, "The wedding thing there" followed by a query, "Is this right?" or "Am I right so far?" Both speakers are oriented towards and contribute to the event*-in-the-making such that it may retroactively be recognized as an instance of the often-vilified feature of classroom talk. Jeannie's initiation is in fact already a response, to the historical situation in which Jeannie (as Mario), institutionally located differentially, responds; and every locution already is a social evaluation. Viewed in a historical context necessary to under-stand the eventness of events, the IRE routine takes on a more positive ethical coloring. A post-constructivist ethics, which abandons the cause–effect reasoning underlying the IRE concept, leads us to a different appre-ciation of certain classroom discourse features.

Saying Is Affecting

There is considerable pausing before Jeannie produces a "but" followed by clearly hearable outward breath ("hh") with an intonation that is close to a sigh.[4] She turns her head away and toward the camera, as if trying to see whether her (affective) expression has been noted. (In this situation, the af-fective expression – i.e., exasperation – likely was produced without being intended, and it is after the fact that Jeannie checks on the camera.) She says, with a rising intonation, "the three dollars?" and then continues, again

---

4   During the 1980s, teachers have been held responsible for the pauses. The present one is of the approximate length that teachers have been said to allow for students to answer. From the present perspective, pausing does not have causal agents, because, as an integral feature of relation*-in-the-making, it is an irreducible *collective* feature.

with rising intonation, "is what exactly?" (turn 080). As any other speaker would do, even though most are not aware of this, she does what we hear as a rephrasing of a question or rearticulation of a statement in the same or different ways when the addressee provides evidence of not having (physically) heard or (conceptually) understood. Mario's face begins to grimace as if in desperation; his hands move upward and cover his face (Figure 7.1b). In this grimace the affective-emotive quality of the event*-in-the-making expresses itself. The expression condensation of the event*-in-the-making marks the being-affected; it directly follows Jeannie's expression of affect, which I gloss here by the term "exasperation." That is, there is a mutual affection, as exasperation is followed by desperation.

There is a long pausing and then Thérèse ("it's the three dollars there that she ..." [turn 82]) and Mario ("she takes each week" [turn 85]), produce in a turn sequence, a constative that can be heard as a candidate for the answer slot. There is further pausing. Thérèse then produces an interjection and at that time, Jeannie turns her head as if gazing over her shoulder right at Mario, as if she were saying "What are you talking about?" (Figure 7.2a). Mario's gaze drops, as if in shame, then the upper body moves up and backward, and simultaneously, the hands are moving forward, the palms open and turn upward, thereby exposing themselves (Figure 7.2b). Mario says with the intonation characteristic of a constative at the same time, "like I don't understand" (turn 090).

From a Metaphysical Conception of Ethics and Its Critique ...

Ethics: ἠϑικὴ ἐπιστήμη [idiké episteme]: knowledge of ἦϑος [idos], of the inner attitude of humans and the manner in which it determines their behavior. (Heidegger, 1961, p. 92)

If we looked at the fragment through one of the common theoretical lenses, which attribute actions to individuals and their agency, we might gloss what is happening in a way that attributes deeds to Jeannie and Mario: As part of the attempt to allow Mario to make the sought-for abstraction – amount = number of weeks * $3 + $6 – Jeannie asks him about the nature of the $3 in the piggybank after week 1, which the children have represented using 3 red chips, but which is marked in the table of values by a yellow highlighted slot. When none of the three children (Aurélie does not even contribute to the conversation here but has given signs of abandoning the task) offer an appropriate answer, Jeannie asks again. Mario then tentatively offers an answer in which he talks about a wedding, though there was nothing in the situation related to a wedding. There is an expression of exasperation, an expression that may be indicative of Jeannie's witnessing the problematic situation and of her evaluative expression. Just as she produces the "buthh" (Fr. *maishh* /mɛ h h/) – exasperation, literally achieved in the forced aspiration transcribed as "hh" – she turns to look at the camera (or operator), who is thereby acknowledged as the witness. She then turns back, reorients towards Mario, and repeats the question about the three (dollars). In this perspective, each speech act is understood as the consequence of the speaker's intentions. Because intentions exist prior to the act, these can be compared to some ethical norm. Characteristic of this orientation are those instances in life where someone is told that "S/he should have thought before acting," "S/he should have known that this is a hurtful comment," and so forth. The origin of this way of thinking about the relation between ethics and practical action comes from the ancient Greeks, who separated abstract, immaterial, and therefore metaphysical ideas (*theoria*) from practical actions in a material world (*praxis*).

In the opening quotation to this section, Heidegger articulates ethics as a form of knowledge (*theoria*) of/about something, here the inner attitude that determines and thereby is external to actual, practical behavior (*praxis*). It is fundamentally a metaphysical position, whereby some knowledge/idea (*theoria*) is said to be responsible for something in the material world (*praxis*). In the metaphysical tradition, ethics is something in the mind of the individual, who, in fact, merely constructs a specific instance of ethical ideas that transcend the human being. The pinnacle of the metaphysical tradition is achieved in Kant's articulation of abstract and practical ethics – he explicitly entitles his project as the "metaphysics of morals" (Kant, 1956a, p. 326). The Kantian approach is constructivist, placing the individual subject at the center of the self-constructed knowledge: "A *person* is that subject, whose actions are susceptible to an *imputation*" (p. 329), where imputation is "the *judgment* whereby someone is seen as the author (causa libera) of an action, which then is called an act/deed (factum)" (p. 334). Acting ethically means to act in a manner without being forced (e.g., by law) so that the underlying rule could serve as a common maxim. Kant formulates ethics as a "doctrine of virtues," that is, as a "doctrine of the duties that are not governed by external laws" (p. 508).

In Jeannie's case, for example, this means that she would not deliberately hurt her students – e.g., by ridiculing them, calling them names, or putting them in stressful situations. However, this Kantian position is naïve and problematic, because it supposes that the individual could know in an unproblematic manner what is good for humanity as a whole (Nietzsche, 1954b). This author also writes about the fact that once we have an understanding of the practical world as it is, then the Kantian pursuit of "things in themselves" will be a harmless and irrelevant endeavor (Nietzsche, 1954a).

Despite the critiques of Kant's ethical position on the part of Nietzsche and other philosophers, the Kantian perspective on knowledge was taken up explicitly in the constructivist formulation of knowing and learning and in recent constructivist formulations of ethics (e.g., von Glasersfeld, 2009). Here, too, the ethical question is something relegated to the solitude of the individual mind, as can be seen from the statement that "we use our construction of 'others,' who seem to have action rules similar to our own, as the foundation of a *second-order viability*" (p. 118). It is evident here, that the constructivist position fails to recognize that collective responsibility is a phenomenon sui generis that cannot be reduced to individual responsibility (Chrétien, 2007): it "cannot be reduced to the sum of individual actions" (p. 194). Without this tie between the two, there is no way that I could answer for myself and answer before the Other (e.g., court, society). There is a difference, however, between Kantian and modern constructivist ethics in that the former leads to a generalized form of ethics whereas the latter leads to an intra-personal ethics taken to be more or less viable in the constructed world. There is, however, no indication about how human beings could ever share an ethical ground or how the individual would ever come to construct ethics in the first place. The constructivist approach, because it is concerned with an ethics constructed in the mind, has actually no place for the individual in its dialectical relation with others and, therefore, for the grounding of morality in historical society and culture. The other is encountered in an open meeting that continues to develop and is co-extensive with life, whereas the use of representations means living in a dead past. The individual, "the one who is actually thinking and who is answerable for his act of thinking," is "not present in the theoretically valid judgment" (Bakhtin, 1993, p. 4). It is not surprising, therefore, that there have been calls for bringing "responsibility … back from the province of specialized ethics, of an 'ought' that swings free in the air, into that of *lived life*. Genuine responsibility exists only where there is real responding" (Buber, 1947/2002, p. 18).

In a constructivist approach to ethics, we would analyze the curriculum generally and the fragment featured here particularly in terms of actions that spring forth from intentions. The opening locution is said to be a question that is attributed to Jeannie independently of what has gone on before, the cultural and historical nature of the setting, and what follows; Mario's locution similarly is totally attributed to him, independently of what has gone on before, the cultural and historical nature of the setting, and what follows (e.g., Roth, 2008). The categorical imperative exists in different forms, but in each case presupposes the act to be founded in an intention that precedes it: "Act only according to that maxim whereby you can at the same time will that it should become a universal law without contradiction."

This formulation of ethics becomes problematic when considered from the perspective of the living curriculum*-in-the-making, where the effect of a locution, whatever the intention might have been, manifests itself in the locution of the respondent. Once an effect has condensated from the relation*-in-the-making, a cause can be attributed – i.e., a locution is a question, an insult, a statement, a request, and so on. That is, in the present approach, the produced act and its intention, on the one hand, and its effect, on the other hand, cannot be separated – especially not into a cause–effect relation because it is only through the effect that a cause can be attributed (see chapter 2). Neither Jeannie nor we can evaluate turn 80 ("but=hh … the three dollars is what exactly?") until we know how it has been heard and how it has affected Mario (or his peers). It is through his verbal and affective expression that we come to know that there has been a negative effect and affect. The traditional formulation of a cause–effect relation is problematic when viewed from the perspective of the event*-in-the-making, which explodes the cause–effect dimension of practical action. Once the cause–effect figure of reasoning is put out of play as a myth, the normal Kantian (constructivist) attribution of responsibility is exploded, too. Thus, in the answer to the rhetorical question "Yet is it really the case that transcendent self-activity is … the self-activity for which I am individually answerable?" (Bakhtin, 1993, p. 6), the author answers: "No one, of course, will claim something like that" (p. 6). We cannot make an ethico-moral judgment based on a single locution, because, as part of living speech in dialogical conversation, it takes a second locution (or other expression) to conclude the act so that we can make, if we so desire at the expense of losing our phenomenon, a determination of causality and causation.

Theoretical cognition alone, as it is considered in the constructivist (Kantian) position, cannot explain why there should be affect involved in ethics in the manner it is observable in the present instance. This is so because theoretical cognition is based on *r*epresentations from which all life has been drained. That is, we see that in and through their relation, Jeannie becomes exasperated and Mario gets frustrated; it is in their own expressions that they make available their evaluations of the affective expressions of the other. If, however, we just looked at the cognitional act, we would lose our phenomenon of interest (Bakhtin, 1993). Thus, "the detached content of the cognitional act comes to be governed by its own immanent laws, according to which it then develops as if it had a will of its own" (p. 7). Bakhtin here refers to the representations by means of which we think (about) the world, and these, in the constructivist position on ethics that he is critiquing, seem to take on an independent life of their own: "Inasmuch as we have entered that content, i.e., performed an act of abstraction, we are now controlled by its autonomous laws or, to be exact, we are simply no longer present in it as individually and answerable active human beings" (p. 7).

The perhaps most advanced solution to the dilemma provided by the cognitive/interpretive position may be in the formulation of practical wisdom, which "consists in inventing conduct that will best satisfy the exception required by solicitude, by betraying the rule to the smallest extent possible" (Ricœur, 1990, p. 312). But this solution does not get us out of the problem, for the subject still would invent behavior before performing the deed and a rational comparison of the rule in the context of the situation at hand. If Jeannie cannot know beforehand what she has done until an effect is available as the condensation of the curriculum*-in-the-making – asked a question, made an evaluation, hurt someone – then she cannot beforehand minimize the distance between abstract ethics and the concrete performance of a deed the effect of which is known only after the fact.

Because listeners open up to the Saying as it unfolds – I note that there is an *active* nature in and to the reception of the Other's speech – they are affected before actually knowing the Said. In the living event of the saying is where we obtain the connection between thinking, irreducibly intertwined with speaking (Vygotskij, 2002), and affect, which alone allows us to understand the "fullness of real life," the "living motives, interests, impulses of the thinker" (p. 54). The constructivist approach makes it impossible to comprehend the influence of affect on cognition and volition. That is, that which transcends the material world*-in-the-making – ideas, intentions, conceptions, or ethics – cannot be that for which I am responsible. Responsibility comes into play when I act in the real world, which is transformed through my act (deed) and therefore is affected irreversibly. Thus, in the real, once-occurent world*-in-the-making, my very presence (acting, being) means responsibility, a responsibility more radical than any responsibility (ethics) we can think of – because it is responsibility for our unavoidable irresponsibility. Because we are inextricably related to the material world*-in-the-making and to the Other and because practical understanding always precedes, accompanies, and en-velops theoretical understanding, there is responsibility more ancient than human memory:

> To maintain that the relation with the neighbor, which incontestably accomplishes itself in the Saying, is a responsibility for the other, and that *Saying* is "answering for the other" means no longer finding a limit or a measure of this responsibility that in "human memory" has never been contracted and which finds itself at the mercy of freedom and destiny. (Levinas, 1971, p. 41)

Levinas here points to the dimension of the association of relation*-in-the-making and living speech that exists as Saying outlined in chapter 6. And it is in the same Saying that we locate responsibility for our irresponsibil-ity. It is in the exposure to the Other (Buber's *Thou*) that comes with speech that we can find the ethical relation that undoes the Kantian (constructiv-ist, metaphysical) ethics: "It is in the risky discovery of oneself, in sincerity, in the rupture of interiority and the abandonment of all shelter, in exposure to trauma, in vulnerability" (Levinas, 1978, p. 82). In a post-constructivist ethics, we view the *Saying* not as an expression of something pre-existing but view the Saying, an expression of the relation*-in-the-making, as a re-source for the speaking subject to discover itself in the Said. It is to such an ethics that we now turn.

... to a Post-constructivist Conception of Ethics

The post-constructivist approach to ethics that I articulate here hinges on the two-sided nature of living speech, whereby (a) any word irreducibly belongs to, and is spread over, speaker and listener simultaneously (i.e., its synchronic dimension) and (b) any Saying unfolds in time and is spread diachronically across two consecutive speakers who also listen to each other. There there-fore exists a two-fold dehiscence, one deriving from the spread over subjec-tivities (subjects*-in-the-making) and the other from the spread over time (curriculum*-in-the-making).

Proposition Is Exposition Is Exposure

> The Saying is *proposition* – proposition to the neighbor, "signification loaned/dealt" to the Other. (Levinas, 1971, p. 40)

> The Saying is exposition of one to the other. Exposition here has a sense very different from thematization. The one exposes itself to the other as a skin exposes itself to that which wounds it, as the cheek offered to the smiter. (p. 44)

We may characterize the traditional conception of the locution as the speakers' making propositions, and, in so doing, their imposition of "meaning" on or contribution of "meaning" to the conversation. In the post-constructivist ethics outlined here, the opposite, if anything, is the case. In the presentation of the fragment, I articulate how speakers and listeners expose themselves to others. Speaking is exposition, possibilities of signification offered up to the other, who imposes signification that shapes the situation – Derrida (1996) denotes this situation as the "monolingualism of the other." The direction of the imposition, therefore, goes the other way, that is, from listener to speaker rather than the reverse, as it does in the constructivist approach. The semantics of the word *exposition* includes "exposure." Thus, I focus our attention here on the fact that exposition names the process of putting something (out) into public view; but such exposition immediately implies exposure, exposing oneself to the public. The French language is in a fortunate position to hear the sound /ekspozisjɔ̃/ (*exposition*) as *ex-peau-sition*, that is, literally translated as "out-of-skin-placing." Being outside oneself, one is (emotionally) affected as much as physically. Exposition therefore names the process of making a statement, of setting forth or declaring in speech (writing). When Mario utters what is a tentative (possible) candidate for a question–answer turn sequence, he puts something into public view – here Jeannie, the teacher, and his two peers.

In attending and listening to Jeannie, Mario also exposes himself. While words furl from Jeannie's lips, all the while her Saying is unfolding, Mario *cannot* know what Jeannie *will have been said* once the locution has ended and the *Said* is available in its entirety. That is, he exposes himself to the unknown, to something that is coming at him, but which he will know as the Said only subsequently. At this instant in the eventing of the event, therefore, there is a double exposure, each interlocutor exposing him-/herself to the Other. In the face of the Other, each participant is vulnerable, subject to being affected, subject and subjected to what is happening. Such exposure brings responsibility, but on the part of the Other. That is, *because* he has been called upon in Jeannie's address, Mario is responsible *prior to his intention* to act. Similarly, Jeannie performs not because she somehow *feels* responsible – which may also be the case; rather, much more originarily, she is always already responsible because she is speaking, calling forth the Other, and thereby affecting him/her. But this speaking already is the second moment of the response*-in-the-making in and to a cultural-historical context rather than an originary beginning. In this position, therefore, Jeannie is already chosen as a respondent, and, therefore, in the role of the patient (see chapter 5). Speaking implies responsibility *one for the other* prior to any conceptualizing of what is to be said.

The exposure that comes with Jeannie's or Mario's speaking constitutes "supreme passivity," an "abandon of the sovereign and active subjectivity posited as 'self-consciousness', as the undeclined subject, or as the subject in the nominative form" (Levinas, 1971, p. 41). This leads us to a form of inversion of intentionality, where the autonomous ("undeclined") speaking subject, rather than acting upon the world, first and foremost is subject to and subjected to the Other. It is also a subject*-in-the-making rather than a finalized (dead) subject. Being a patient, the one who is subject to affect and suffering, the subject*-in-the-making *first* appears in the accusative form. It constitutes an inversion of the constructivist (Kantian) subject, which is the origin of its cognitive structure, the viability in the world of which is the intentional project of the autonomous subject. Thinking speech from the perspective of the autonomous subject would "amount to a prior representation ... as though speaking consisted in translating thoughts into words and consequently in having been first *for-oneself* and *at home with oneself*" (Levinas, 1978, p. 81). The proposed post-constructivist ethics thereby overturns the primacy of the subject and its mind, a view that also changes how we are led to think subject, subjectivity, and identity (see chapter 5).[5]

The transcription of the lesson fragment shows that when Jeannie speaks, Mario is listening; when Mario is speaking, Jeannie is listening. They are committed to the dialogue; their meeting is the practical instantiation of the figure or motif that is co-extensive with life itself. As we can see from the emotional dimensions of their replies, they are affected in and through this exposure.

---

5   The complexity involved in such a rethinking certainly is one of the reasons why it takes Ricœur (1990) an entire book to articulate the questions of Self, Other, and their ethical nature of their relation.

Each, therefore, in his/her turn opens up to receive, and this opening up is part of their *response*. Here response is understood as a category that unites listening and replying into one single process, because "listening is an act of speech, and even the first of all" (Chrétien, 2007, p. 31). It would be impossible to *reply* – etymologically derived from Middle French *reploier*, to send back – if there had been no listening to the original locution; and this reply is grounded in and inseparable from the listening. This orientation toward the speaker on the part of the listener constitutes part of the *active* reception, understanding*-*in-the-making*, which occurs at the level of inner speech (Bakhtine [Volochinov], 1977). Here an "utterance is received, comprehended, and evaluated" (p. 165). There are two dimensions to the active orientation of the listener. First, "the utterance of another is replaced in the context of a factual commentary (which confounds itself partially with what is called the apperceptive ground of the utterance)" (p. 165). *At the same time*, an answer forms itself – as Saying unfolds, so does understanding*, inherently, therefore, in the making. These two parts are irreducible moments of the same phenomenon: the diastatic and dehiscent nature of the response. These two moments "can be isolated only in abstract terms" (p. 166). In this way, "the listener becomes the speaker" (Bakhtine, 1984, p. 274).

The specificity of the kind of ethics Levinas proposes arises from the fact that the one who makes a proposition exposes a text, and in this exposition thereby also exposes him-/herself: Addressing the Other is speaking-*for*-the-Other. Jeannie does not just summon Mario, but exposes herself; Mario does not just expose himself in the response (listening, replying), but, in replying, summons Jeannie simultaneously. Here, those who expose themselves, who thereby are vulnerable, also are those who speak for and address the Other for whom they thereby bear responsibility. They are also those who, in responding, socially evaluate the other. The hyperbolic nature of the Levinasian ethics comes from the fact that it is the vulnerable, "the persecuted one [who] is liable to answer for the persecutor" (Levinas, 1978, p. 175). It is here where the absoluteness of passivity and the responsibility lies. In the relation*-in-the-making, I am always chosen and choosing, suffering and act[ing] in one" (Buber, 1937, p. 11). Speakers, who expose themselves in their Saying, and, therefore, are the equivalents of the persecuted ones, have to answer for the persecutors, the ones whom they address in and during Saying – because they not only call on the Other but also call for the response of the Other (which begins with their listening/attending and ends in their own completion of a Said).

Exposure and the associated passivity are fundamental to the post-constructivist ethics I propose in conjunction with understanding curriculum as a living, unfinalized event*-in-the-making. Thus, the passivity of the Saying is "an exposure to the other, it is signification, is signification itself, the-one-for-the-other to the point of substitution – but a substitution in separation, that is, responsibility" (Levinas, 1978, p. 92). Here we can hear in the "substitution" a substitution of the traditional subject, conscious of its actions that it deploys while doing so to the dialectical construction of the subject, which is also subject and subjected to the condition. It is not Jeannie who determines the "meaning" of her locution "why is the three in yellow?": It is what Mario is hearing – condensed in his reply, which incorporates and reports the speech of the Other even in the absence of direct or indirect discourse – that will set up the next speaking turn and, therefore, determine the movement in and of the conversation.

Relative to the constructivist approach, it is not Jeannie but Mario who "calls" the nature of the sequentially ordered turn pair. (Pertinent here, the baseball umpire Bill Klem is often quoted to have said, "It [throw] is nothing [ball or strike] until I call it.") There is therefore a substitution of the traditional subject: Jeannie is in the position of the accusative. The subject is subject*-in-the-making that arises from the transition from the accusative "me" to the nominative "I." Maintaining that the relation*-in-the-making with the other accomplishes itself in the unfolding Saying also means "glimpsing an extreme passivity, a passivity without assumption, in the relation with others and, paradoxically, in the pure saying itself" (Levinas, 1971, p. 41). "Without assumption" here means that the passivity is not taken on actively; it is passivity more radical than any passivity that we can think of or take because it pre-exists and we find ourselves in it (see chapter 5). That is, the *Saying* in general signifies the turning toward and opening up to the Other, intimacy; and opening up means opportunities to be affected, vulnerability.

Speaking exposes itself to the listening, and listening is exposed to the speaking. That is, there is not merely a sequentially ordered taking of turns as theorized in classical conversation analysis, but both Jeannie and Mario are implied in the turns of the respective other. Each word, therefore, represents a reciprocal relation rather than the one typical for the constructivist (intentional) approach, where the locution is taken as a representation of the conceptual structure in the mind. Levinas (1978) denotes this reciprocal relation by the term of the "one-penetrated-by-the-other" (p. 85), which leads him to unfold a discourse that includes the persecutor and the persecuted, the violence of denuding and being denuded: a traumatic form of violence. The special and sometimes difficult to understand nature of Levinasian ethics derives from this interpenetration of the interlocutors, here Jeannie and Mario. We do find this interpenetration in speech, where each locution is from the Self, in reply to the Other, taking up the Other's speech, to which it thereby returns. There is always an "interpenetration of reported and reporting speech" (Bakhtine [Volochinov], 1977, p. 175). As a result, the "psyche ... is a social entity that penetrates inside the organism of the individual person" (p. 65).

In the constructivist literature on pedagogy and curriculum, there is an emphasis on the "meanings" that speakers articulate, make, or have. Thus, Mario would have said to have (not) made sense of Jeannie's "question," and Jeannie would have been said to construct the "meaning" of Mario's responses – him not understanding and, as a consequence, reiterating the question. In the post-constructivist ethics proposed here, the issue of signification is reversed, or, perhaps better, it is but a moment of the whole "being-as-event" or "world-as-event." For one, the Saying prevents sense to be attributable to the speaker him-/herself. This is so because in the Saying, "the *for-the-other*, the passivity more passive still than any passivity, the emphasis of sense, is kept from being *for-oneself*" (Levinas, 1978, p. 85). In this formulation, sense (a word which in many Anglo-Saxon texts might appear as "meaning") is kept from being for-oneself, which renders illegitimate to talk about "Jeannie's sense ['meaning']" or "Mario's sense ['meaning']" in the way we find it in many analyses of classroom talk. Vygotskij (2002) agrees with this position when he says that the "word is in consciousness that which according to Feuerbach is absolutely impossible for the individual but possible for two" (p. 467). When Jeannie speaks, it is not for her, it is for Mario. She seeks an expression *for* Mario, rather than for herself, and this is especially salient in her repeated attempts – when summoned – to rearticulate the locution so that it becomes an intelligible first moment of a question–answer pair.

Affect and Affectation: Exasperation and Frustration

In the exasperation she is expressing through her body movements (posture change, voice), we come to see the second moment of Jeannie's response to the situation, which also constitutes the social evaluation of the situation as a whole. It includes and pertains to both Mario's apparent difficulties in producing a sought-for answer and her own inability to ask in a manner that would allow a satisfactory question–response pair to evolve. That is, the first locution (turn 069) is not such that it allows a second locution to come forth so that it produces the premise for a positive evaluation, the third turn of an IRE sequence. Similarly, Mario allows us to glimpse his response, which includes an emotive evaluation of the situation in the fragment. We might gloss this evaluation as a form of frustration with the situation as a whole tending toward despair, for there now have been repeated joint attempts at producing what would become the premise of the next pedagogical move to explain the amount of money (number of chips) in the second goblet.

In this fragment, we therefore observe how the interlocutors affect each other in and through their talk and other forms of bodily expression including prosody; and this affectation is reflected in affective expressions. Thought, realized in and being the condensation of the Saying, and affect, realized in the various bodily expressions including intonation, no longer are separate but constitute different moments of the same unfolding event irreducible to Jeannie's or Mario's individual or collective agency. Moreover, the participants Jeannie and Mario do not merely deliver some (cognitive) content, as this would be in the constructivist framework, but they provide these expressions *for* each other and make available how another's expression has affected them. Thus, for example, the intonation that goes with "but" together with the hearable expiration "hh" (turn 080) followed by the third instantiation of what can be heard as a question about the nature of the "three" (dollars, yellow chips) evolves into Mario's grimace and the covering of his face with his hands. This is a change from earlier locutions and expressions that have been much more assertive. We therefore have a double effectuation, whereby a first turn pair affects the first moment of the response, and the second turn pair, the second moment of the response, affects the first speaker, which is made visible as the second part of the second turn pair, for which the second locution is the first turn.

The importance of theorizing affect as an integral part of the relation and of bringing affect into the analysis becomes very clear in this brief fragment from a classroom episode. Both participants orient to and engage the other. Speakers are not mere dispassionate cognitive devices, but the situation, which we may gloss as a failure to ask the right question and to give the right answer, is associated with affect made available publicly through emotional expressions upon which the participants themselves act. These expressions are reflections of the material situation but at a level that differs from cognitive consciousness. We most clearly see this in the sequence where Mario, in providing a locution as candidate for the second slot in the question–answer sequence, offers up a candidate answer (turn 078). It is an offer that the rising intonation marks in a way that we may gloss as, "Here is my answer but I am not certain about it" or "Is this the answer you are looking for?" The expression of exasperation and the repetition of the question, which constitute the social evaluation part, the effect (perlocution), mark the answer as inappropriate.

Jeannie is not just asking for the nature of the three dollars ("the three dollars is what exactly?") but, in its repetition, in asking the same question again, the locution also marks that the preceding answer is not the expected one. The term "but" functions as adversative conjunction and as interjection that expresses opposition, objection, or protest (Oxford English Dictionary [OED], 2012). There therefore is a double evaluation, the totality of which is negative – not because we, the observer participants "interpret" the instant in this way but because the participant concerned, Mario, produces a concomitant expression as the second member of a turn pair characterized by a negative evaluation across both cognitive and emotive dimensions: He has been affected in attending to Jeannie's expressions, and his evaluation expresses itself in his grimacing, as in desperation, and his covering of his face.

From the aforesaid we learn that Saying is contact and, therefore, already wounds or caresses (Levinas, 1971). Because of the two-sidedness of tact, within and outside the body, it also is associated with denuding, penetration, wounding more than the outside, and going to the very heart of being. With contact, there also is tact, contingency, and contamination, all with etymological roots in the Latin verb *tangere*, to touch. When we listen to someone else, we may be touched by the Said and we are affectively contaminated, i.e., touched without being aware of it, by the intonational forms of the Saying – which sometimes moves us to tears even though we may not want to cry.

Answerability

Because transaction participants affect each other by definition – and, emotionally speaking, infect each other, since affect spreads like contagion and fuels the affect of others – there is a form of responsibility that is prior to any intention. This responsibility comes from the very praxis of speaking, which is why both Levinas and Bakhtin include it as lynch pin in their ethics. The latter uses the term answerability to characterize the ethical dimensions for each act/deed that we produce: We solicit answers but also are answerable for the solicitation. He does not make an explicit link to the answer in a speaking situation. Such a link is made when we constitute the Saying as the paradigm of ethics. In the French language, the verb *répondre* (to respond), in the same way as the English verb *to answer*, has a different dictionary sense in different constructions. *Répondre à* is equivalent to "to answer (someone)" or "to answer to (a charge)"; *répondre de* translates as "to answer for [charges in regard to]." That is, in providing responses, speakers not only answer to but also answer for something. These two aspects are irreducible and therefore cannot be separated, as stated in the third introductory quotation to this chapter. Whereas Bakhtin attributes this responsibility to the person producing the locution, Levinas actually theorizes the beginning in the reception, thereby making the listener answerable for the Saying of the speaker. But because any speaker is already responding to a cultural-historical situation, s/he is responsible in the very act – not in the least because speaking means participating in once-occurrent and irreversible life.

In Bakhtin, every act is answerable, not just the act of speaking. This is so not in the least because the answerable act or deed is "the actualization of a decision – inescapably, irremediably, and irrevocably" (Bakhtin, 1993, p. 28). The answerable act/deed "is this affirmation of my non-alibi in Being that constitutes the basis of my life" (p. 42). We can hear this answerability in two ways. First, the author of the act or deed is answerable, that is, responsible for the act, which, in an ever-changing "world-as-event" – i.e., world*-in-the-making in terms of the concepts developed here – is once-occurrent and therefore cannot be taken back. This world is not abstract, but, qua practical and inhabited world that conditions us and that we condition, is at our "mutual disposition" (p. 54). Thus, my act contributes to the changes of the world*-in-the-making, thereby also making it a different world at the disposition of the Other. But answerability also means that the author of the act/deed is answerable for making an answer possible, that is, in being intelligible on the part of the other. That is, the utterance is *for-the-other*, and to have this characteristic, the address needs to be such that the other actually *can* understand and answer.

A relation always is a relation*-in-the-making (chapter 6); and a living relation*-in-the-making is mutual. This allows us to suggest that there is "an architectonic interrelationship of two valuatively affirmed others" (Bakhtin, 1993, p. 74). The basic moments of the architectonic are "I-for-myself," "the-other-for-me," and the "I-for-the-other" (p. 54). The synchronic structural and diachronic temporal dimensions of the practical world are captured in the notion of "world-as-event," inherently diachronic, and in terms of an architectonic (i.e., inherently synchronic structure). Values are inherent in the way that this architectonic is structured: The "valuative architectonic ... is something-*given* as well as something-to-be accomplished, for it is an architectonic of an event" (p. 75). Events, in their eventness, are diachronic. In fact, the whole world is unitary in content because it is to be conceived in the category of "world-as-event" (p. 32). Bakhtin notes that the contraposition of *I* and the *Other* has not been stated explicitly (at the time he composed his essay); but it has indeed occurred in the works of Levinas and Buber generally.

Bakhtin develops an ethics in the context of art and the relationship between the author of a piece of work and those who render social evaluation. This allows us to extend the post-constructivist ethics articulated here from speaking to writing and any other form of human expression. The mutual responsibility and guilt of the author (of an utterance) and respondent are expressed in terms of the relation between artist (poet) and the consumer of art (reader). The artist and writer have to keep in mind that their creation, "bears the guilt for the vulgar prose of life" (Bakhtin, 1990, p. 2). The everyday person, on the other hand, "ought to know that the fruitlessness of art is due to his willingness to be unexacting and to the unseriousness of the concerns in his life" (p. 2). The "architectonics of answerability" refers to the fact that the reader is giving life to the art (text) produced by the artist. Translated back to the communicative relation with which this article begins, it is the listener who gives life to the text produced by the artist; it is the relation between the author and recipient that affirms the diachrony (dehiscence) of the word.

The *Saying (le Dire)* as Paradigm for a Post-Constructivist Ethics

> Responsibility always remains a response to that which precedes us and to that which surrounds us. (Chrétien, 2007, p. 195)

In the post-constructivist ethics proposed here, Saying always is a response and a beginning simultaneously. We can then understand the ability to respond, that is, response-ability, as the foundation of responsibility. Considered in this way, responsibility is not something that I take. Responsibility is integral to the relation*-in-the-making that we enter in the encounter with the Other. Because the Saying also is a commentary on what has preceded, there is an integral relation between evaluation and signification:

"every actualized word not only contains a theme and a signification in the objective sense ... but also an evaluative accent" (Bakhtine [Volochinov], 1977, p. 147). Every word that Jeannie utters in the conversation, as every word that Mario produces, contains this evaluative accent. Every locution takes up and is a reply to a preceding situation. Even Jeannie's first question in this fragment is in response to something that precedes the instance, Mario's raised hand that summoned her to the group of desks in the narrow sense and a response to the institution and her institutional role in a larger sense. Jeannie asks the question because she is a teacher, whose role in this lesson is to assist children in learning mathematics. As a consequence, without evaluative accent, the word as such does not exist. "The most obvious level, which at the same time is the most superficial of the social evaluation contained in the word is transmitted by means of the *expressive intonation*" (p. 147). "Being-*for*-the-other, in the manner of the Saying, is therefore exposing *to* the other that signification itself" (Levinas, 1971, p. 42). This is to say that this reversal of the ethical question involves the exposition rather than imposition of signification ("meaning").

Each Saying is an irreducible moment of conversation, which can be viewed as the exchange of signs (words) that are or are made common to the interlocutors. Precisely because Mario signals a problem with understanding Jeannie's opening locution, the communication is shaped to deal with this "incomprehension" so that the exchange eventually is enabled. Both parties are committed to the relation*-in-the-making and, thereby, responsible for themselves and for the other because "collective responsibility and co-responsibility form a constitutive dimension of social existence" (Chrétien, 2007, p. 196). In the economic exchange process, the things exchanged have equal value, which in fact is different value – use-value and exchange-value (Marx/ Engels, 1962). Marx's insights can be metaphorized (literally "transferred") to ethics, for in his theory, the value of a thing only stands proxy for the value of a person. For example, the difference between the cost of materials and the cost of a garment is the value of the tailor's work. In positing the equivalence of values of the things they exchange, human beings posit the equivalence of their mutual labor, and, therefore, the mutual equivalence of themselves as human beings. Thus, "value is a relation between people ... a relation hidden under material cover" (p. 88).[6] Bakhtin's (1993) theory of ethics, consistent with his (sociological) theory of language, takes on this dialectical (dialogical)

---

6   An analysis that replaces the term "commodity" in Marx's *Capital* with the linguistic term
     "sign" and examples of commodities with examples of signs produces texts that exhibit

perspective of the Marxian exchange, which, by being about the value of human beings, inherently takes on deontological dimensions.

The Saying is an event*-in-the-making, and events*-in-the-making are diachronic and dehiscent – spread out across time and space – which, from a dialectical perspective, cannot be captured in nominal categories. The verb is much more appropriate to capture the eventness of the event, particularly in constructions such as "there is pausing" where the attribution of causation is prevented. It is in the very diachrony of the Saying – a direct consequence that it is a real, practical and temporal act – that the possibility for being affected enters the picture. Understanding the response as beginning with listening, as developed in chapter 2, also is a way of conceptualizing post-constructivist ethics in a diachronic and dehiscent way. That is, as soon as we take the practical action – a real, once-occurrent, and irreversible process – as the point of reference, we introduce the same deontological dimension that we get when we attempt to understand being and the world as (historical) events*-in-the-making. However, when we consider the Said, which, in its denominative form, presents the world in asynchronic manner, we end up with an a-temporal and abstracted structure and metaphysical ethics.

Across his work, Bakhtin (1993) builds a non-reductionist, dialectical (he prefers the adjective dialogical even though his work is deeply influenced by Marxian thought) theory of the world*-in-the-making. Understanding the world as event*-in-the-making requires us to think the eventness of the event. For Bakhtin, as for Vygotsky, the spoken/written word (utterance) is such a category. Post-constructivist ethics therefore arises from the fact that "every word has *two faces*. It is determined as much by the fact that it proceeds *from* someone as by the fact that it is directed *towards* someone. It precisely constitutes *the product of the interaction of speaker and listener*" (Bakhtine [Volochinov], 1977, p. 123). Any word that Jeannie utters in this encounter is *for* Mario, and any word Mario utters in this encounter is *for* Jeannie. As a result, the word is the bridge *between* and *common to* participants – not just "taken-as-shared" as constructivists hold it. We may also say that the word is the same and different simultaneously; it symbolizes the inner difference of the same. This inner difference manifests itself in very different ways – diachrony (speaking, responding) and dehiscence (differences in speech intention and speech effect [social

structural and semantic family resemblances with post-constructivist philosophies of language and ethics (Roth, 2006).

evaluation]). It is, as some commentators point out, an explicit attempt to build on Karl Marx's philosophical writings to establish an understanding of humans in their flesh and blood who, in real praxis, not only are subject to the reigning conditions but also simultaneously transform these conditions. It is an explicit attempt to understand life as a moving, continuously self-transforming, Heraclitean flux.

Kant (1956b) pins moral value to action, which he derives from its formal properties, and associates it with the moral value of the person. As part of a discursive act, the word therefore is associated with moral value of the person (Kant, 1956a). From this perspective, the value of Jeannie or Mario as persons derives from the particular acts ascribed and imputed to them qua agential subjects. But in the post-constructivist ethics articulated here, the word is attributed to both interlocutors simultaneously. This leads to the fact that the non-coincidence of the word-sign with itself begins in the Saying (Rus. *vyskasivanie*, statement or utterance for Bakhtin). Differences in understanding*-in-the-making of the word that exist between two speakers are not a result of two subjectivities, each "interpreting" the word in its own way, but are a result of the originary non-self-identity of the word-sign with itself, which manifests itself in different understandings. This is a straight analogy to the situation of Marx's category of value, which manifests itself as use-value or exchange-value of the same commodity to buyer and seller, respectively. In fact, we may pin value directly to the word (signification), which, in analogy to economic value, is use- and exchange-value simultaneously.[7] Again, the differences are not the results of different individuals – as constructivist, metaphysical ethics would consider the issue – but an inner difference of the thing.[8] The dehiscence of the word, itself a diachronic moment spread in and producing time, also is a reflection of diachrony of all processes. It is a diachrony made salient in the notion of the *one-for-the-other* characteristic not only of philosophical thought but also apparent in the theories of social psychologists for whom any consciousness of and for self always already is consciousness for the other. This double relation of consciousness, being

---

7   The co-translator and author of the introduction to *Art and Answerability* points out the close relations between Bakhtin and Marx (Holquist, 1990).

8   This idea is difficult to understand when we imprison ourselves – a choice, and therefore responsibility – in the perspective of/from the individual subject and when objects are considered irrespective of the unfolding events in which they are constitutive parts.

for the other and being for the self, is reflected in the word "like the sun in a water droplet" (Vygotskij, 2002, p. 467).

To conclude, the post-constructivist ethics articulated here is grounded in the aliveness of the Saying in speech. Whereas the Said, as some*thing* non-living, can be manipulated in a system of non-living representations, the Saying is part of the Heraclitean flux that never returns in a self-identical way. But the Saying is not just affecting others, it also implies opening up, a transcendence of the Self in the direction of the Other. The speaking subject "approaches the other by *ex-pressing* itself," "in the literal sense of the term by expelling itself out of any locus, neither *inhabiting* nor stomping any ground" (Levinas, 1978, p. 83). The passivity and ethics in living speech therefore do not arise from the fact that we use language that is not our own – we always appropriate it from the other – and, therefore, that anything we can express is but a realization of possibilities that already exist in culture or "ex-appropriation." The radical passivity and the special ethical nature of the relation*-in-the-making encompassing Jeannie and her students come with Saying, which, in its performative, living dimensions, manifests itself as agency and passivity. This allows us to understand ethics and responsibility as inherent moments of once-occurrent life as event*-in-the-making rather than as a mentally constructed feature in some immaterial, *metaphysical* world that has to find its ground.

· 8 ·

THE PLANNED, LIVING, AND
ENACTED CURRICULUM

Curriculum is all the planned, guided and implemented learning that occurs in a
school. Queensland state schools develop school curriculum plans using the Key
Learning Area syllabuses or New Basics organisers. (Aussie Educator, 2012)

[W]hile the course of action can always be projected or *reconstructed* in terms of prior
intentions and typical situations, the prescriptive significance of intentions for situated action is inherently vague. (Suchman, 1987, p. 27, emphasis added)

All teachers learn to write lesson plans to specify what students are to learn.
Teachers then implement these plans on a particular day and time as a way
of guiding students so that they may learn what the plans intend them to
learn. The result of the lesson leads to the "implemented learning." Whether
students have learned what has been stated as the intended learning outcome
in the planned curriculum is evaluated by comparing the stated goals and objectives with students' actual responses on some assessment. A plan for one or
several lessons may be specified as represented in Figure 8.1. Although lesson
plans vary in structure and detail, what is common to them is the specification
of learning outcomes. Underlying such a specification is the idea that learning
can be planned and anticipated on the part of the teacher. This, of course,
flies into the face of any teacher's observation in an actual classroom where

Subject: Mathematics

Grade: Grade 2

Topic: Characteristics of three-dimensional objects

Content: Geometric objects are not distinguished by color and size but rather shape.

   Three-dimensional objects differ in the number, shape, and curvature of their faces.

Goals: Students will be able to:

   1. know the characteristics of the different kinds of objects

   2. understand the definition of the types of objects

   3. identify an object by its category name

   4. compare different types of objects

Objectives: After completing this lesson, the student will state the differences between

   types of three-dimensional geometric objects such as cubes, rectangular prisms,

   pyramids, cylinders, and spheres. They will list and describe the major categories of

   three-dimensional objects.

Materials: Three-dimensional objects in a black plastic bag; colored construction paper

Introduction: Mathematics words about shape. Not using color and size as properties for

   classifying objects. Describe the game of grouping "mystery objects."

Development: Teacher places a first object from the plastic bag to begin a group by placing

   it on a piece of colored construction paper. The first student will take an object and

   either group with the teacher's object or create another group. Once several objects

   are on a sheet, names for the group will be elicited.

Practice: The whole class will contribute to the classification. Students will be asked to

   explain their thinking.

Figure 8.1: A typical lesson plan, here for a lesson fragments of which are analyzed in this chapter, includes grade level, goals, objects, and a description of how the lesson will be implemented.

students do not learn what the curriculum specifies. Moreover, such thinking leads to attributing the deviations from the planned curriculum outcomes to unwilling or incapable students or poor teachers. Programs intended to "fix" the problems exist for both types of participants in classroom lessons in the form of remedial lessons, student help forums, or staff training programs. What the approach does not recognize is that a living curriculum*-in-the-making is not in the hands of any individual. It is a societal phenomenon that is available in and arises from the living, joint practical work of the collective. What individual actors do are but one-sided manifestations of the collective work of the relation*-in-the-making, and this work cannot be reduced to individuals because of its *sympractical* nature.

The featured lesson plan is premised on the idea that learning generally and students' responses on assessments can be planned ahead of time independent of the particulars of the setting, and its history, independent of the biographies and competencies of its participants. It also places particular institutional accountability on the teacher, who has constructed the plan according to the specifications of some higher organizational unit (school board, province) and who has to answer for students' attainment of the goals and for any deviations from the stated objective of observing certain student performances (e.g., "the student will state the 4 differences ..."). Learning thereby is equated with teaching, for the latter is to bring out (cause) the former (effect). In those cases where students do generally exhibit what is stated in the objectives and teachers are held accountable for it, a clear cause and effect relation is assumed on the part of the administration that effectuates the accounting procedure.

A critique begins by acknowledging the fact that curriculum plans effectively make the teacher the true subject of the process, who, in planning the lesson, simultaneously plan learning (Holzkamp, 1992). A specific quantum of teaching is correlated with a quantum of learning – apart from interferences that principally are of two kinds: (a) interferences that fall under the jurisdiction of the school and its administration and (b) students' abilities, over which the school and its administration do not have control and fall outside of what they can be held (juridically) accountable for. To make the conditions of a match between planned and actual curriculum outcomes as propitious as possible, school staffs enact extended sets of practices that minimize possible variance in the body of those who are to receive teaching. These practices include the homogenization according to age and ability, instituting forms of order and regimes that resemble those of the military and prisons (Foucault, 1975), emphasizing "equal" treatment of all irrespective of the biographical, emotional, cognitive and other differences, and so on. Whatever variation remains is used in a dialectical fashion to produce hierarchization of the student body all the while claiming equality and fairness.[1] When teachers, while standing back for a second, can attribute deviations from the planned curriculum and what has

---

1 Even if every student were to obtain a PhD, there would be a large number of unemployed and non-seekers of employment, because optimal market economies require around 7% unemployment and an equal number of healthy individuals who have given up looking for work.

happened so far in the lesson, they might "call to order" or implement some disciplinary strategy – call for attention, removing students, etc.

When plans are thought of as determinants of actions, then we are already employing a cause–effect figure. Although the problematic of curriculum plans as determinants of action could have been subsumed under a more general critique of the cause–effect figure, the special role of these plans in curriculum theory and practice warrants some more detailed considerations. In this chapter, I begin with a general discussion of several important texts concerning the relation between plans (instructions) and situated action. Plans and instructions are an important topic because these do not only appear in the form of lesson plans but also in the form of instructions students are asked to follow when doing some (hands-on) task or constructed-response item on a worksheet. I then take a closer look at a particular lesson as a basis for reflecting on the role that curriculum plans may have and the problematic of the idea that outcomes could be planned – an issue that appears in a special light when the living curriculum is considered as an open-ended, unfinalized event*-in-the-making.

Plans, Instructions, and Situated Action

The traditional conception of the relation between plans and situated actions is that of a cause–effect relation (Suchman, 1987). In this way, plans are thought as a representation of an action that the actor has made prior to actually engaging in the action. This is why Nietzsche considers representations to be integral to his conception of the "will to power," the specifically human desire to change life conditions rather than just being subject to them (Marx/Engels, 1958).[2] Agents may not actually make the plans for future actions themselves but use a set of instructions, such as those (a) provided in a recipe for preparing a dish, (b) that come in the "user manual" with a new electronic device we have purchased, (c) describe how to assemble some do-it-yourself piece of furniture, or (d) in a field guide describing how to recognize birds, mushrooms, trees, or edible plants. Instructions do not have to be based on words alone, as in most recipes and user manuals, but, as in the case of many assembly instructions,

---

2   Buber (1947/2002) comments, "man – as Nietzsche finally expresses it in the notes which were brought together under the title *The Will to Power* – is 'as it were an embryo of the man of the future,' of the real man, of the real species of man" (p. 177).

may consist entirely of pictorial material. In all these instances, the instructions constitute a representation of the materials and things to be done to arrive at some goal: a finished dish for dinner, a pre-programmed TV recording device, or an IKEA kitchen table to be assembled. But, as representations, plans and instructions are of the past, dead, projected into the future, it should be immediately clear in the context of this book why there is a gap between plans or instructions and situated action: it is precisely the same gap that we find between the event*-in-the-making and its condensation in the finalized event.

All readers will have had experienced the frustrations that come with trying to follow instructions or that ended up with a dish that does not quite look or taste like as the dish anticipated. Inevitably, users of such instructions complain about the nature of the instruction, about "the problems of clarity, or consistency, or completeness, or followability, or factual adequacy" (Garfinkel, 2002, p. 198). Such complaints are not restricted to certain individuals but they are ubiquitous; and even highly trained engineers and scientists often have been shown to have trouble following sets of instructions, for example, those that are provided by an "intelligent" photocopier, come with a kit for doing genetic analysis, or are described in a scientific journal for observing a particular scientific fact. The difference between plans and situated action (as inner-worldly fact) can be attributed to the local relations that arise from the relation between actor and circumstance.

The gap between plans and instructions, on the one hand, and situated action, on the other hand, derives from the relation between the representation, which is inherently general, and the situated action, which is inherently unique, integral to the once-occurrent event*-in-the-making. It takes into account the specifics of the unforeseen and unforeseeable contingencies that inherently come with the event*-in-the-making. Precisely because plans and instructions have been produced to be valid across and independent of a great many situations, they must be abstract and lack the specifications of dealing with every possible contingency. Because the number of contingencies is infinite, a set of instructions that would take into account all possible contingencies also would have to be infinitely long, providing a catalogue of entries each responding to another "what if ...?" The problem with instructions is not that they somehow fail to provide everything needed to make them followable; the problem arises from the fact that we assume the cause-effect figure to be the appropriate way for thinking the relation of plans to actions. This way of thinking is inappropriate, or, to use Nietzsche's categorization, it is a myth. Thus, even scientists with 30 years of experience in dissecting fish eyes may find themselves after working for an entire day with the results from a dissected fish eye only to conclude that they had done something wrong during the dissection (Roth, 2009).

To take into account the role of contextual particulars as constituents of the nature of practical action, an alternative way of thinking about plans and instructions considers these to be resources that describe, always in approximate and generic terms, what has to be done. In any actual instant, however, it is up to the agent to find a course of action that after the fact can be said to have minimized the difference between what a plan projects to happen and what actually was happening. In this case, plans no longer are treated as the causes that determine the outcomes (effects); rather, someone following a plan or set of instructions for a first time finds the relevance of what is described in their own practical action in the course of the event*-in-the-making. After finalization of the event, the object*-to-be-made, now existing in and as representation, may be compared to the plan, another representation. That is, this comparison is only possible after the fact, when the event*-in-the-making has condensed into the event. Thus, when we follow the instruction "knead until smooth" we do not know how long this will take, how to determine when the dough is "smooth," and even what to do so that my actions can be said to have been "kneading."

An example of the relation between instructions and the event*-in-the-making is illustrated in the following case. In one study, a sociology graduate student assisted a quadriplegic student in completing a chemistry experiment by doing what the latter told him to do (Lynch, Livingston, & Garfinkel, 1983). Even in this case, where the person giving the instructions was present and could articulate them in more and more detail, the relationship between these and the practical actions turned out to be precarious and ambiguous: "These written instructions were simply not adequately descriptive of the work of doing an experiment since they omitted the embodied engagement of the students with the table-equipment" (p. 211). However, the students have not had previously experienced these practices, so that "it was up to them to discover them" (p. 211).

Descriptions of what actually has happened are denoted by the term *account*. In the context, the *event* is an account of what has been an event*-in-the-making that becomes graspable in and through its finalization. For example, if the ultimate texture of the bread I have been making looks and feels like the one anticipated, then what I have done may be described as having "kneaded until [the dough was] smooth." When the bread comes out of the oven, that is, when the recipe*-in-the-making has come to an end, the recipe may be used retroactively as a description of what has been done. We are then said to have followed the recipe (plan, set of instructions). When the anticipated results are not achieved, then the plan or set of instructions cannot be used as the (causal) account what actually has happened. In this case, blame is attributed to the instructions or to the agent. When a lesson does not achieve what the lesson plan sets out as goals and objectives, then teachers or "unruly" or "incapable" students tend to be blamed. Similarly, when students do not do what some task description asks them to do or do not achieve what the laboratory instructions set out to be done to observe some specific phenomenon, students tend to be blamed.

Such accounts of actions are condensations of the living Heraclitean flux into theoretical terms – even when done on the part of participants themselves (Bourdieu, 1980). But once such a condensation from the real living act into discourse has occurred, a possibility "owing to the ambiguity of language" (Bakhtin, 1993, p. 39), we have lost our phenomenon: the living work in a living world under continual flux. The representation into which the living event*-in-the-making has condensed presupposes the "unity of apperception" and the "entire apparatus of cognitional unity" (p. 39). In the end, all that appears in a "theoretical description *after the fact*" but "remains unknown to a living and act-performing consciousness" (p. 39). All of these after-the-fact accounts, whether participants or researchers articulate it, are "no more than the technical apparatus of the performed act" (p. 39). The more there is theoretical unity in the description, the farther away we get from the actual uniqueness of the performance in the unique and once-occurrent world*-in-the-making.

Thinking about plans as resources for practical action the relevance of which has to be worked out in any specific case already is better than thinking about the relationship between plans and situated actions using the cause–effect figure. However, whereas this approach might be valuable for describing what might occur when an individual uses a plan or set of instruction that does not involve others, it is not useful for describing, thinking about, and theorizing events*-in-the-making that involve others, that is, for a relations*-in-the-making. Already in the individual case, the event*-in-the-making comes with advantages, because it allows us to theorize how the unexpected arises within the horizon of the person, thereby leading to the unpredictable nature of event trajectories. For example, if students were to work on pre-specified physics projects or chemistry experiments on their own, the trajectories of these through the lens of the event*-in-the-making would understandably differ even though all students are said to follow the same set of instructions. To capture the emergent nature of what happens in a classroom when students follow instructions and what happens in a classroom where teachers have written detailed lesson plans, it is more advantageous to use the event*-in-the-making as a lens. In the following, I use fragments from two lessons to elaborate on the issues raised so far.

Case 1: Following Instructions in Science Laboratories

Lesson plans, instructions for getting students to learn something, may actually include other instructions to achieve what the lesson plan states as goals and objectives. For example, students may be instructed to model the process of saving money by entering a constant amount each week to arrive at a mathematical generalization (chapters 4, 7), or they might be asked to do some investigation to understand the role of the center of mass in the movement of an object. In this section, I provide examples of what happens in a classroom when students are asked to follow sets of instructions through the lens of the event*-in-the-making. I draw on classroom materials from a physics course where students investigated rotational motion (e.g., Roth, McRobbie, Lucas, & Boutonné, 1997a, b). Instructions are not something given once and for all, but what precisely the instruction says comes to be an outcome (effect) of the event*-in-the-making.

Finding Relevance in Practical Action

Teachers often provide students with written or verbal laboratory instructions. It is generally assumed that the relationship between a good instruction and the action it describes is simple: "Good" instructions are unambiguous and lead social agents to do exactly what the instructions indicate. However, even the simplest instruction is ambiguous because inherently and unavoidably generic and decontextualized. As the event*-in-the-making unfolds, those following the instructions are confronted with local contingencies that they cannot anticipate and that unforeseeably arise within their horizon. The definitiveness of instructions as inner-worldly facts is itself a product that arises from the collective performances and work of students and teachers alike. As teachers are interested in students' production of specific phenomena, the question therefore has to be posed, "How do students know that what they have done is what they were supposed to do?" The following episode illustrates the relationship between a teacher instruction and the videotaped actions in one group consisting of Belinda, Geoff, Rachel, and Theon.

Mr. Russell had asked students to "mark dead center of the baton[3] and give it a strike with, perhaps, a meter ruler. I just want you to comment later about the motion of the body [baton]." Rachel produces what we will hear as a prediction: "maybe the mass, the center of mass stays in one path, it doesn't move, like the center of gravity." Theon looks up, "A bit like what Jim said (earlier in the lesson)." "Strike it with a ruler," he continues and provides slight blows from the top to the pipe. Belinda, Geoff, and Rachel watch Theon change the blows' directions, now from the side so that the loaded pipe ("baton") rolls to the left and to the right. "It rolls around in a circle, it's like a fish," Rachel says to describe the movement.

Geoff picks up the pipe and rolls it down the inclined table. Theon comments, "It rolls straight." Rachel countered, "But if you push it with a ruler, it was not going straight" but acknowledges the straight movement caused by Theon's gentle push with "Yes it does." Theon realizes Belinda's suggestion to hit the pipe in the middle. Rachel greets the resulting motion, "You see," and Geoff comments, "It's changing on an angle." Mr. Russell passes by and tells the students, "What I'd like you to do is just mark the center of strike and give me your comments." Theon strikes the pipe (baton) and engages Mr. Russell to check if what he is doing is what he is supposed to do. "Is that working?" "You just make a short sharp shot, just as in billiards," replies Mr. Russell. Theon obliges and observes, "It is not working." But Mr. Russell already has moved to another group. Geoff then suggests, "I s'ppose. But that's what we are s'pposed to do." A few seconds later, Mr. Russell brings the event*-in-the-making to a close by calling the class to order.

If this were an isolated episode or an episode involving low-achieving students, many educators would easily dismiss it. However, the other five groups in this class could be seen responding to the task in very similar ways.

---

3   A metal pipe, one-half of which is filled with a substance so that the center of mass is not in the geometric center of the object.

CURRICULUM*-IN-THE-MAKING

Some were spinning the loaded pipe ("baton"), others rolled it on the table, still others struck it from above. In fact, one might say that Theon and his group came closest to observing what Mr. Russell had planned for them to see. Other observers might be tempted to blame Mr. Russell for giving poor instructions. Again, this would miss the mark for I observed similar student behavior in situations where they had detailed written instructions in their hands.

To the observers of the episode, the four students – who represent a cross section of the class in terms of their achievement in Mr. Russell's class – appeared baffled. The four might be glossed as wrestling with many questions: "What does Mr. Russell want us to do?" "What could it mean, 'dead center,' 'give it a strike,' and 'perhaps with a meter ruler'?" "Are we to mark the geometric center or the center of mass?" "Which of these possible 'dead centers' are we asked to strike?," "What sort of strike?," "From which direction?," and "What has the meter ruler got to do with the strike?" But before they may reply to this multitude of questions, students have to begin a situated inquiry from which, because something is significant, they can elaborate the meaning of the teacher's original question.

In the course of my analysis, however, I realize that this question does not seem to be independent of another one, "*What* is it that Mr. Russell wants us to see?" The two questions are interrelated and in fact interdependent, for, to assess what they have to do, the students need to be able to assess what they have done, that is, they require an account, a representation of the finalized micro-event*-in-the-making. In the course of their inquiry, the four students need to know whether what they have observed was in fact what they were supposed to observe. To make such an assessment, both what they will have seen and what they have anticipated to see must exist as representations – otherwise comparison is impossible. Somehow, students have to find the significance in what they have done. They have to have a phenomenon, something that has condensed from the curriculum*-in-the-making. When they come to the conclusion that they have no phenomenon, they cannot know if the problem lies in their preparations or in their observations. It is the outcome, the observed phenomenon as an effect, on the basis of which the appropriateness of an action as the cause; and the match between the two serves as the basis for assessing whether the instruction was followed.

At the moment Theon and his group mates are predicting and producing the motion of the loaded pipe (baton), they do not know if what they have seen is the sought-after phenomenon. Other groups moved on to other tasks, although their striking of the pipe has not produced what the teacher has intended them to produce and see. Towards the end of the lesson, Mr. Russell says that he wants students to verify that the loaded pipe moves in a straight line when the center of mass is struck. Two students in the class strike the pipe at the center of mass once, produce and thus reify the desired observational fact, and return to their seats. Although they have not produced the sought-after motion previously, they now appear satisfied that striking the center of mass produces straight-line motion. At this point they appear certain that what they have observed is what they were supposed to observe.

It has been suggested that rule following implies a competence that is described in ethnomethodological studies as an "ad hoc" elaboration of rules in use (Suchman & Trigg, 1993). Accordingly, the maintenance of "any rule of action requires the local elaboration by participants of just what the rule could mean in relation to specific circumstances of its application" (p. 167). Students in this physics laboratory tentatively elaborate, in very situated and contingent ways what the instructions received from the teacher might mean relative to the specific context (including such things as the current curriculum, teacher's talk prior to the activity, the conversations and activities emerging against an open horizon of possible events). If it is not clear whether what students observe is significant, that is, match events as they would be seen by the teacher (who in an ideal situation is the representative of canonical physics), students change their actions to produce a variety of responses from the objects under study. They "fiddle" with and adjust objects and instructions to make them fit the contingencies of the setting. They then assess whether their accounts make the event significant relative to the present context. For example, Theon describes the situation as inappropriate ("It doesn't work") possibly against the teacher's comment, "just as in billiards." Geoff's comment, "But that's what we are s'pposed to do" opens the possibility that what they have seen is what they are supposed to see, an ascribed consequence of appropriate prior actions. When one of the responses can be seen and understood as significant, students can then engage in repetition by means of which order arises through the consistency of the observed response.

It might be argued that students do not understand how to produce and observe phenomena because of ineptitude, lack of skill, or simply lack of interest. Such an approach might be a reasonable explanation if failure to produce and observe phenomena was isolated to students. However, scientists are subject to the same predicament. The problem of producing phenomena reproducibly and its dependence on embodied laboratory practices has also been demonstrated among highly trained university researchers using the polymerase chain reaction (Jordan & Lynch, 1993) and constructing TEA lasers (Collins, 1982). Investigators in different laboratories could not reconstruct phenomena despite elaborate instructions and information about the setups. In these cases, not seeing a phenomenon was linked to the associated embodied laboratory practices. Faraday already knew about the problem of seeing a phenomenon (Gooding, 1992) and, therefore, to make as sure as possible others would see *his* phenomenon, sent his scientific colleagues throughout Europe copies of his apparatus with instructions of what to do and what to look for.

Students' Fundamental Dilemma

This micro-analysis of students ordering activities in a traditional physics laboratory shows how most students do produce phenomena and arrive at a finalizing understanding even in a "cookbook" laboratory. They observe, structure their field of experience and come up with reasonable results from their perspective; they also turn instructions into actions through situated inquiries into possible movements. However, a few students tried to refrain from throwing themselves into the process of understanding*-in-the-making – i.e., making a commitment to the open-ended and uncertain nature of the event*-in-the-making. Without such a commitment, however, no understanding can condensate. A finalized understanding precisely requires living through the process of understanding*-in-the-making, with all of its contingencies and uncertainties. The above analysis cannot yield the motivation for such student actions. Here, the analysis has to go to a different level and investigate the larger context in which students conduct their inquiries. At this new level, the students' fundamental dilemma emerges as shown by the following lesson fragment from a conversation recorded during the investigation with the rolling objects.

Craig, Erin, Karis, and their frequently silent partner Angela had described the outcomes of their races between a sliding cylinder (on a trolley) and a rolling cylinder. Therefore, they decide to think about the phenomenon as a statistical one. Mr. Russell approached the group just as the students

THE PLANNED, LIVING, AND ENACTED CURRICULUM

conducted one run and observed that the rolling cylinder had a greater acceleration than the "sliding" equivalent.

Fragment 8.1

```
01 R:   i am a little disappointed keep going keep going.
02 K:   we are doing the best of five.
03 E:   its a little slow.
04 R:   try it again, put that ((weight)) right in the middle. ((Karis obliges))
        yea; right. but i know what i=m expecting and i havent tried the trolleys.
        ((Karis conducts a race between the trolley loaded with a large
        hollow cylinder against a rolling large hollow cylinder))
05 R:   it is not doing as I want, so I'll have to.
06 E:   what is it meant to be?
07 R:   well i tell you later.
08 K:   its a surprise.
09 R:   yeah; its a surprise; but its not quite living up to expectations.
```

In this conversation, Mr. Russell indicates his disappointment. He wanted students to see that the objects accelerated faster when they are "sliding" than when they are rolling but he had not tried the investigation himself (turn 04). The students, however, had no means to judge the outcome in the same way; they have to take objects as as they will have appeared to them. From this perspective, "doing the best of five" (turn 02) is not unreasonable. The students' dilemma becomes clear in Mr. Russell's assessment that the experiment is "not doing as [he] wants" and what "[he] is expecting." He manifests already knowing what is still concealed and withheld from students. Mr. Russell does not want to tell students what the problem is (turn 07), and they are left on their own to make sense of the event*-in-the-making.

Students know that the correctness of the knowable in their laboratory exercises is prefigured in advance. They were not asked to elaborate an order helpful to their understanding*-in-the-making that is part of *their* lifeworld, from which a finalized understanding may fall out as a sediment. But they are asked to seek an order that they know the teacher is hiding from them. In other words, independently of students' doing, outcomes are to be assessed against a normative order that is more or less compatible with standard physics depending on the teacher's own finalized understanding. Whereas the students have to work before an open horizon of possible objects*- and events*-in-the-making, they are asked to disclose the one yet unknown possibility against which their work is judged. This form of inquiry is closed and distinctly different from the "ordinary situation of discovering research where the search for an 'answer' to a 'question' can arise within an open horizon of inquiry" (Lynch et al., 1983, p. 217).

It is here that I situate the fundamental dilemma and difference of students' living curriculum*-in-the-making. Whereas I show that their inquiries occur within the open horizon of the event*-in-the-making – leading to results often quite different from those of standard science – the frame that situates their living work also forces them to search for a hidden order. But to see this order, because of the relation between representation and finalized perception, students already have to know science in the way that they are designed to learn by means of the lesson. To see and understand what the planned curriculum anticipates students will see and understand, they already have to know what the planned curriculum sets out for them to learn. It appears as if such dilemmas exist even in the most well-meaning student-centered instruction. Teachers still shape the format and content of lessons and produce fine-grained definitions of what is done, said, and understood. As a result, the students are required to expose themselves in and to understanding*-in-the-making all the while knowing that what they come to understand when everything is said and done may vary from a normative understanding against which the teacher measures their own achievements.

Case 2: Unexpected Turns of the Living Curriculum

We have already been following Mrs. Winter and her students in some of the preceding chapters. In the course of their classification lesson, they move from a floor where there is only Mrs. Winter's object (Figure 8.2a) to one where all the mystery objects have found a place (Figure 8.2b). A lot of *collective, sympractical* work is required to get from the former to the latter situation. The resulting categorization scheme is itself is the what has settled out from the living work with the particular objects. That is, if we consider is happening between the two instances as categorization*-in-the-making, what we see in Figure 8.2b is the account. In the course of this categorization*-in-the-making, each move both categorizes and establishes what will have been the categorization scheme according to which the mystery objects have been classified. Each action is an open-horizoned micro-event*-in-the-making that submits a mystery thing to an order, thereby making it a finalized object, and constitutes this order simultaneously. This double nature of each action – submitting

Figure 8.2. The classroom floor before the building a categorization scheme for the "mystery objects" (a) just after Mrs. Winter has placed the starting object and (b) after all students have had their turns.

something to and making the categorization scheme simultaneously – reflects the flow of the living curriculum*-in-the-making.

The final state of the objects on the floor and the way in which they are grouped may serve as an account of the curriculum. This account stands in an asymmetrical relationship with respect to the work that actually has been leading to it. Mrs. Winter and Mrs. Turner have prepared the lesson plan but are not the cause of what is on the floor. The arrangement cannot be attributed to them. But the children, too, cannot be considered to be the causal agents whose actions caused the configuration to emerge. It is also not the action of the children who have been "guided" or "scaffolded" (see chapter 6). Although we might be tempted to reduce the living curriculum to such statements, they do not capture what actually eventuates during the curriculum*-in-the-making. This actual eventuation and the ways in which participants witness it constitute how subjects, objects, tools, and so on eventuate and, therefore, what they are qua inner-worldly, finalized facts. It is therefore not the difference between initial and final state of the objects on the floor that allows us to understand collective and individual change – i.e., "co-construction" or construction in social space and "individual construction" – but the actual performance changes and transforms the constituents of the event*in-the-making. Because a teacher-student relation*-in-the-making cannot be reduced to individual participants, the living work is sympractical and a societal phenomenon sui generis. The finalized categorization irreducibly is a collective, *emergent* achievement rather than the determined outcome of the planned curriculum (Figure 8.1).

Lesson Fragment 8.2 begins just after Jane, whose turn it currently is to pick and place a mystery object, has placed a larger, blue cylinder with a smaller yellow cylinder. Using iconic gestures, she has placed her fingers around the circumference of the cylinder tops and then, using the palm of her hand held against these tops, says: "this one ((hers)) has the same way." "Okay," Mrs. Winter says and adds: "anybody else want to add something to that?" In this turn pair, a constative is immediately affirmed "okay." The saying continues soliciting others to add. There is pausing, that is, the solicitation is not being treated (yet) as such. Mrs. Winter takes the floor again: "Connor, what do you think?" That is, in saying his name, she specifically makes an offer to summon Connor and, thereby, produces the first part of what is a possible request–acceptance pair. In speaking, Connor responds to the summons but offers up an opening of a question–x pair, "like you mean different?" (turn 02), where the "x" is yet to be determined as something that has been said. In restating that it can be different, the next locution completes and actualizes a question–response pair and then offers an expansion: "it can be the same." Connor moves forward until his hand comes to hover above the larger cylinder; and, while moving his hand from above the taller cylinder to the lower, its relatively smaller size comes to be exhibited in the changing distance for everyone to see. He says: "this one's taller" (turn 05). Something unexpected and apparently inappropriate has occurred, as, following a pause, Ethan's turn will have completed an affirmation–negation turn pair. There is pausing, then two simultaneous turns, both apparently having size as content, the second one produced by Connor offering an assertion about the circular surfaces being different in size. He then uses a hand gesture to show a circular shape (turn 11).

Fragment 8.2

01	W:	^connor. <<all>what dyou> think.
02	C:	lI:ke you mea:n; dIFFrent?
03		(0.76)
04	W:	WELL it can be dIFFrent or the same.
05		(3.17) ((*Connor moves forward to the blocks.*))
06	C:	[UM: thisone:s taller

(.)
[(((*Connor touches the tops of the
taller cylinder and then moves hand
over shorter cylinder.*))

07		(0.85)
08	E:	<<p>but its not size>
09		(0.47)
10	E:	[and size would]
11	C:	[and this ones] sort of a bigger [cIRclE

[(((*Connor places hand over top of cylinder in a
grasping shape and keeps circular grasp shape in the air and then draws a circular
shape in the air.*))

12	M:	[but not size as THAT]
13	C:	[like like like] like that

[(((*Connor makes a circle shape
by holding both hands together.*))

14		<<pp>like that>
15		(1.66)
16	W:	thATs right. and so we ARe we ARe talking about [size

[(((*Mrs. Winter holds hands
apart at a distance.*))
but when we make nEW categories [we are NOT going to make new
[(((*Mrs. Winter opens palms wide a certain
distance from each other and repeats the motion quickly with tiny pulses*))
[CAtegories out of SIze. (0.17) there IS ONe that IS
[(((*Mrs. Winter again opens palms wide a certain distance from each other and repeats
the motion quickly with tiny pulses*))
[taller than the other.
[(((*Mrs. Winter points to a shape*))

There is pausing, and then Mrs. Winter says, "That's right," which actualizes the saying as the second part of a constative–confirmation pair. This comes to be elaborated in the following words, which state that "we are talking about size." But this statement is followed by its negation in the context of "making new categories," "we are *not* making new categories out of size" (turn 16).

Here, the curriculum*-in-the-making has taken an unforeseen turn, marked by two constative–negation pairs. From the beginning, there have been assertions and confirmations that size (or color) is not a characteristic of geometrical objects and therefore must not be used in constative statements about grouping the mystery objects. That is, although there has been a curricular plan that specifically negated size and color as grouping properties and despite the repeated instructions disallowing such constative statements, we find it here again. Thus, despite all the planning Mrs. Winter and Mrs. Turner have done prior to the lesson and despite repeated reiterations of the interdiction, there has been another statement of this type. Those present now find themselves confronted with a world* where something has occurred that now needs to be addressed, because it has indelibly changed the factual world. Perhaps unsurprisingly, peers and teacher produce next turns that negate the constative about size as a specification of category.

In this instance, then, the living curriculum is not moving straight forward from some incipit to the end (Figure 8.2b), where all mystery objects have been classified according to recognized and recognizable geometric properties. To use an analogy, the planned curriculum is not a roadmap that specifies the shortest or a few alternative routes to the destination; if it is a map, then it is one in which there are no roads and where the path has to be laid in walking (Figure 8.3). If the use of color and size properties has been ceasing in the course of this lesson, this is not because students effectuated the teacher-stated interdiction but precisely a result of the living sympractical work that all those present have completed. Students are learning about the inappropriateness of using color and size not because the teacher tells them – she has done so and yet their use continues for a while – but because the classification that emerges from their collective work includes objects of different sizes and colors in the same group, so that the distinguishing property is to be found in something else. It is also in the emergent result that the students are afforded to find the relevance of the instruction, "we are not using size or color" (Mrs. Winter).

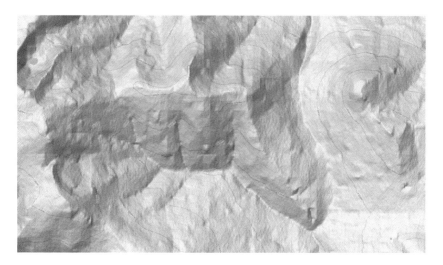

Figure 8.3. This map of a wilderness area where there are no roads serves as an analogy for a curriculum*-in-the-making. (Map data © 2012 Google)

Inherently, the plans cannot determine with any certainty what will happen. This is so not merely because there are contingencies and unforeseeable student responses. Rather, this is so because the plan does not and cannot specify what emerges from the *collective* work, which is irreducible to individual performances and the relations thereof. The symplactical work itself is confronted with contingencies that emerge within its horizon so that its trajectory is out of the hands of the individual participant. In other words, the sources of these contingencies are the turn *pairs*, in and from which new, previously unseen and unforeseen possibilities arise; and these are dealt with through subsequent turn pairs, each of which is evidence of the *collective* nature of the work that is both in and out of the hands of the individual. As participants in the unfolding event*-in-the-making, Connor and Mrs. Winter are changed, they are in fact subjects*-in-the-making. But because the work is collective, the content of the change also is in and out of the hand of the individual (see chapter 5).

Of Accounts: Curriculum as Inner-Worldly Fact

After nearly an hour and 20 minutes of work, all 23 objects had found a place on the colored construction paper sheets on the floor (Figure 8.2b). This configuration on the floor is the result of irreducible living symplactical work, and it reflexively points back to the living work even though it cannot be used to recover what has happened (although educators often take such remnants as evidence for the *kind* of thinking that has occurred). The ordering is performatively produced, and, in the objective quality of what is emerging on the floor, there is a normative force: further order is produced as subsequent actions are constrained by the already existing assemblage. The categorization scheme that ultimately comes to be found on the floor has a contingent history, which itself cannot be seen but only exists in and as the living work of its production. As a consequence, many other schemes have been possible, including a non-existent one.[4] The normative force can be observed at work when groupings that already include cubes of different size or color constitute evidence that color and size are distinct but not distinguishing properties. The final configuration, as traced by a recording and record of the event*-in-the-making, can be used as an account and to account for the curriculum. Because the configuration matches the goals that Mrs. Turner and Mrs. Winter have met what they had stated as the objective for this lesson: to arrive at a classification of the given set of three-dimensional geometrical objects the goal of which is to allow students (a) to know the characteristics of the different kinds of objects, (b) to understand the definition of the types of objects, (c) to identify an object by its category name, and (d) compare different types of objects.

As it is available on the floor, the account not only constitutes a recorded trace of the work but also constitutes a classification scheme. This is so because we can see it as a shorthand notation of the experimental materials that have been used in classical concept learning paradigms; the structure of these materials is produced with materials from two-dimensional geometry in Figure 8.4. All of those on the same construction paper are squares, but none of the others, individually or pair-wise from the other groups, constitutes a square. The relevance of the instructions can be seen precisely when the performative dimensions are consistent with classical geometry that this grouping emerges; and precisely when there is recognition of the perceptual commonality of the objects (collection in Figure 8.2b labeled "cubes"; upper collection in Figure 8.4) that geometry is reproduced as an objective science accessible in the same way to anyone. The living sympractical work involved to get this configuration emerge on the classroom floor is not that of the teacher(s) alone nor that of the students (alone) nor that

---

4   I have repeatedly witnessed situations where teachers, because a class was "unruly," ended the event*-in-the-making and punished students in one way or another, for example, by having to sit on their seats or place hands on the desk, without being allowed to say a word.

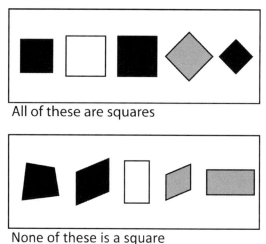

All of these are squares

None of these is a square

Figure 8.4. Classical concept learning tasks included sets that are said to consist of members of the concept to be learned (a) and sets that are said to consist of non-members of the concept.

of some mystical and mythical *inter*action: it is the irreducibly *joint* work of all participants. It is the result of a collective work that is irreducible to individual participants precisely because no speaking turn is an isolated fact but constitutes only part of an irreducible higher order unit that reflects the collective nature of events*-in-the-making.

The emerging configuration of groups of objects, a category system, is a witnessable and witnessed collective achievement, produced in and through the practical work and practical reasoning objectively available to all those present. The witnessing is itself an integral aspect of this work, as can be seen in the turn pairs where an assertive statement is confronted with its negation. We therefore do not just have Connor make an assertion, which is subsequently judged to be wrong. The collective work of asserting also involves the active reception and evaluation of an assertion*-in-the-making, which begins at the moment that the locution begins (when it is yet to be established what kind of locution it will be). But in the end, the category system on the floor constitutes a mathematical object, which can be understood only when it is tied to its origin in the naturally witnessable, accountable, and analyzable collective work in and from which it has sprung forth. This object arises as the local achievement of the in situ collective living, continually unfolding work. This geometrical category system and the work of its production together constitute a pair (e.g., Husserl, 1939). As is the case of all other mathematical objects, this one, as objective collective achievement on the floor that any one witnessing can inspect, comes to be independent of the living work of categorizing. It is in this collective work that "mathematics, as a professional discipline, is sustained and renewed" (Livingston, 1986, p. 15). It is also here that mathematics "evolves, is revitalized, and is taught on the occasions, and critically on the occasions, when provers come together and do, for and among each other, the recognizably adequate work of doing recognizably adequate mathematics" (p. 15).

We may characterize the pairing of the text that accounts for the emergence of the mathematical object as "categorizing objects according to the rules of three-dimensional geometry" and as the living work of categorizing in this way: "doing [categorizing objects according to the rules of three-dimensional geometry]" (see Garfinkel & Sacks, 1986). Here, the "doing" refers to the work for which the notational particulars, "categorizing objects according to the rules of three-dimensional geometry" constitute the proper gloss. In the same way, the mathematical object on the floor and the work of performing/seeing its mathematical adequacy together constitute a pair. Thus, the geometrical categorization is like a geometrical proof, which "is not the disengaged, material argument, but it is always tied to the lived-work of that theorem's particular proving; a proof is this inextricable pairing of the proof and the associated practices of its proving" (Livingston, 1986, p. 14). Whereas research in curriculum studies focuses on the structures of the second part of the pair, the gloss or account of the work (its achievement), the perspective on the living curriculum developed here is interested in the work from within the unfolding event*-in-the-making when the ultimate achievements are not yet available and the very nature of what is unfolding is not yet available.

Curriculum scholars tend to define the enacted curriculum as "what actually takes place in the classroom" (Stein, Remillard, & Smith, 2007, p. 321); such scholars tend to point out that "research has revealed that a substantial difference exists between the curriculum as represented in instructional materials and the curriculum as enacted in the classroom by teachers and students" (p. 321). Although such definitions suggest that researchers are looking at classroom events, *what* takes place as inner-worldly fact is available only after an event*-in-the-making has come to an end and, in so doing, comes to be "in hand." We inherently cannot know that there is a difference between the curriculum, as represented in a written plan (e.g., Figure 8.1) and the enacted curriculum, unless the nature of the latter is available to the analysis, that is, as another object or inner-worldly fact.

It is precisely here that we are missing whatever is *living* about the curriculum, for we only compare two glosses. Thus, for example, the final configuration on the floor may be used as an indication that at least part of the planned curriculum has been attained. Moreover, teachers and observers may state, but only after the fact, that "Connor has had some trouble getting away from categorizing according to size," based on the observations that he has repeatedly pointed out size differences. But all such statements are possible only afterwards, because at the moment Connor opens his mouth and articulates words, we know nothing about the kind of event*-moment that we witness in its unfolding. That is, when researchers claim to be looking at the "enacted curriculum" to intimate that they are interested in curriculum as event, they are actually not taking the appropriate first-time-through perspective required for understanding the curriculum as an event*-in-the-making. The "enacted curriculum," as treated in the literature, is in fact an account or gloss of the living work that has come to an end. The "substantial differences" between planned (intended) and enacted curriculum continue to be blamed on (attributed to) the teacher, who is held accountable for what has happened in the classroom.

Even when we may be tempted to say that students "have trouble," such as Theon and his group in the above-cited classroom episode, we have no indication as to the understanding*-in-the-making of these students that will condense as affirmed understanding. When asked on an examination, they may or may not respond as stated in the curriculum goals and objectives. Whatever the outcomes of such an examination, it will not have captured the totality of the changes students undergo while participating in the lesson*-in-the-making.

Sometimes researchers also introduce the notion of the "experienced curriculum." But this notion does not eliminate the problem – whether researchers attempt to get at the experience through student interviews following the lesson or during the lesson (directly asking them about a relation that they have had with the teacher or using clickers). In each case, students can only respond to and articulate (account for) what has already happened rather than what is in the process of happening, which is inherently incomplete and therefore inaccessible and only forthcoming as an inner-worldly fact. Now some readers might suggest that the lesson is unfolding, which is true. But we do not know from within the curriculum*-in-the-making whether it is in the course of achieving the goals and objectives. It is only when the lesson is completed, and, therefore, no longer in the making that we can make an assessment about the relationship between what has been achieved and what the plan for the lesson has projected as achievement.

When there is a fit rather than difference between the planned and enacted curriculum, the plan can (and often is) used as an account of what has happened much as a recipe is used to account for what we have done when asked by a guest how to make the dish (or the guest may directly ask for the recipe). But in the same way as the recipe, the actual living work does not come with the curriculum plan, which, in contrast to the cooking, refers to the work of a collective. It would be inappropriate, therefore, to blame Mr. Russell or Theon and his mates for not achieving a definitive response to the investigation with the baton. It is just as inappropriate to attribute the success of the geometry lesson to Mrs. Winter, Mrs. Turner, the class, or the transaction of any of these reified subjects.

· 9 ·

RESEARCHING THE
LIVING CURRICULUM AS
EVENT*-IN-THE-MAKING

Bakhtin … is seeking to get back to the naked immediacy of experience as it is felt from within the utmost particularity of a specific life, the molten lava of events as they happen. He seeks the sheer quality of happening in life before the magma of such experience cools, hardening into igneous theories, or accounts of what has happened. And just as lava differs from the rock it will become, so the two states of lived experience, on the one hand, and systems for registering such experience on the other, are fundamentally different from each other. (Holquist, 1993, p. x)

In this book, I offer up a new conceptualization of the living curriculum and the associated learning that occurs; in this, the book is a contribution to the effort of overcoming the problems that come with all metaphysical approaches – including all kinds of constructivism (e.g., Radford & Roth, 2011). I introduce to the curriculum discourse a way of talking/writing about classrooms that retain the very mobility of the event*-in-the-making, of what we live without ever being able to (fully) *comprehend* what is happening; and we do comprehend after the fact only because (a) the situation *comprehended* (comprised) us as witness (b) the event is no longer living and therefore holds steady to be prehended. This requires us to think the living curriculum as pure mobility but its comprehension in terms of process and outcome. Such a discourse moves us towards acknowledging the unpredictability of teaching and learning *in the way we live it in situ*. I do so, for "it is impossible to modify the interpretation of particular phenomena without at the same time modifying the language in which it is expressed" (Romano, 1998, p. 2). I describe and analyze lesson fragments from a perspective that does not (attempt to) destroy their event-ness and then develop associated concepts. The fundamental argument in this book therefore can be stated in this way: An event*-in-the-making *is not* – for eventing is synonymous with unfinished-unfolding, advening-to-advenants, taking-advenants-by-surprise, opening-possibilities-in-annihilating-them, and eventuating-demise-of-the-event. The preceding analyses lead us to a number of implications, including how we analyze data that record events (audiotape, videotape).

From a methodical perspective, to analyze events*-in-the-making requires us, as intimated in the descriptions and analyses presented throughout this book, to take a first-time-through perspective, where we move through an episode step by step without drawing on anything that subsequently occurs as analytic resource. The analyses of the lesson fragments presented throughout the foregoing chapters implement precisely this recommendation. In this way, the analytic stance is similar to that of the participants, who, at any one instant, do not know what will be the case only seconds or minutes hence. The problem with traditional ways of analyzing data is that they presuppose the actor (cause) → effect figure of reasoning. That is, the *individual* is presupposed as the unit of analysis. But if we want to understand happenings through the lens of the event*-in-the-making, then the unit of analysis has to change.

Events are not the results of the addition of individual people, things, tools, rules, relations, and so on. Rather, an event*-in-the-making – as any social fact in the course of its making – is a phenomenon *sui generis* that cannot be reduced to any of its manifestations. Different authors use different terms to refer to this whole that exceeds the individual social actor: "world-as-event," "life-as-event" (Bakhtin, 1993) or "plenum" (Garfinkel, 2002). If we are interested in understanding life-as-event, then our analytic methods have to recover the mobility of the event*-in-the-making, which we do not get when we take every action as a unit from which events are built up. Instead we need to have units that embody mobility. We find such an orientation in two well-known approaches to the analysis of language in use – though scholars referencing those approaches generally do not emphasize the irreducible unit but instead return to the individual agent: conversation analysis and Bakhtin's dialogism. The purpose of this chapter is to highlight some of the policies and suppositions we need for getting at the eventness of events.

Common Reduction of Conversations and Speculations about Mind

Throughout this book, I underscore that events*-in-the-making are irreducible unitary and unique events that cannot be reduced to specific agents, who, alone or as collections, act and bring about effects. Typically, when scholars analyze conversations, they tell us what this person said, then what the response is, what the next person says, who makes "meaning" of what, and so on. Take the following quotation from a chapter that presents and analyzes a whole class relation in which a teacher and seventh-grade students talk about experiments

Teacher:	because sometimes when you know you're drinking a lot of alcohol it inadvertently affects the way you act. But they didn't know, so then they got these reaction times on them.
Jerod:	They didn't know?
Teacher:	They didn't know how much was in there.
	Jerod asked a clarifying question pertaining to the way in which the data were created. By asking, "They didn't know?" he seemed to indicate his understanding that if the participants had known how much alcohol they were drinking, their performance on the reaction time test could have been affected. (Cobb & Tzou, 2009, p. 149)

In this excerpt, the authors analyze the conversation from the perspective of the individual, suggesting that Jerod "asked a question" although the locution "They didn't know" might just as well be a constative confirming what has been said before using indirect discourse. It is indirect speech because the original "they didn't know" is not merely reported but already – if the authors are right in having heard a question as indicated by the question mark – a social evaluation. The original constative statement "they didn't know" is paired with a next turn locution consisting of the same words but with rising intonation. We therefore may entertain, for the moment, that we are seeing a constative–question pair*-in-the-making, which means, what is being stated is questioned.

Jerod's locution then is analyzed as the first turn in the next turn pair, which includes the very same words as its beginning "They didn't know," followed by "how much was in there," which in fact is heard as taking up an earlier locution, "they didn't know how much alcohol was in it" (Cobb & Tzou, 2009, pp. 146–147). Here then, we entertain the hypothesis of a question–affirmation pair, because the repetition of the "they didn't know" is articulated with falling intonation, which is typical for constatives. In this turn pair, the "they didn't know" is treated as a question about the content of an earlier locution that comes to be confirmed. There is nothing else that we see playing out in the public space of this discussion reported and described.

The authors, however, treat Jerod's locution as an indication, pointing us to something that is actually not there: an understanding. This understanding is taken as a thing indexed by another thing, the word. The authors then move to speculate what this understanding is about: had the participants in the story that the conversation is about known how much alcohol there was in their drinks, they also would have known that their performance on the reaction time test would be affected. The individualistic approach is evident from the fact that the authors speculate about the contents of mind, which are not available in their description of the fragment (e.g., transcription). All we have are the words Jerod says, and none of these words is about understanding or its content. We find here a separation of what is actually said from thought (understanding); the authors might have alternatively written about what Jerod meant to say, the meaning of his utterance.

This example is not a singular aspect of the chapter as can be seen that in the next sentence and following the next piece of transcription, the authors engage in another speculation: "The question Belinda asked … suggests that she might have been aware of the importance of testing a representative group of people" (Cobb & Tzou, 2009, p. 147). All Belinda said, however, was "Did they know they were drinking alcohol?" In any event, the authors do what a pragmatic position does not allow us to do: to look for things attached to or indicated by words independent of their use. Belinda's locution, however, is another second turn paired with the teacher's earlier locution and about the protagonists in the story knowing that they were drinking alcohol. In fact, as seen from the next turn (teacher), we have exactly the same type of confirmative that was also observable in the sequence involving Jerod: "They signed up for a test in which they know that they could be given an amount of alcohol" (p. 147). The authors therefore speculate about something in Belinda's mind – i.e., here an "awareness" – that is at the origin of the locution "Did they know they were drinking alcohol?" from which the original awareness, not itself available in the locution, could be recovered.

This approach, typical for the way in which recordings from classrooms are analyzed, is dangerous. It treats language in a manner that "has its place in a primitive idea of the way language functions" (Wittgenstein, 1953/1997, p. 3). Moreover, it does not get at what is alive in the living curriculum, because it attributes essences to individual locutions, such as treating them as questions irrespective of their place in the diachronic conversation. What the students and teachers say are but pointers to something else, that is, representations. Throughout this book I cite authors who tell us that representations point us to the now-dead past. In this analysis, the entire dynamic of the conversation as an irreducible social phenomenon gets lost, including its dynamic nature and the excess of the relation*-in-the-making over individual intentions. The ([socio-] constructivist) approach fails to capture the eventness of the living curriculum, reducing instead the conversation to individual locutions, which in turn are only reflections of the contents of the speakers' minds. To get at the event*-in-the-making, we need a different approach, one in which analysts place themselves in the same kind of situation that characterize what they analyze. That is, the analysts must not draw on what comes after in the tapes – e.g., a locution has become a question – but have to do their analysis from the perspective of the ignorance about the future. It is a method that does not allow the analyst to surreptitiously bring their unacknowledged cultural competence in the analysis – by denoting something as a question just because the analyst or transcriber has heard it so. This way of analyzing tends to be characterized by the adjectival "first-time-through."

In conversation analysis,[1] the first-time-through perspective is already implemented, as two consecutive turns form one irreducible unit. That is, two turns are the minimal unit that makes sense, which means, we cannot reduce this unit to individual speakers. The turn pair is a social phenomenon sui generis. The immediate consequence is that we operate with a unit that harbors an inner contradiction: this unit is not self-same but diastatic, dehiscent, spread across time and agents. At its heart, there are two speakers; but there are two listeners as well, though we have only her voice in which the voice of the other is refracted, commented upon, and evaluated.

In taking this approach, we thereby arrive at a unit of the kind required for understanding the flow of an event*-in-the-making with its *internal* dynamic rather than one that requires an external engine to come alive. Ordinary methods of analyzing conversation do require such an external engine, as they take each locution as saying something more or less definitive, having

---

1 Conversation analysis cannot be reduced to the analysis of conversations, though, of course, it does precisely this. Rather, conversation analysis is a method and a subdiscipline of linguistics interested in understanding properties of sequentially ordered turn taking routines in and from which conversations emerge.

some shared or not shared "meaning." But this way of approaching conversation loses the very phenomenon we are after. Think about this analogy: sentences are like the photographs that make a film real. Getting movement back into the conversation is like taking a film projector to move the photographs in quick succession through the path of the light. But this does not make the people in the movie move again. The projection creates an *impression* of movement, which is due to the motor of the projector and not to the movement of the people. This is precisely the critique Bakhtin articulated in his analysis of the novel and its historical evolution. We cannot understand the evolution of the novel from its Greek antecedents to the modern day by somehow aligning all novels in sequence and then animating them like movies that play the pictures on the reel fast enough to create the illusion of movement (Bakhtin, 1981). Rather, to understand the development of the novel, we need to situate ourselves in "contemporary reality," which serves as its subject and provides the linguistic resources. Moreover,

> since it is constructed in a zone of contact with the *incomplete events* of a particular present, the novel often crosses the boundary of what we strictly call fictional literature – making use first of a moral confession, then of a philosophical tract, then of manifestos that are openly political, then degenerating into the raw spirituality of a confession, a "cry of the soul" that has not yet found its formal contours. These phenomena are precisely what characterize the novel as a *developing genre*. (Bakhtin, 1981, p. 33)

Language, then, is something alive; and being alive means change, for constancy is death: languages are dead precisely when no longer spoken. Therefore, "language constitutes an uninterrupted process of evolution, which realizes itself by means of the *social interaction of the speakers*" (Bakhtine [Volochinov], 1977, p. 141). The laws of linguistic evolution are in essence sociological laws, and the idea of an "individual speech act (in the narrow sense of the word individual) is a *contradictio in adjecto*" (p. 141). Thus, "signification does not reside in the word or in the soul of the speaker or in the soul of the listener. Signification is the effect of the *interaction of speaker and recipient, imposing itself on the material of the given sonorous complex* (pp. 146–147, original emphasis, underline added, my translation).[2]

---

2   The official English translation uses the word "meaning" instead of signification; but the French version reproduces the term *signification* de Saussure had used in the work to which Bakhtin and Vološinov have written their book as a reaction.

In this quoted excerpt, the idea of signification (i.e., "meaning") as something associated with words or something in the head (soul) of speaker and listener is abandoned. If there is any sense to the concept of "meaning," then it refers us to the effect of the societal relation involving speaker and listener. This, therefore, is precisely the position that Wittgenstein (1953/1997) takes in suggesting to abandon the idea of "meaning" and to focus instead on what is being done with it (i.e., its effect) as evidenced in the voice of the second speaker in the turn unit. This effect cannot be recovered other than in the irreducible relation*-in-the-making. The response may actually include an action as a second turn, such as when students write following the instructor's exclamation "Write!"

The stipulated unity of content and performance of the practical act also is at the heart of the ethnomethodological approach (Garfinkel & Sacks, 1986). The formal structure of practical action – e.g., of asking a question about the nature of the group – is represented in this way: "doing [asking a question about the nature of the group]" or "doing [having difficulties in comprehending]." Here, the bracketed part of the unity is the accountable text (proper gloss) that participants and others, after the fact, may use to describe or name the already-made event. "Doing" refers to the living, sensuous work that contributes to bringing the event about, thereby emphasizing that the "accountable-conversation-as-a-practical-accomplishment consists only and entirely in and of its work" (p. 172). What is in the brackets constitutes the "natural thesis," the way in which a social phenomenon is named and noted. But this natural understanding, which could also be scientific understanding, needs to be bracketed to get at the living work by means of which the named is phenomenalized (Husserl, 1976).

Getting at the Eventness of Events*-in-the-Making

[T]he aesthetic reflexion of living life is, in its very principle, not the "self-reflexion" of life in motion, of life in its actual aliveness: it presupposes another *subiectum*, a *subiectum* of empathizing, a *subiectum* situated outside the bounds of that life. (Bakhtin, 1993, p. 15)

We may gloss the fragment presented in chapter 2 in this way: Mrs. Winter and Connor *do* something that the other practically understands as "asking a question" – e.g., orienting toward and addressing Connor, using a particular grammatical form, or raising the pitch toward the end of the locution – or as "exhibiting non-understanding" – e.g., by not replying or by asking "What do you mean?" But this living *doing* is prehensible and comprehensible only once it is completed. At issue is this: What is the work that others recognize as "asking a question and replying with a counter-question"? To get at what is living in the curriculum*-in-the-making, we need to get at the work rather than at the bracketed gloss, whether this gloss is produced by just plain folks or by scientists.

The classical way to think about a conversation has been formalized in speech act theory. Speech acts come in three kinds: locutions, illocutions, and perlocutions (or, equivalently, locutionary, illocutionary, or perlocutionary acts). The approach attributes the illocutionary (intention) act to the current speaker, who, in speaking, performs a locutionary act and, thereby, brings about an effect (i.e., the perlocutionary act of the recipient). The locutionary act refers to the production of sound-words; the illocutionary act is the intent behind and cause of the locutionary act. The effect of the locutionary act on the recipient is the perlocutionary act.

Clearly, this way of thinking about a conversation is consistent with a constructivist approach whereby each speaker is theorized to have an intention or reason for saying what s/he says prior to actually saying it. Speech act theory, therefore, is built on the same cause–effect figure on which constructivist theory generally draws between thinking and acting (doing, saying). This is precisely one of the points of contention in the lengthy discussion and exchanges between Searle and Derrida, in detailing the problems in speech act theory (Derrida, 1988). It is a model built on the individual as the unit of analysis, and a conversation is thought as the result of two or more speakers who, each with their own intentions and thoughts, externalize the latter to make them available to others.

The model is already problematic, however, at the level of the individuals, because in conversations, such as those that evolve in the classrooms, participants do not know beforehand what they will be saying. In such situations where speakers do not merely articulate some planned or memorized text, it is better to think about a mutually constitutive relation between thought and speech (Merleau-Ponty, 1945; Vygotskij, 2002). Thus, at the beginning of the Saying, there is only a seed of a thought; this seed is related to the thought expressed in the ultimately Said as a grain and the mature tree that will have grown from it. As speaking unfolds, thought forms in response to what is said; and each saying is in response to the thought that forms.

Although this analysis already is closer to the way in which we actually speak, it does not yet address a major issue: speech addresses itself to the other, and, therefore, to be intelligible, shapes itself in form and content as a function of the other. A teacher such as Mrs. Winter speaks about the intended curriculum very differently if her recipients are the students in her second-grade mathematics class ("We're beginning a brand new unit in math today ... and we talked a little bit last week about some of the things that we already know about geometry") than if her recipients are the two researchers present, with whom she is developing a new way of teaching three-dimensional geometry (the text in Figure 8.1 is proxy for this type of discourse). Again, although this revised way of thinking about a conversation better accounts for the nature of what contributors to a conversation say, it still lacks in a very important way: Participants in (true) conversations are not in control over their course. In staff meetings we may have or in any classroom conversation has a dynamic of its own. To understand and appropriately theorize this dynamic, we need to change the unit of analysis from the individual speaker to the societal phenomenon.

Now that we articulated our interest in recovering the internal dynamic of the *conversation*, the aspect of language as part of the event*-in-the-making, we cannot take the individual locution as the unit. We always have to take the turn pair.

Fragment 9.1

```
01  W:    em an ↑what did [we say that [group was about.]
                          [((points toward objects on the floor,
          maintained until turn 06))
                                       [((makes tiny circular movement
          with index finger))
02        (1.00)
03  C:    <<p>what do you [mean li[ke?>]
                          [((touches "his" cube))
                                  [((looks up to Teacher))
```

Strictly speaking, therefore, we cannot say that Mrs. Winter is asking a question and refer to Turn 01. The minimum unit is the turn pair, which here includes Turns 01–03. We may view what is happening through the lens of the realization of possibilities, which makes possibilities disappear while creating new ones simultaneously. Thus, Mrs. Winter's locution (turn 01) is a possible offer of a question; a next turn that will have been confirmed as a suitable reply then actualizes the possible question–reply pair and thereby opens up new possibilities. If, on the other hand, this possibility is not actualized, Mrs. Winter may repeat the offer (in a different way) and continue to do so until the question–reply sequence will have occurred. In either case,

Connor's locution both actualizes a possibility – that of replying to a question with a counter-question – and opens up new possibilities one of which will have been actualized in and with the subsequent turn. As readers can see, this way of approaching conversation keeps its internal dynamic open, never taking anything as definitive and always against the open horizon of the future, with its unforeseeable contingencies and always emerging and disappearing possibilities. In this way, we never grasp what is happening until after the happening has come to an end, which enables us to talk about "what has happened," that is, to talk in past tense. In speaking, the theme is continuously in the making as a possible theme comes to be actualized opening up its own demise.

As soon as we take this approach, we no longer can say Mrs. Winter does this and Connor does that. We have to ask, what kind of unit is this? For the present, we may take it, because of the grammatical and intonational values as a question–question pair. There are then at least two inner contradictions. First, the moments of this turn pair are question and question rather than question and its answer. Second, the constituent moments of this pair, the locutions, are diastatically spread across voices, and they are diachronic, spread out across time. In fact, time is made for an answer in Turn 02, and the work of this making is again sympractical and distributed across Mrs. Winter and Connor: *She gives him time to answer as much as he takes his time to answer*. This time is irreducible to the individual, Mrs. Winter or Connor, much as an economic exchange that involves buying and selling cannot be reduced to buyer and seller because it requires both. The exchange involves buying and selling simultaneously and irreducibly: buying and selling are but different ways in which the economic exchange manifests itself. The expression "there is pausing" institutes this decentering of agency to the eventness of the pausing.

In fact, if we were to take for an instant the perspective of Connor, then his response begins in Turn 01, as to do anything like he does in Turn 03, he has to orient and listen to Mrs. Winter. It is in this period of orienting and listening that understanding (even understanding that he does not understand subsequently expressed in "what do you mean like?") forms and the answer takes shape. This is also the period of transformation of the locution,[3] which, in reception, no longer is what it would be if we were to take Mrs. Winter as

---

3   Locution refers to the embodied act of speaking, which is singularized in the person; the utterance is an irreducible social fact, requiring locution and its social evaluation.

its center. The locution therefore is already an utterance, spread across speaker and recipient; but the second moment is not available until it takes shape in public (turns 02, 03). Thus, the "nervous center of any locution, of any expression, is not at the inside but at the outside: it situates itself in the social milieu that surrounds the individual" (Bakhtine [Volochinov], 1977, p. 134). This turn pair embodies change: it is not only in time but makes time, it is spread across locations and locutions. It is out of this tension that the second turn also is the first moment of the next pair; it concludes one and simultaneously opens another pair.

We may now take a look at the next turn pair: turn pair 03–04. Again, it is irreducible. The pair in fact involves an overlap in that the second moment already begins while the first is still unfolding. Here, we may observe a question–answer pair, where the second turn, is a projected answer to the question – at least for the moment, because we do not know whether the "answer" is an answer until we find out from its pairing with the next turn whether we can find something like a confirmation of some sort.

Fragment 9.2

```
03  C:   <<p>what do you [mean li[ke?>]
                     [((touches "his" cube))
                        [((looks up to Teacher))
04  W:                    ^[WHAt ] ↑was the (0.15) ^WHAt
         ↑did we put for the name of that group.
```

When we take this perspective, then our analysis becomes independent of the individual and his/her intentions, understandings, etc. We obtain societal facts, here available as turn pairs that are linked like a chain (Figure 9.1). Each link in the chain is equivalent to a turn pair – the chain is made of these chain links. But the individual turn is the point of linkage from one pair to the next. The turn, which is not an element but a node, simultaneously belongs to two turn pairs: It not only is Janus-faced but constitutive of the change, as its function differs in the two pairs. The changeover from one function to the next, which coincides with the locution, is what captures the living aspect of language-in-use. The locution constitutes change, as it does not *express* – push out – what is in the mind of the speaker. It simultaneously is *in response to* one speaker, oriented backward, and *for the benefit* of another speaker, oriented forward. The links are the recurrent, the perpetual (eternal) return of what is alike (*das Gleiche*); and what is alike is precisely not the self-identical same, because each link differs from the preceding one: in form, content, function, location, or time.

Figure 9.1. In a chain, each link participates in the constitution of two connections.

In this way, our method takes us to the level of the societal. We are no longer able to attribute the conversation to individuals. The unfolding conversation is our event*-in-the-making. One of the characteristics of conversation is that it is open ended, precisely what we expect for and from the event. When we participate in a conversation, even in a business or faculty meeting, we do not know where the conversation is heading. We may have inarticulate and unarticulated intentions preceding our speaking, but these do not determine the trajectory of the conversation or its end. What will have been said, the contents of the conversation, is a result of the path that the Saying is laying in saying.

We thereby also have rid ourselves of the individual as the causal agent – in the way Nietzsche (1954c) suggests we need to do to get at the eventness of the event. We cannot attribute the end result, the content of the conversation and its effect, to individual speakers. It is an irreducible *societal* fact, attributable only to the relation, itself irreducible to individual, independent actors or the sum total of their actions. We also have rid ourself of cause–effect thinking about societal events, because the effect of a locution is inseparable from the locution: both are integral part of the minimum unit that makes sense.

We thereby also come to understand the way in which ethnomethodologists articulate social facts, such as queues. These consist not of individual actions or the sum or enchainment thereof (Garfinkel, 2002). Queues are societal facts, not understood in the traditional way of inner-worldly things, but structured structuring events that are *staffed* by some cohort. We may therefore observe queues in the bank, at the ticket counters of the latest blockbuster movie, in walk-in clinics, the offices of driver's license agencies, or supermarket counters. Independent of the local staff, we observe queues as societal facts that maintain themselves even when the individual staff changes as those who are currently served and those who leave are replaced by others in the queue or that arrive. Queues are organized and organizing societal work precisely in the same way as conversations are; this work does not belong to individuals, such as the speaking and required listening are irreducible synchronous processes spread across locations and staff. It is sympractical work at a collective level that cannot be reduced to individuals, This then allows us to understand the curriculum as something living, which is alive because it is changing precisely while sustaining and repeating. If it were not returning, it would be dead; but it can return only as something different, because otherwise it were not alive.

Subject*-in-the Making

In the conversation analytic approach, the effect of the speech comes to be known through the second turn in a turn pair, which means that we cannot know what a locution is doing until after its effect (perlocution) is known. In choosing the turn pair as the minimal unit, conversation analysis implements the "modification without change," the "phase shift of the identical," which philosophers suggest is required for capturing the eventing of the event. When we attempt to understand the living mathematics curriculum through the verb to *event*, then there are neither causes nor effects (Nietzsche, 1954c). Causes and effects are but discursive resources for attributing rationality and (legal) responsibility after the fact. That is, in conversation analysis, the diachronic and dehiscent nature of eventing is captured in the understanding of the speech act as comprised of locution, illocution, and perlocution. Whereas the first of these three moments of the speech act is made available in the utterance, its second moment, the illocution (intent), is generally immanent and invisible. The third moment of the speech act, the perlocution or effect, is available only in and through the subsequent locution. It cannot be otherwise because the content of the Saying is available only in the Said, which, in its entirety, is available only once the Saying has ended. In a strong sense, therefore, understanding*-in-the-making and the diachrony of Saying and Said are one and the same. Understanding always is delayed with respect to the living understanding*-in-the-making. And this delay is without remedy. Our understanding of the mobility of the conversation, therefore, no longer focuses on causes and effects but understands the effect (perlocution) as that aspect that allows a cause (illocution) to be attributed. ("You are insulting me" [perlocution, effect], "I was only joking" [illocution]).

In this take on analytic method, we therefore have already abandoned the detrimental cause–effect reasoning, and, with it, the idea of the subject that is the origin of change. In fact, the subject is an effect of the *societal* relation. Thus, for example, Mrs. Winter *is* a questioner only if the turn pair turns out to be a question–answer turn pair. As questioner she therefore can be only after the fact. To bring out this important distinction even further, consider the situation where Mrs. Winter might say directed toward her husband, "Did you dust the bedroom?" The traditional way of taking this is to say that she has asked a question. But if the response were to be, "Why are you always criticizing me?," then the locution attributable to Mrs. Winter is, from the perspective of the irreducible conversation, a critique; and this is what the conversation then has to address. There is no question at all but a critique, which becomes available as such in the social space in and through the second locution. If such incidences recur, both at home and in other societal spaces, then Mrs. Winter might be classified as a nagger, niggler, or criticizer.

The upshot of these comments is that whatever scholars refer to as "constructed identity" is the effect or condensation of relations*-in-the-making, abstracted from societal relations. Subject positions and identity are not essences, are not things that we can construct but are abstractions made in the finalization of events*-in-the-making, themselves motilities that would require denotations such as identity*-in-the-making, subject*-in-the-making, and so on. These event*-like processes *have to be* without end, for their very stability would mean that they have come to an end. Change is absent only in and with death (e.g., dead languages are those that nobody speaks). Our method, thereby, has allowed us to overcome the fallacy of the "subject in itself," "thing in itself," or "substance in itself," all of which have been the subject of Nietzsche's (1954c) critique that I have placed in the epigraph of this book. All of these are event-related complexes that cannot be reduced, as the understanding thereof is inseparable from the event*-in-the-making, characterized by the same open-ended horizon that also characterizes the event*-in-the-making.

Mrs. Winter is not an all-knowing teacher, for she would not have had to do what we may gloss by "reformulating her *question* repeatedly until Connor understood." If anything, there is what conversation analysts call a *repair*, which, qua societal phenomenon, again requires collective work. This collective work is irreducible to the work of individuals; it is not the sum total of the individual work but precisely collective work, a societal phenomenon sui generis. But the residue in these changing exchanges is that subsequent exchanges no longer take the same trajectory, which is in fact a common experience of teachers when they walk from group to group in student-centered lessons. They no longer perform the same locutions but perform some of those that have emerged from exchanges such as those between Mrs. Winter and Connor. That is, *exchanges* change those that staff them. Mrs. Winter is not a stable subject, but a constantly changing moment of an event*-in-the-making. We have cultural-historical devices, tracers, to track and reduce these changing moments to the *same* in the face of inevitable change. We may talk about Mrs. Winter as a person with a specific identity, when in fact there are observable changes even in the course of a three-week unit on three-dimensional geometry in a second-grade class. The pedagogies before and after the unit are different, the result of the intervening events; and those performances that we can pin to Mrs. Winter are no longer the same even though she has undergone the changes rather than actively brought them about (see chapter 5 on the advenant, patient, and witness).

Once we take such a perspective, we may understand why Mrs. Winter may say that a lesson was successful or unsuccessful, why she might feel good or bad about what has been effectuated. It also allows us to understand that in the very process of participating, Mrs. Winter is changing, evolving, and developing as a teacher. Often this may not be noticed immediately. But we do note change over time. It also allows us to understand why, in and through participation in the living curriculum, other teachers become burned out and drop out of teaching altogether. Such effects of participating in the living curriculum cannot be anticipated and are generally not thought about in the literature on learning. Most teachers who come to a point of abandoning teaching have not gotten into it with the intention of dropping out. They have chosen the profession because of a calling or because it promised a stable income and a good life. It is precisely the participation in the living curriculum, as a result of which the intended plans do not jibe with the actually enacted curriculum once finished, that teachers *become* burnouts, dropouts, and the likes.

Objects*-in-the-Making

From the perspective of method, we need to take the same approach to objects specifically and to the material world more generally. We may not take an object as a "thing in itself," for from the perspective of the event*-in-the-making, even objects are effects of events*in-the-making and, therefore, have to be thought as objects*-in-the-making. Initially, something (some "thing") in the room may not be salient at all, and, therefore, it is nothing (no thing). "It's nothing until I call it!" is a perceptive statement the philosophical dimensions of which may have exceeded its speaker, the baseball umpire Bill Klem, referring to whether a throw is a "ball" or a "strike." The pitcher's throw and its social evaluation are the irreducible minimum unit that makes sense when we take a baseball game from the perspective of event*-in-the-making. We do not know which team will win, but understanding who won and who lost is a function of the unfolding event*-in-the-making, which cannot be attributed to the pitcher, who threw a ball, or to the umpire, who called it. There are many instances in sports history where the umpires, referees, and linespeople are said to have pro-duced the final outcome. But in fact, they *always* are part of the production of the outcome, only that in most cases it is easier to attribute a goal to the player rather than the one or the other member that staffs the social event.

We now have in place an analytic method that allows us to understand the curriculum as a living event*-in-the-making. The curriculum is not an inner-worldly thing. Both the curriculum plan and the curriculum finished once a lesson is over are abstractions, as much as the lived curriculum that is abstracted from teachers' and students' recollection of what a class or course was like. The approach makes problematic the identification of what are treated as things, such as "knowledge," "understanding," and "meaning." We can only say that Connor has or does not have a mathematical understand-ing or knowledge if we abstract from the event*-in-the-making, when we, for example, remove all locutions and other actions Connor performs during this lesson and then construct a model of his mental structure. This mental structure ("his" "constructions") would be taken as the *cause* "behind" or "un-derlying" the locutions, the articulation of which are effects of thinking and the speaking that make the thinking available on the outside.

Living versus Lived Curriculum

Once-occurrent uniqueness or singularity cannot be thought of, it can only be partic-ipatively experienced or lived through. (Bakhtin, 1993, p. 13)

[O]ur life with men. There the relation is open and in the form of speech. ... [O]ur life with intelligible forms. There the relation is clouded, yet it discloses itself. (Buber, 1937, p. 6)

The living curriculum – "our life with men," where "the relation is *open*," that is, unfinalized, "and in the form of speech" – frequently is reduced to accounts of curriculum in the narratives' participants – the "life with intelligible forms," which has clouded the living, open relation. In these narrative accounts, the event is already available as an inner-worldly fact. Although the curriculum is no longer living, it and the relation on which it is based "disclose itself." That is, although these narratives no longer are those of witnesses of events*-in-the-making, they contribute to the articulation of otherwise invisible form in the flux of life. The problem is that these accounts overemphasize the figure of causes and effects. Such figures are possible only when the effect is itself available as inner-worldly fact, that is, after the event no longer is open but closed and completed. It allows attributions of the who-did-what-with-which-effect kind.

Narratives are not some "pure" reflections of now finalized events*-in-the-making but they have their own constraints and affordances. It is precisely because of narrative constraints that "[i]n principle, there exists no clear demarcation between *autobiography* and *biography*, and this is an essential point" (Bakhtine, 1984, p. 157). The relationship between the protagonist and author "is not a constitutive and organizing element of the artistic form" (p. 157) and "the coincidence of hero and author is a *contradictio in adjecto*" (p. 158). Rather, the organizing principle is the narrative, which has a plot and its hero. The narrative has a dynamic of its own; it is of social nature, for, being directed toward a recipient, it has to be intelligible to have any function in conversation.

The event*-in-the-making is not subject to a narrative plot, in which the hero brings about certain effects in his life, those of others, and in the material world. But the narrative accounts that teachers and students produce after the events, while constituting a form of understanding, are subject to the requirements of hero and plot. These narratives therefore are not direct reflections of the living curriculum qua event*-in-the-making. From within the event*-in-the-making, even the nature of an action is not available until after the fact – which is a lesson that we learn every time when following an instruction (in a cookbook, programming a recording device, assembling a piece of furniture, pruning trees) does not yield what we had anticipated. This situation is without remedy. The coherence or incoherence of plans, actions, and effects can be achieved only after the fact.

The problem of the relation between event* and account has been related to the "coroner's problem," which is one of reconstructing events when effect – a dead person – is known.

> The coroner begins with the remains at hand. With what the corpse looks like as his point of departure he imagines alternative ways the deceased could have lived so that as a phase of the way he lived he came to look the way he does. The corpse's actual appearances are problematic as *events*-to-start-with. They take on their demonstrable facticity in the course of his inquiries. (Garfinkel, Lynch, & Livingston, 1981, p. 136)

The authors therefore accept as suitable account of the work of discovery neither a historical rendering in terms of causes (e.g., the quasar that manifests itself in the astronomers' instruments) or the astronomers' actions (e.g., those that they describe in their notebooks, the methods section of their scientific publication announcing the first sighting of a quasar, self-reports, interview responses, anecdotal reports, and so on). Rather, the authors recommend the first-time-through perspective when the effects that events eventuated are not yet available as inner-worldly facts. This then allows understanding the work from which emerges, in these authors' case, such a thing as a pulsar, or, in the present book, something like the enacted curriculum, student learning, teacher development, knowledge, and so forth. The first-time-through perspective allows us to witness how something eventually known as a fact is taking shape so that it can be abstracted to become an inner-worldly fact. It is a way of coming to understand how anything related to the curriculum becomes *performatively* objective, so that it is recognizable as an irreducible social fact that is independent of its production staff (i.e., specific students and teachers).

> Our policy, and the point: We want to examine the pulsar for the way it is *in hand* at all times in the inquiry. We want to see the way in which it is "performatively" objective. We did *not* and we want *not* to examine the end-point object for its correspondence to an original plan. We want to disregard, we want *not* to take seriously, how closely or how badly the object corresponds to some original design ... that is independent of their embodied work's *particular occasions* as of which the object's production – the *object* – consists, only, and entirely. (Garfinkel et al., 1981, p. 137)

In this quotation, the authors precisely make the point articulated in chapter 8, where I highlight the difference between planned curriculum and enacted curriculum, the latter referring to what the living curriculum has effectuated: the inner-worldly fact of a lesson (curriculum) that has been completed. It can be compared to what had been planned, whereas the living curriculum, which as event*-in-the-making is unfinished and therefore does not and cannot exist as ob-ject, some thing thrown before and against the subject. This latter would be the metaphysical approach, whereby the subject is thought of the representation of the present, when in fact only something that already has object-nature can be made present again (represented). Thus, the pulsar, as independent Galilean object, is an effect of the astronomers' sympractical work that comes about *in the course* of one night's work. We see it taking shape, as a signal comes to be observed under some but not other conditions. As a result, a story of the kind we read in the research article can be produced: If you do this, then you see the pulsar. Any other doing does not allow the pulsar to emerge from practical work. In any case, the observation of a pulsar is irremediably tied to laboratory work. To see a pulsar, one has to do the work or look at a sedimentation of such work, for example, at a "photograph" published in a scientific journal or the news media. In the same way, curriculum is the result of work, which, in many instances, remains hidden and invisible. As soon as we focus on this work, with all of its vagaries, successes and failures, the curriculum remains living unfinished, open, and in the making, just as all its different moments, the particular staff populating the setting observed, the things the work gives rise to, and the subjects that emerge.

This position is consistent with the approach Bakhtin takes throughout his work, where he emphasizes that participative thinking does not detach the performed act from its performance.

> To those who wish and know how to think participatively – that is, those who know how not to detach their performed act from its product, but rather how to relate both of them to the unitary and unique context of life and seek to determine them in that context as an indivisible unity – it seems that philosophy … fails to speak of what it ought to speak. (Bakhtin, 1993, p. 19)

Why does such an approach get at the eventness of events? It is because social structure is not thought as something that is separate from the performance, and, therefore, has to be recovered by the analysts. The specific nature of a queue or a second-grade mathematics lesson lies in the performance (work), part of which is the recognition of the structure performed. This is why teachers can walk into another classroom and recognize that there is a geometry lesson in progress although they had not previously known anything that might have allowed them to anticipate what kind of lesson they would be stepping into. In the same way, we may step into a situation and recognize that there is a lineup in the making; and if we do not, someone on its current staff will remind us that there is one and to get the back and wait as everyone else does. That is, the lineup is a collective phenomenon that organizes itself; it recognizes when something is going awry, and self-corrects it. The structure, therefore, is performatively objective rather than something added to the queue.

The approach articulated here actually is consistent with the statement quoted in the volume's epigraph, whereby dropping the concepts of subject and object also leads to the dropping of the concept of substance and its modifications, including mind and matter and, therefore, their differentiation. If societal structure is performatively objective, that is, available in the concreteness of what can be observed, then we do not require the distinction between mind and what appears in the public space, such as a performance. We no longer require thinking about "meanings" and "understandings" that are somewhere in the mind and are only indicated by what is said and done. The living curriculum is in the performance, and observable as performance.

APPENDIX A

For the transcriptions, I follow a commonly used system based on conversation analysis adapted for the inclusion of prosodic features (Selting et al., 1998). In the rules implemented here, everything is lowercased, and sound words that run into each other are transcribed that way unless the run-in sign "=" is used when it would be difficult to distinguish pronunciation (e.g., "a=one"). The transcription is phonetic such that if a participant pronounces the words "this" or "that" in the way a French or German speaker often does, that is, with a soft "d" or "s," the transcription will read something like "ze other one is to read dis ze whole branch."

Notation	Description	Example
(0.14)	Time without talk, in seconds	more ideas. (1.03) just
(.)	Pause in speech less than 0.10 seconds	011 C: o:kAY (.) could be a double cone
((turns))	Verbs and descriptions in double parentheses and italics are transcriber's comments	((modifies graph))
*	Asterisks marks the instant in speech that corresponds to the video image on the right	
(??)	Marks inaudible words, about one word per question mark	042 T: <<p>but dat (??) in the positions here
::	Colons indicate lengthening of phoneme, about 1/10 of a second per colon	si::ze
[ ]	Square brackets in consecutive lines indicate overlap	011 C: o:kAY (.) could be a double cone sidewa[ys]. 012 T: [yea]
<<f> >	Forte, words are uttered with louder than normal speech volume	<<f>um>
<<p> >	Piano, lower than normal speech volume	042 T: <<p>but dat (??)
<<pp> >	Pianissimo, much lower speech volume	009 T: <<pp>under way>
<<dim> >	Diminuendo, becoming weaker	<<dim>i donno>
<<len> >	Lento, slower than normal	<<len>square?>
prETty	Capital letters indicate louder than normal talk indicated in small letters.	looks prETty grEEN to mE
hh	Noticeable out-breath	
.h	Noticeable in-breath	021 T: <<dim>hu hu hu hu hu>.hhfs
–,?;.	Punctuation is used to mark movement of pitch (intonation) toward end of utterance, flat, slightly and strongly upward, and slightly and strongly downward, respectively	C: okay; save that. (0.27) do you want me to blEACH it?
=	Equal sign indicates that the phonemes of different words are not clearly separated	i=ll
`, ´, ˇ	Diacritic indicates movement of pitch within the word that follows – down, up, down up	ˇsimilar.

APPENDIX B

Appendix B1: The killer whale hidden in Figure 3.4.

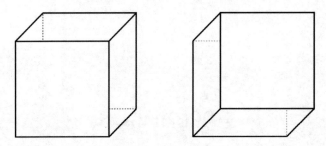

Appendix B2: The two ways to see a three-dimensional cube when there are only lines on a flat white plane.

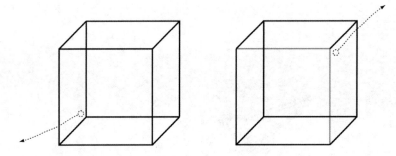

Appendix B.3. Placing the focus at a circle and then making the eyes move along the trajectory indicated by the arrows will produce the two three-dimensional Necker Cubes that research subjects report to be seeing in psychological experiments.

REFERENCES

Aussie Educator. (2012). A total education page for Australia. Accessed March 5, 2012 at www. aussieeducator.org.au/curriculum/curriculum.html.

Bakhtin, M. M. [Medvedev, P. N.} (1978). *The formal method in literary scholarship: A critical introduction to sociological poetics.* Baltimore, MD: Johns Hopkins University Press.

Bakhtin, M. M. (1979). *Estetika slovesnogo tvorchestva* [Aesthetics of verbal creation]. Moscow, Russia: Iskusstvo.

Bakhtin, M. (1981). *The dialogic imagination.* Austin, TX: University of Texas Press.

Bakhtin, M. (1984). *Problems in Dostoevsky's poetics.* Minneapolis, MN: University of Minnesota Press.

Bakhtin, M. M. (1990). *Art and answerability* (M. Holquist & V. Liapunov, trans.). Austin, TX: University of Texas Press.

Bakhtin, M. (1993). *Toward a philosophy of the act* (V. Liapunov, trans., V. Liapunov & M. Holquist, Eds.). Austin, TX: University of Texas Press.

Bakhtine, M. (1984). *Esthétique de la création verbale* [Esthetics of verbal creation] (A. Aucouturier, trans.). Paris, France: Éditions Gallimard.

Bakhtine, M. [Volochinov, V. N.] (1977). *Le marxisme et la philosophie du langage: essai d'application de la méthode sociologique en linguistique* [Marxism and the philosophy of language: Essay on the application of the sociological method in linguistics] (M. Yaguello, trans.). Paris, France: Les Éditions de Minuit. (Original: Vološinov, 1930)

Benveniste, É. (1966). *Problèmes de linguistique générale, vol 1.* [Problems of general linguistics]. Paris, France: Éditions Gallimard. (First published in 1950)

Bergson, H. (1908). *L'évolution créatrice 4ième ed.* [Creative evolution, 4th ed.]. Paris, France: Libraries Félix Alcan et Guillaumin Réunies. (First published in 1907)

Bourdieu, P. (1980). *Le sens pratique* [The logic of practice]. Paris, France: Les Éditions de Minuit.

Bourdieu, P. (1997). *Méditations pascaliennes* [Pascalian meditations]. Paris, France: Seuil.

Brown, T., & McNamara, O. (2011). *Becoming a mathematics teacher: Identity and identifications.* Dordrecht, The Netherlands: Springer.

Buber, M. (1937). *I and Thou* (R. G. Smith, trans.). Edinburgh, UK: T. & T. Clark.

Buber, M. (1979). *Das dialogische Prinzip* (The dialogical principle). Heidelberg, Germany: Lambert Schneider.

Buber, M. (2002). *Between man and man* (R. Gregory-Smith, trans.). London, UK: Routledge. (First published in 1947)

Chrétien, J.-L. (2007). *Répondre: Figures de la réponse et de la responsabilité* [To respond: Figures of response and responsibility]. Paris, France: Presses Universitaires de France.

Cobb, P., & Tzou, C. (2009). Supporting students' learning about data creation. In W.-M. Roth (Ed.), *Mathematical representation at the interface of body and culture* (pp. 135–171). Charlotte, NC: Information Age Publishing.

Collins, H. M. (1982). Tacit knowledge and scientific networks. In B. Barnes & D. Edge (Eds.), *Science in context: Readings in the sociology of science* (pp. 44–64). Cambridge, MA.: MIT Press.

Czarnocha, B. (2008). Ethics of teacher-research. In B. Czarnocha (Ed.), *Handbook of mathematics teaching research: Teaching experiment – a tool for teacher-researchers* (pp. 79–86). Rzeszów, Poland: University of Rzeszów.

Deleuze, G., & Guattari, F. (2005). *Qu'est-ce que la philosophie* [What is philosophy]? Paris, France: Les Éditions de Minuit. (First published in 1991)

Derrida, J. (1967). *L'écriture et la différence* [Writing and difference]. Paris, France: Éditions du Seuil.

Derrida, J. (1988). *Limited inc.* Evanston, IL: Northwestern University Press.

Derrida, J. (1996). *Le monolinguisme de l'autre ou la prothèse d'origine* [Monolingualism of the Other; or, The prosthesis of origin]. Paris, France: Galilée.

Derrida, J. (2000). *Le toucher, Jean-Luc Nancy* [On touching – Jean-Luc Nancy]. Paris, France: Galilée.

Descartes, R. (1679). *Les passions de l'âme* [Passions of the soul]. Paris, France: Michel Bobin.

Dewey, J., & Bentley, A. F. (1999). Knowing and the known. In R. Handy & E. E. Hardwood, *Useful procedures of inquiry* (pp. 97–209). Great Barrington, MA: Behavioral Research Council. (First published in 1949)

Foucault, M. (1975). *Surveiller et punir: Naissance de la prison* [Discipline and punish: Birth of the prison]. Paris, France: Gallimard.

Garfinkel, H. (1967) *Studies in ethnomethodology,* Englewood Cliffs, NJ: Prentice-Hall.

Garfinkel, H. (1996). Ethnomethodology's program. *Social Psychology Quarterly, 59,* 5–21.

Garfinkel, H. (2002). *Ethnomethodology's program: Working out Durkheim's aphorism.* Lanham, MD: Rowman & Littlefield.

Garfinkel, H., Lynch, M., & Livingston, E. (1981). The work of a discovering science constructed with materials from the optically discovered pulsar. *Philosophy of the Social Sciences, 11,* 131–158.

Garfinkel, H., & Sacks, H. (1986). On formal structures of practical action. In H. Garfinkel (Ed.), *Ethnomethodological studies of work* (pp. 160–193). London, UK: Routledge & Kegan Paul.

Gooding, D. (1992). Putting agency back into experiment. In A. Pickering (Ed.), *Science as practice and culture* (pp. 65–112). Chicago, IL: University of Chicago Press.

Hegel, G. W. F. (1979). *Werke - Band 3: Phänomenologie des Geistes* [Works, vol. 3: Phenomenology of mind/spirit]. Frankfurt/M, Germany: Suhrkamp-Verlag. (First published in 1807)

Heidegger, M. (1961). *Nietzsche Erster Band* [Nietzsche, vol. 1]. Pfullingen, Germany: Neske.

Heidegger, M. (1977a). *Gesamtausgabe. I. Abteilung: Veröffentlichte Schriften 1914–1970 Band 5: Holzwege*. Frankfurt a/M, Germany: Vittorio Klostermann.

Heidegger, M. (1977b). *Sein und Zeit* [Being and time]. Tübingen, Germany: Max Niemeyer.

Heidegger, M. (1984). *Gesamtausgabe. II. Abteilung. Vorlesungen 1923–1944. Band 53: Hölderlins Hymne "Der Ister"* [Complete edition. Part 1: Published writings 1923–1944 vol. 53: Hölderlin's hymn "The Ister"]. Frankfurt/M, Germany: Vittorio Klostermann.

Heidegger, M. (1997). *Gesamtausgabe. I. Abteilung: Veröffentlichte Schriften 1910–1976. Band 10: Der Satz vom Grund* [Complete edition. Part 1: Published writings 1910–1976, vol. 10: The proposition on ground/reason]. Frankfurt/M, Germany: Vittorio Klostermann.

Heidegger, M. (2006). *Gesamtausgabe. I. Abteilung: Veröffentlichte Schriften 1910–1976. Band 11: Identität und Differenz* [Complete edition. Part 1: Published writings 1910–1976, vol. 11: Identity and difference]. Frankfurt/M, Germany: Vittorio Klostermann.

Henry, M. (1988). *Voir l'invisible: Sur Kandinsky*. Paris, France: Presses Universitaires de France.

Henry, M. (2000). *Incarnation: Une philosophie de la chair*. Paris, France: Éditions du Seuil.

Holquist, M. (1990). Introduction: The architectonics of answerability. In M. M. Bakhtin, *Art and answerability* (M. Holquist & V. Liapunov, trans.) (pp. ix–xlix). Austin, TX: University of Texas Press.

Holquist, M. (1993). Foreword. In M. M. Bakhtin, *Toward a philosophy of the act* (V. Liapunov, trans., V. Liapunov & M. Holquist, Eds.) (pp. vii–xv). Austin, TX: University of Texas Press.

Holzkamp, K. (1992). Die Fiktion administrativer Planbarkeit schulischer Lernprozesse [Administrative planning of learning processes at school – A fiction]. In K.-H. Braun & K. Wetzel (Eds.), *Lernwidersprüche und pädagogisches Handeln* (pp. 91–113). Marburg, Germany: Verlag Arbeit und Gesellschaft.

Husserl, E. (1939). Die Frage nach dem Ursprung der Geometrie als intentional-historisches Problem [The question of the origin of geometry as intentional-historical problem]. *Revue internationale de philosophie, 1*, 203–225.

Husserl, E. (1973). *Husserliana Band I. Cartesianische Meditationen und Pariser Vorträge* [Husserliana, vol. I. Cartesian meditations and Paris lectures]. The Hague, Netherlands: Martinus Nijhoff.

Husserl, E. (1976). *Husserliana Band III/1. Ideen zu einer reinen Phänomenologie und phänomenologischen Philosophie: Erstes Buch: Allgemeine Einführung in die reine Phänomenologie* [Husserliana vol. III/1. Ideas to a pure phenomenology and phenomenological philosophy, vol 1. General introduction to a pure phenomenology]. The Hague, Netherlands: Martinus Nijhoff.

Husserl, E. (1980). *Vorlesungen zur Phänomenologie des inneren Zeitbewusstseins* [Lectures on the phenomenology of internal time consciousness]. Tübingen, Germany: Max Niemeyer.

Inhelder, B., & Piaget, J. (1958). *The growth of logical thinking from childhood to adolescence*. New York, NY: Basic Books.

Jordan, K., & Lynch, M. (1993). The mainstreaming of a molecular biological tool: A case study of a new technique. In G. Button (Ed.), *Technology in working order: Studies of work, interaction, and technology* (pp. 162–178). London and New York: Routledge.

Kant, O. (1870). *Kritik der reinen Vernunft* (2nd ed.) [Critique of pure reason]. Berlin, Germany: Heiman.

Kant, I. (1956a). *Werke Band II: Kritik der reinen Vernunft* [Works, vol. 2: Critique of pure reason]. Wiesbaden, Germany: Insel Verlag.

Kant, I. (1956b). *Werke Band IV* [Works, vol. 4]. Wiesbaden, Germany: Insel Verlag.

Kant, I. (1956c). *Werke Band V* [Works, vol. 5]. Wiesbaden, Germany: Insel Verlag.

Kirshner, D., & Whitson, J. A. (Eds.). (1997). *Situated cognition: Social, semiotic, and psychological perspectives*. New York, NY: Routledge.

Lakoff, G. (1987). *Women, fire, and dangerous things: What categories reveal about the mind*. Chicago, IL: University of Chicago Press.

Lakoff, G., & Johnson, M. (1980). *Metaphors we live by*. Chicago, IL: University of Chicago Press.

Lave, J. (1993). The practice of learning. In S. Chaiklin & J. Lave (Eds.), *Understanding practice: Perspectives on activity and context* (pp. 3–32). Cambridge, UK: Cambridge University Press.

Leontyev, A. N. (1981). *Problems in the development of mind*. Moscow, USSR: Progress Publishers.

Levinas, E. (1971). *Le Dit et le Dire* [The Said and the Saying]. *Le Nouveau Commerce, 18/19*, 21–48.

Levinas, E. (1978). *Autrement qu'être ou au-delà de l'essence* [Otherwise than being or beyond essence]. The Hague, The Netherlands: Marinus Nijhoff.

Levinas, E. (1996). Martin Heidegger and ontology. *Diacritics, 26*, 11–32.

Livingston, E. (1986). *The ethnomethodological foundations of mathematics*. London, UK: Routledge and Kegan Paul.

Luria, A. R. (1970). *Traumatic aphasia: Its syndromes, psychology and treatment* (D. Bowden, trans.). The Hague, The Netherlands: Mouton.

Luria, A. R. (1973). *The working brain: An introduction to neuropsychology*. New York, NY: Basic Books.

Lynch, M., Livingston, E., & Garfinkel, H. (1983). Temporal order in laboratory work. In K. D. Knorr-Cetina & M. Mulkay (Eds.), *Science observed: Perspectives on the social study of science* (pp. 205–238). London, UK: Sage.

Maine de Biran, P. (1841). *Œuvres philosophiques tome premier: Influence de l'habitude sur la faculté de penser* [Philosophical words, vol. 1: Influence of habitude on the capacity to think]. Paris, France: Librairie de Ladrange.

Maine de Biran, P. (1952). *Mémoire sur la décomposition de la pensée* [Dissertation on the decomposition of thought]. Paris, France: Presses Universitaires de France. (First published in 1852)

Maine de Biran, P. (2006). *Influence de l'habitude sur la faculté de penser*. Paris, France: L'Harmattan.

Marion, J.-L. (1988). "L'Interloqué." *Topoi, 7*, 175–180.

Marion, J.-L. (1996). *La croisée du visible* [Crossing of the visible]. Paris, France: Presses Universitaires de France.

Marion, J.-L. (1998). *Étant donné: Essai d'une phénoménologie de la donation* [Being given: Essay of a phenomenology of givenness]. Paris, France: Presses Universitaires de France.

Marion, J.-L. (2004). *The crossing of the visible*. Stanford, CA: Stanford University Press.

Marion, J.-L. (2005). *Le visible et le révélé* [The visible and the revealed]. Paris, France: Les Éditions du CERF.

Marion, J.-L. (2010a). *Certitudes négatives* [Negative certitudes]. Paris, France: Éditions Grasset & Fasquelles.

Marion, J.-L. (2010b). *De surcroît: Études sur les phénomènes saturés* [In excess: Studies of saturated phenomena]. Paris, France: Quadrige/Presses Universitaires de France. (First published in 2001)

Marx, K./Engels, F. (1958). *Werke Band 3: Die deutsche Ideologie* [Works, vol. 23: The German ideology]. Berlin, Germany: Dietz.

Marx, K./Engels, F. (1962). *Werke Band 23: Das Kapital* [Works, vol. 23: Capital]. Berlin, Germany: Dietz.

Marx, K., & Engels, F. (1983). *Werke Band 42* [Works, vol. 42]. Berlin, Germany: Dietz

Maturana, H. R. (1988). Reality: The search for objectivity or the quest for a compelling argument. *Irish Journal of Psychology, 9*, 25–82.

Maturana, H. R., & Varela, F. J. (1992). *The tree of knowledge: The biological roots of human understanding*. Boston, MA: Shambhala Publications. (First published in 1987)

Merleau-Ponty, M. (1945). *Phénoménologie de la perception* [Phenomenology of perception]. Paris, France: Gallimard.

Merleau-Ponty, M. (1964). *Le visible et l'invisible* [The visible and the invisible]. Paris, France: Gallimard.

Nancy, J.-L. (2000). *L'intrus* [The intruder]. Paris, France: Galilée.

Nancy, J.-L. (2005). *The ground of the image*. New York, NY: Fordham University Press.

Nietzsche, F. (1954a). *Werke Band 1* [Works vol. 1]. Munich, Germany: Hanser.

Nietzsche, F. (1954b). *Werke Band 2* [Works vol. 2]. Munich, Germany: Hanser.

Nietzsche, F. (1954c). *Werke Band 3* [Works vol. 3]. Munich, Germany: Hanser.

Noddings, N. (2003). *Caring: A feminine approach to ethics and moral education*. Berkeley, CA: University of California Press. (First published in 1984)

Oxford English Dictionary (OED) (2012). Online version. Accessed January 18, 2012 at www.oed.com.

Piaget, J. (1970). *Genetic epistemology*. New York, NY: W. W. Norton.

Piaget, J., & Inhelder, B. (1966). *La psychologie de l'enfant* [Child psychology]. Paris, France: Presses Universitaires de France.

Radford, L., & Roth, W.-M. (2011). Intercorporeality and ethical commitment: An activity perspective on classroom interaction. *Educational Studies in Mathematics, 77*, 227–245.

Ricœur, P. (1990). *Soi-même comme un autre* [Oneself as another]. Paris, France: Éditions du Seuil.

Romano, C. (1998). *L'événement et le monde* [Event and world]. Paris, France: Presses Universitaires de France.

Rorty, R. (1989). Contingency, irony, and solidarity. Cambridge, UK: Cambridge University Press.

Roth, W.-M. (1998). Starting small and with uncertainty: Toward a neurocomputational account of knowing and learning in science. *International Journal of Science Education, 20,* 1089–1105.

Roth, W.-M. (2006). A dialectical materialist reading of the sign. *Semiotica, 160,* 141–171.

Roth, W.-M. (2008). The nature of scientific conceptions: A discursive psychological perspective. *Educational Research Review, 3,* 30–50.

Roth, W.-M. (2009). Radical uncertainty in scientific discovery work. *Science, Technology & Human Values, 34,* 313–336.

Roth, W.-M. (2010a). Incarnation: Radicalizing the embodiment of mathematics. *For the Learning of Mathematics, 30* (2), 2–9.

Roth, W.-M. (2010b). *Language, learning, context: Talking the talk.* London, UK: Routledge.

Roth, W.-M. (2011a). *Geometry as objective science in elementary classrooms: Mathematics in the flesh.* New York, NY: Routledge.

Roth, W.-M. (2011b). *Possibility: At the limits of the constructivist metaphor.* Dordrecht, The Netherlands: Springer.

Roth, W.-M. (2012). *First-person method: Towards an empirical phenomenology of experience.* Rotterdam, The Netherlands: Sense Publishers.

Roth, W.-M. (2013a). An integrated theory of thinking and speaking that draws on Vygotsky and Bakhtin/ Vološinov. *Dialogical Pedagogy, 1,* 32–53.

Roth, W.-.M. (2013b). *Meaning and mental representation: A pragmatic approach.* Rotterdam, The Netherlands: Sense Publishers.

Roth, W.-M. (2013c). To event: Towards a post-constructivist approach to theorizing and researching curriculum as event*-in-the-making. *Curriculum Inquiry, 43,* 388–417.

Roth, W.-M. (2013d). Toward a post-constructivist ethics in/of teaching and learning. *Pedagogies: An International Journal, 8,* 103–125.

Roth, W.-M., & Hsu, P. (2012). Analyzing verbal data: An object lesson. In B. J. Fraser, K. Tobin and C. McRobbie (Eds.), *Second international handbook of science education* (pp. 1501–1513). Dordrecht, The Netherlands: Springer.

Roth, W.-M., & Lee, Y. J. (2007). "Vygotsky's neglected legacy": Cultural-historical activity theory. *Review of Educational Research, 77,* 186–232.

Roth, W.-M., McRobbie, C., Lucas, K. B., & Boutonné, S. (1997a). The local production of order in traditional science laboratories: A phenomenological analysis. *Learning and Instruction, 7,* 107–136.

Roth, W.-M., McRobbie, C., Lucas, K. B., & Boutonné, S. (1997b). Why do students fail to learn from demonstrations? A social practice perspective on learning in physics. *Journal of Research in Science Teaching, 34,* 509–533.

Roth, W.-M., & Middleton, D. (2006). Knowing what you tell, telling what you know: Uncertainty and asymmetries of meaning in interpreting graphical data. *Cultural Studies of Science Education, 1,* 11–81.

Roth, W.-M., Pozzer-Ardenghi, L., & Han, J. (2005). *Critical graphicacy: Understanding visual representation practices in school science*. Dordrecht, The Netherlands: Springer-Kluwer.

Roth, W.-M., & Radford, L. (2010). Re/thinking the zone of proximal development (symmetrically). *Mind, Culture, and Activity, 17*, 299–307.

Roth, W.-M., & Radford, L. (2011). *A cultural-historical perspective on mathematics teaching and learning*. Rotterdam, The Netherlands: Sense Publishers.

Scherer, K. R. (1989). Vocal correlates of emotion. In H. L. Wagner & A. S. R. Manstead (Eds.), *Handbook of psychophysiology: Emotion and social behavior* (pp. 165–97). London, UK: Wiley.

Selting, M., Auer, P., Barden, B., Bergmann, J., Couper-Kuhlen, E., Günthner, S., Meier, C., Quasthoff, U., Schlobinski, P., & Uhmann, S. (1998). Gesprächsanalytisches Transkriptionssystem [Conversation analytic transcription system]. *Linguistische Berichte, 173*, 91–122.

Shchyttsova, T. (2003). Das menschliche Ereignis in der Philosophie von M. Bachtin [The human event in the philosophy of M. Bakhtin]. In C.-F. Ceung, I. Chvatik, I. Copoeru, L. Embree, J. Iribarne, & H. R. Sepp (Eds.), *Essays in celebration of the founding of the Organization of Phenomenological Organizations*. Accessed March 11, 2012 at www.o-p-o. net/essays/ShchyttsovaArticle.pdf.

Sheets-Johnstone, M. (2011). *The primacy of movement: Expanded second edition*. Amsterdam, The Netherlands: John Benjamins.

Stein, M. K., Remillard, J., & Smith, M. S. (2007). How curriculum influences student learning. In F. K. Lester Jr. (Ed.), *Second handbook of research on mathematics teaching and learning* (vol. 2, pp. 319–369). Charlotte, NC: Information Age Publishing.

Suchman, L. A. (1987). *Plans and situated actions: The problem of human-machine communication*. Cambridge, UK: Cambridge University Press.

Suchman, L. A., & Trigg, R. H. (1993). Artificial intelligence as craftwork. In S. Chaiklin & J. Lave (Eds.), *Understanding practice: Perspectives on activity and context* (pp. 144–178). Cambridge UK: Cambridge University Press.

Tiberghien, A., & Malcoun, L. (2009). Construction of physics knowledge in classroom and students' learning. In B. Schwartz, T. Dreyfus, & R. Hershkowitz (Eds.), *Transformation of knowledge through classroom interaction* (pp. 42–55). London, UK: Routledge.

Tobin, K., & Roth, W.-M. (2006). *Teaching to learn: A view from the field*. Rotterdam, The Netherlands: Sense Publishers.

Varela, F. J. (1996). Neurophenomenology: A methodological remedy for the hard problem. *Journal of Consciousness Studies, 3*, 330–350.

Varela, F. J., & Shear, J. (1999). *The view from within: First-person approaches to the study of consciousness*. Thorverton, UK: Imprint Academic.

Vološinov, V. N. (1930). *Marksizm i filosofija jazyka: Osnovie problemi soziologicheskogo metoda v nauke o jazyke* [Marxism and the philosophy of language: Essay on the application of the sociological method in linguistics]. Leningrad, Russia: Priboii.

von Glasersfeld, E. (1989a). Cognition, construction of knowledge, and teaching. *Synthese, 80*, 121–140.

von Glasersfeld, E. (1989b). Facts and the self from a constructivist point of view. *Poetics, 18*, 435–448.

von Glasersfeld, E. (2001). Scheme theory as a key to the learning paradox. In A. Tryphon & J. Vonèche (Eds.), *Piaget: Essays in Honour of Bärbel Inhelder* (pp. 141–148). Hove, UK: Psychology Press.

von Glasersfeld, E. (2009). Relativism, fascism, and the question of ethics in constructivism. *Constructivist Foundations, 4*, 117–120.

von Weizsäcker, V. (1973). *Der Gestaltkreis* [The gestalt circle]. Frankfurt/M, Germany: Suhrkamp.

Vygotskij, L. S. (2002). *Denken und Sprechen* [Thinking and speaking]. Weinheim, Germany: Beltz Verlag.

Vygotskij, L. S. (2005). *Psykhologija rasvitija cheloveka* [Psychology of human development]. Moscow, Russia: Eksmo.

Vygotsky, L. S. (1978). *Mind in society: The development of higher psychological processes.* Cambridge, MA: Harvard University Press.

Vygotsky, L. S. (1986). *Thought and language* (A. Kozulin, trans., ed.). Cambridge, MA: MIT Press.

Vygotsky, L. S. (1989). Concrete human psychology. *Russian Psychology, 27* (2), 53–77.

Vygotsky, L. S. (1997). *Educational psychology.* Boca Raton, FL: St. Lucie Press.

Waldenfels, B. (2006). *Grundmotive einer Phänomenologie des Fremden* [Basic motives of a phenomenology of the foreign/strange]. Frankfurt/M, Germany: Suhrkamp Verlag.

Walshaw, M., & Brown, T. (2012). Affective productions of mathematical experience. *Educational Studies in Mathematics, 80*, 185–199.

Wittgenstein, L. (1997). *Philosophische Untersuchungen / Philosophical investigations.* Oxford, UK: Blackwell Publishers. (First published in 1953)

INDEX

A

Accountability, 2, 22, 109, 173, 191, 201
Accusative, 20, 24, 107, 108, 111, 112, 115, 158, 160
Actor, 16, 41, 87, 174, 175, 196
  independent, 206
  individual, 122, 172, 206
  social, 196
  solipsistic, 138
Actualization, 17, 33, 38, 89, 119, 164, 166, 186, 188, 203–204
Adonné (gifted), 19, 20, 21, 106, 109, 111, 114–117
Advenant, 20, 21, 34, 35, 36, 43, 106–108, 111, 114, 119, 196, 209
Affect, 19, 21, 89–95, 107, 108, 119, 141, 147, 151, 154, 155, 158, 161–163
Affectability, 35, 94, 108
Affectation, 62, 161, 162
Affection, 107, 151
  auto-affection, 92
  other-affection, 113
Affectivity, 4, 92
Agency, 43, 62, 100, 113, 114, 136, 142, 151, 162, 169, 204
Answerability, 163–165, 168
Architectonic, 82, 164–165
Arrivage, 47, 48, 92, 95–98, 101, 108
Asynchrony, 167

B

Being (*Sein, Être*), viii, xi, 15, 29, 31, 34, 53, 54, 55, 73, 82, 83, 105, 119, 131, 142, 157, 164, 166
Bergson, H., xii, 1, 2
Biography, 173, 211
Bourdieu, P., 5, 77, 177

Bracketing, 24, 201, 202
Buber, M., 1, 2, 22, 54, 71, 105, 108, 118,
    121, 122, 133, 136–140, 142, 145, 153,
    156, 159, 165, 174, 210

C

Cause–effect, composition, 120
    dimension, 154
    figure, 2, 3, 4–13, 24, 37, 39, 45, 53, 154,
        174, 175, 177, 196, 202, 211
    reasoning, 150, 208
    relation, 35, 40, 45, 47, 49, 52, 54, 83,
        154, 174
    thinking, 2, 45, 55, 138, 206
Certainty, 21, 33, 35, 48, 49, 50, 89,
    101, 189
Contingency, 66, 11, 138, 163, 175, 178,
    181, 182, 189, 190, 204
Conversation analysis, 51, 87, 128, 160,
    196, 199, 207, 208
Corporeity, 9, 10
Curriculum, enacted, vii, 17, 18, 20, 22, 45,
    48, 143, 171–194, 209, 212
    lived, 18, 23, 33, 34, 210–214
    planned, vii, 2, 17, 22, 23, 30, 35, 82,
        108, 145, 171–194, 212

D

Defensive learning, 81
Dehiscence, 18, 36, 50, 135, 156, 159, 165,
    167, 168, 199, 207
Delay, 51, 53, 83, 90, 207
Deleuze, G., 29
Deontology, 142, 167
Derrida, J., 18, 29, 34, 50, 66, 131, 145,
    157, 202
Descartes, R., 47, 86
Diachronicity, 22, 24, 36, 51, 95, 134,
    135, 137, 156, 164, 165, 167, 168,
    199, 204, 207

Diastasis, 18, 22, 36, 38, 95, 137, 159,
    199, 204
Différance, 131, 132
Disciplinary strategy, 192
Dynamic, 15, 51, 87, 121, 138, 199, 203, 211
    approach, 102
    internal, 203
    system, 102, 131

E

Embodiment (theory), 87, 102, 113, 143
Emotion, viii, 19, 81, 89, 92, 93, 96, 107,
    143, 147, 157, 158, 162, 163, 173
Emotioning, 92
Empathy, 9, 66, 106, 142, 201
Enactivism, 86, 87, 98, 101, 102, 112,
    113, 143
Ethnomethodology, 23, 31, 87, 181, 201, 206
Eventness, 3, 26, 28, 31, 33, 34, 128, 136,
    137, 140, 150, 165, 167, 196, 199,
    201–207, 213
Euclid (Euclidean), vii, 125, 138
Exchange-value, 134, 166, 168

F

Fallacy, 208
    constructivist, viii, 13–16
Familiar, 35, 68, 70, 92, 99, 102
Finalization, 26, 51, 80, 134, 176
    Being, 105
    categorization, 186
    closure, 51
    curriculum, 23, 46
    effect, 22
    entity, 29
    event(*-in-the-making), 3, 18, 24, 25, 40,
        50, 80, 130, 149, 175, 176, 208, 211
    fact, 186
    knowledge, 85
    lesson, 109

locution, 39
"meaning," 52
micro-event, 180
movement, 80
object, 18, 75, 76, 80, 184
other, 118
perception, 184
phenomenon, 89
question–reply, 130
result, 76
Said, 24, 130
social fact, 24
subject, 20, 111, 120, 136, 158
thing, 105
thinking, 2
understanding(*-in-the-making), 86, 89, 92, 123, 129, 133, 182, 183
unit, 109
First-time-through, 31, 193, 196, 199, 212
Flesh (*Leib, chair*), 9, 10, 11, 92, 113, 168
For-the-other, 141, 159, 161, 164, 166, 168
Foucault, M., 124, 173

G

Galileo, G., 71, 72, 91, 213
Gift (*don*), 20, 62, 111, 114, 115, 116
Gifted (*adonné*), 19, 20, 21, 106, 109, 111, 114–117
Givenness, 49, 61, 99, 114
God's-eye view, 53, 117, 118

H

Hegel, G. W. F., 14, 46, 91
Heidegger, M., 29, 35, 45, 53, 61, 73, 131, 151, 152, 153, 174
Heraclitean flux, 3, 7, 15, 18, 56, 58, 60, 67, 136, 168, 169, 177
Hero, ix, 120, 211
Husserl, E., 3, 7, 56, 57, 73, 75, 191, 201

I

Ideality, 9, 51
Identity, 20, 29, 30, 45, 51, 53, 97, 108, 118, 158, 209
    constructed, 208
    identity*-in-the-making, 208
    non-self-identity, 134, 168
    self-identity, 6
Illocution, 202, 207
Incomprehension, xii, 1, 37, 89–92, 149, 166
Inner-worldly fact, 16, 18, 20, 22, 23, 28, 46, 53, 90, 107, 117, 175, 179, 186, 189–194, 206, 211, 212
Interloqué, 20, 21, 106, 111–112
Intersubjectivity, 138
Invisible, 61, 64, 69, 82, 85, 108
    body, 9
    curriculum, 213
    equation, 100
    feature, 72
    form, 211
    illocution, 207
    knowledge, 86
    new, 2
    seen, 68
    thing, viii, 91
    understanding*-in-the-making, 100, 103
    unseen, 68
    work, 57
IRE, 41, 51, 128, 150, 162
Irreversibility, 1, 144, 156, 164, 167

K

Kant, I., 5–9, 12, 13, 20, 28, 46, 50, 65, 86, 105, 119, 143, 152–154, 156, 158, 168
Khôra, 50

L

Learning paradox, ix, 17, 18, 56, 57, 61, 74, 82, 86, 100
Levinas, E., 31, 33, 34, 36, 51, 52, 54, 107, 108, 141, 144, 156–161, 163–169
Living work, 23, 24, 57, 75, 86, 177, 184, 186, 189, 190, 192–194, 201

M

Maine de Biran, P., 10–12, 45, 77
Marx, K., ix, 13–15, 45, 119, 134, 135, 166–168, 174
"Meaning," 5, 16, 38, 45, 52, 97, 132, 142, 145, 157, 160, 161, 166, 180, 197, 198, 200, 201, 210, 214
Merleau-Ponty, M., 9, 117, 202
Metaphysics (metaphysical), 28, 29, 120
  approach, 7, 44–46, 143, 195, 212
  belief, 52
  ethics, 151–156, 167, 168
  level, 142
  logician, 52
  mind, 143
  thinking, 35
  world, 143, 169
Mobility (pure), 3, 6, 7, 15, 17–19, 21, 22, 23, 24, 28, 30, 33, 195, 196, 207
Motive, 3, 13, 45, 81, 86, 98, 99, 119, 151, 155

N

Narrative, 211
  account, 3, 211
Nietzsche, F., xii, 3, 4, 28–29, 35, 45, 49, 52, 55, 106, 120, 131, 133, 138, 143, 147, 174, 176, 206, 207, 208
Nominative, 20, 24, 158, 160, 167

O

Objectification, curriculum, 2
  empathizing, 142
  images, viii
  other, 118
  structure, 97
  subject, 136
  understanding, 123
  zone, 135
Objectivity (objective), 117
  achievement, 2
  activity, 102
  availability, 52, 191
  body, 9
  case, 24
  collective achievement, 191
  content, 45
  cube, 75
  existence, 72
  experience, 10
  fact, 16
  geometry, 77
  life, 102
  life activity, 102, 103
  performative, 212, 213, 214
  phenomenon, 9
  presence, viii, 64, 79
  science, 3, 7, 75, 198
  sense, 166
  sequence, 8
  world, 75, 80
Once-occurrent, actuality, 119
  becoming, viii
  Being, 54, 55, 119, 142
  event, 34, 49, 113, 119, 175
  life, 164, 169
  participation, 31
  process, 167
  uniqueness, 1, 210
  unity, 45
  whole, 83
  world, 16, 164, 177

Other, 31, 105, 108, 122, 136, 138, 145, 153, 156, 157–161, 164, 165, 169

P

Participative, consciousness, 15, 16
  describing, 53
  experiencing, 1, 55, 106, 210
  thinking, 2, 14, 15, 47, 49, 50, 52, 54, 117, 213
  witnessing, 18
Passibility, ix, 17, 19, 22, 35, 60, 107, 114
Passivity, ix, 17, 22, 35, 39, 61, 107, 108, 113, 114, 116, 142, 158–161, 169
  radical, 114, 169
Pathos, 19, 36, 39, 61, 82, 92, 95, 100, 106–108
Patient, 20, 21, 106, 109, 111, 112–114, 116, 118, 158, 209
Pedagogy (pedagogical), 21, 48, 138, 161, 162, 209
Performance, 10, 15, 34, 41, 45, 54, 155, 173, 177, 179, 186, 189, 201, 209, 213, 214
Performative, 169, 190, 212, 213, 214
Perlocution, 47, 163, 202, 207
Persecution, 108, 159, 160
Phenomenalization, 19, 62, 64, 66, 72, 73, 74–77, 116, 201
Phenomenology, viii, 10, 17, 22, 23, 28, 51, 68, 86, 87, 94, 101, 102, 107, 108, 113, 114, 145
Post-structuralism, 28, 29, 142
Power-knowledge, 124, 133
Pragmatism (pragmatic), perspective, 132
  position, 198
Praxis, 14, 45, 126, 144–147, 152, 163, 168

R

Rationality, 35, 207
  irrationality, 81
  rational comparison, 155

rational property, 88
Rationalization, 14, 56
Reality, xii, 10, 12, 123, 136, 200
Recipe (instruction), 75, 100, 174, 177, 194
Responsibility, viii, 22, 141–169, 207
Ricœur, P., 155, 158

S

Self, 22, 115, 136, 138, 158, 161, 168
Sensibility, 13, 107
Signification, 78, 97, 103, 131, 132, 139, 157, 160, 161, 165, 166, 168, 200, 201
  historical, 123, 135
Situated action, vii, 12, 17, 143, 171, 174–178
Sound-word, 65, 116, 131, 202
Space, public, 129, 214
  social, 186, 208
  symmetrical, 134, 139
Speech act, 152, 200, 202, 207
Spontaneity, 27, 28
Stream, 1, 13
  downstream, 7
  streaming, 1
  upstream, 7
Subjection (subject to, subjected to), 6, 12, 13, 20, 37, 46, 47, 48, 69, 91, 101, 106, 107, 109, 112, 113, 114, 117, 119, 136, 158, 168, 174, 182, 211
Subjectivity, 98, 107, 112, 115, 116, 134, 141, 144, 158
Subjectivization, 29
Substitution, 160
Suffering, 82, 108, 112, 136, 158, 159
Sympathy, viii, 9
Sympraxis (sympractical), 126
  relation*-in-the-making, 124
  word, 123
  work, 173, 184, 186, 188, 189, 190, 204, 207, 213

Synchrony, 51, 156, 164, 165, 207

T

Teleology, xi, 35, 53
Transcendence, 9, 10, 11, 13, 90, 101, 112, 113, 116, 119, 152, 154, 155, 169

U

Uncertainty, 30, 34, 53, 81, 97, 130, 182
Unfamiliarity, 60, 81, 102
Unfinalizability (unfinalized), 120
    consciousness, vii
    curriculum(*-in-the-making), 3, 23, 142, 210
    depth, 120
    event*-in-the-making, 3, 18, 33, 39, 47, 49, 52, 85, 107, 160, 174
    hero, 120
    individuals, 119
    man, 120
    object(*-in-the-making), 2, 54
    participant, 118
    process, 115
    product, 120
    protagonist, 120
    Saying, 24
    subject(*-in-the-making), 120
    thing, 38
    transition, vii
    word(*-in-the-making), 123
    world-as-event, 15
Unforeseeable, xii, 22, 61, 107, 109, 115
    ascent, 19
    contingency, 117, 175, 204
    creation of form, 2
    equation, 100
    fashion, 107
    future, 3
    knowledge, 2

outcome, 30
possibility, 17
response, 189
result, 116
understanding*-in-the-making, 86
what, 110
word, 117
Unforeseen, 22, 30, 38, 109, 114
    contingency, 175
    event, 48
    future, 3
    knowledge, 18
    learning object, 98
    manner, 19
    possibility, 17, 188
    turn, 188
    understanding*-in-the-making, 86, 97
    unseen, 68
    what, 47, 110
    word, 116
    yet-to-be-known, 80
Unit of analysis, 196, 202, 203
Unknowable, 31
Unpredictability, 3, 18, 30, 49, 99, 134, 178, 195
User manual, 174
Use-value, 134, 166, 168

V

Vulnerability, 22, 35, 92, 107, 108, 146, 156, 157, 159, 160

W

Will to power, 4, 174
Wittgenstein, L., 91, 198, 201
World-as-event, 15, 26, 43, 142, 161, 164, 165, 196
Writing [écriture], 29, 65
    erasing, 66, 67
    re/writing, 24–26, 106, 111

CRITICAL PRAXIS AND CURRICULUM GUIDES

Shirley R. Steinberg and Priya Parmar
Series Editors

Critical Praxis and Curriculum Guides is a curriculum-based book series reflective of theory-creating praxis. The series targets not only undergraduate and graduate audiences but also tenured and experienced teachers of all disciplines. Research suggests that teachers need well-designed, thematic-centered curricula and lessons. This is accomplished when the school works as a community to meet its own needs. Community in this sense includes working collaboratively with students, parents, and local community organizations to help build the curriculum. Practically, this means that time is devoted to professional development workshops, not exam reviews or test preparation pointers but real learning. Together with administrators, teachers form professional learning communities (PLCs) to discuss, analyze, and revise curricula and share pedagogical strategies that meet the needs of their particular school demographics. This communal approach was found to be more successful than requiring each individual teacher to create lessons on her/his own. Ideally, we would love it if each teacher could create his/her own authentic lessons because only s/he truly knows her/his students—and we encourage it, because it is possible! However, as educators ourselves, we understand the realities our colleagues in public schools face, especially when teaching in high-needs areas.

The Critical Praxis and Curriculum Guides series provides relief for educators needing assistance in preparing their lessons. In the spirit of communal practices, the series welcomes co-authored books by theorists and practitioners as well as solo-authored books by an expert deeply informed by the field. Because we strongly believe that theory guides our practice, each guide will blend theory and curriculum chapters, creating a praxis—all, of course, in a critical pedagogical framework. The guides will serve as resources for teachers to use, expand upon, revise, and re-create.

For additional information about this series or for the submission of manuscripts, please contact either Shirley R. Steinberg at msgramsci@aol.com or Priya Parmar at priyaparmar_24@hotmail.com. To order other books in this series, please contact our Customer Service Department: (800) 770-LANG (within the U.S.); (212) 647-7706 (outside the U.S.); (212) 647-7707 FAX; or browse online by series at www.peterlang.com.